Sacred Therapy

Sacred Therapy

Jewish Spiritual Teachings on Emotional Healing and Inner Wholeness

Estelle Frankel

SHAMBHALA
Boston & London
2005

SHAMBHALA PUBLICATIONS, INC.
HORTICULTURAL HALL
300 MASSACHUSETTS AVENUE
BOSTON, MASSACHUSETTS 02115
www.shambhala.com

9 8 7 6 5 4 3 2 1

First Paperback Edition

Printed in the United States of America

♾ This edition is printed on acid-free paper that
meets the American National Standards Institute Z39.48
Standard.

Distributed in the United States by Random House,
Inc., and in Canada by Random House of Canada Ltd

THE LIBRARY OF CONGRESS CATALOGUES THE PREVIOUS
EDITION OF THIS BOOK AS FOLLOWS:

Frankel, Estelle.
Sacred therapy: Jewish spiritual teachings on emotional healing
and inner wholeness/Estelle Frankel.
p. cm.
Includes bibliographical references and index.
ISBN 1-57062-997-8 (hardcover)
ISBN 1-59030-204-4 (paperback)
1. Spiritual life—Judaism. 2. Healing—Religious
aspects—Judaism. 3. Self-actualization
(Psychology)—Religious aspects—Judaism.
4. Repentance—Judaism. 5. Cabala. I. Title.
BM723.F675 2003
296.7'1—dc21
2003002498

Sanctity is not a paradise but a paradox.
—*Rabbi Joseph Soloveitchik*

Contents

Preface

The ideas in this book are the product of my long and often zigzag journey as a student and teacher of Jewish mysticism and as a psychotherapist. So that you have some idea where I am coming from, I would like to share a bit of my story with you. Perhaps you will find aspects of your own journey mirrored by mine.

My spiritual journey began in 1969, when I had the good fortune of meeting Rabbi Shlomo Carlebach and a group of hippies who were exploring the boundaries of religious ecstasy through song, dance, prayer, and meditation at the House of Love and Prayer in San Francisco. I have always considered this meeting auspicious, as it profoundly influenced the course of my life at a rather vulnerable point in my youth.

Though both my parents grew up in Hasidic households in pre-war Poland, they lost touch with their Orthodox roots after the war. They chose, instead, to raise my brother and me in a community that identified itself with Conservative Judaism. By the time I finished my bat mitzvah, the sixties had arrived, and I was becoming increasingly turned off to conventional Judaism. The deep spiritual longings I felt were not being addressed by organized religion, and the vision and music of universal love that filled the streets of San Francisco in the late sixties were far more compelling to me than the ethnocentrism and chauvinism I encountered at home and in the synagogue. At that time in my life, I found hiking in the California redwoods and along the rocky coastlines far more spiritually nurturing than any time I had spent in synagogue.

I had just graduated from high school a semester early in order to travel to Canada with a few friends, some of whom were heading north to dodge the draft, when, by chance, I was invited to spend a Sabbath at the House of Love and Prayer in San Francisco's Haight Ashbury district. I entered to find a roomful of people ecstatically singing and dancing, with light and love radiating from their faces. The incredible feelings of universal love and connection that were the hallmark of the sixties were fused with the spirit and light of *Shabbos*—the Jewish Sabbath.

Rabbi Shlomo Carlebach, may his memory be a blessing, had an amazing gift for making people fall in love with God and with Judaism. He also had a way of making each of us feel beautiful, special, and loved. A true *tzaddik* (a realized, righteous being) and wounded healer, Reb* Shlomo, as he is affectionately known by his disciples, had the gift of seeing people through God's eyes, mirroring back to each of us our highest potential. In many ways I owe my life to Reb Shlomo's love and his profound understanding of Judaism, for the peak spiritual experiences I had at the House of Love and Prayer opened up the possibility that my spiritual longings could find expression in Jewish form. Instead of heading north as I had planned, after a few months at the House of Love and Prayer, I was inspired to journey east, to Jerusalem, to explore my roots.

For the next eight years I lived immersed in the world of simple pious Jews, Hasidic mystics and scholars, and kabbalists of North African or Sephardic (Spanish) descent. I spent both day and night in study, prayer, and meditation, soaking up the words of ancient sacred texts, entering the dreamtime of my ancestors. In addition to the four years I spent studying at Machon Gold Teachers' College and Jerusalem's Michlalah College for Jewish Studies, I was blessed to sit at the feet of many great teachers, including the late Reb Gedalia Koenig, may his memory be a blessing, Rabbi Adin Steinzaltz, Rabbi Gedalia Fleer, and Rabbi Meir Fund, all of whom introduced me to different aspects of Jewish mystical thought. I also continued to study Hasidic thought with Reb Shlomo Carlebach over the next twenty-five years whenever our lives intersected geographically.

---

*The titles "Reb" and "Rebbe" are often used in place of the more formal title "Rabbi" when describing a spiritual master. The Hasidic masters were typically called Rebbe rather than Rabbi.

As with any long-term relationship, my relationship with Judaism has not been without ambivalence. Since falling in love, I have been through periods of personal doubt, boredom, and disillusionment. Perhaps the most painful period of disillusionment occurred following my divorce from my first husband, when I was in my early twenties. (See chapter 1 for a more detailed account.) It was during that time, when I was experiencing a loss of faith in Judaism and in myself as well, that I entered into psychoanalysis. I was extremely fortunate to find an analyst in Jerusalem who happened to be both a skillful clinician and learned in Jewish mysticism. Having an appreciation for Judaism himself, he was able to skillfully guide me through that difficult time, pointing out my emotional blind spots without devaluing my spirituality.

In analysis I became aware of ways that I and many others around me had been using spirituality defensively to avoid dealing with emotions and childhood pain. The *ba'al teshuvah* world of newly religious Jews seemed to host a disproportionately high number of wounded souls who, like me, were seeking healing through spirit. Unfortunately, as I found out, emotional problems don't go away unless they are addressed psychologically as well as spiritually. As psychologist John Welwood has pointed out, we cannot spiritually "bypass" our unfinished emotional business without its interfering with our clear vision of the spirit.

Inspired by the healing process I had gone through in analysis, I decided to return to the States to study psychology. It was clear to me that getting into mysticism without adequate psychological and emotional grounding had undermined my personal development. Surrendering to God's will without also owning my own personal power had gotten me into trouble and led to some poor decision making.

While in graduate school, I worked with a therapist who was very helpful in guiding me to reclaim my personal power and work through childhood issues but who unfortunately did not understand my spiritual life. True to Freudian form, he saw my religiosity as serving a purely regressive function. He felt that through Judaism, the great Father religion, I was unconsciously attempting to resurrect my father, who had died when I was a child. On several occasions he interpreted my love affair with Judaism as part of my "search for the lost love object" of my childhood.

Though I could acknowledge that Judaism provided me with a needed sense of structure that I had lost when my father died, my therapist's purely reductionistic understanding of my spirituality felt rather devaluing and unhelpful. I promised myself that when I became a therapist, I would never discount my clients' spiritual life. I was determined to find an approach to healing that would integrate healthy ego development with spiritual authenticity, honoring the view from the roof of higher consciousness while not denying that gremlins live in the basement! Creating this integration of psyche and spirit has been the focus of my work for the past twenty-five years.

As I was starting my psychology practice in Berkeley in the early eighties, I became involved in the emerging movement known as Jewish Renewal. In the spirit of the early Hasidic masters who re-infused Jewish religious life with passion and new meaning, Jewish Renewal is actively promoting the evolution of the Jewish mystical tradition through the creative blending of ancient teachings with the contemporary wisdom available to us through depth psychology, science, feminism, ecology, and holistic medicine, as well as the other great spiritual traditions of the world. Rabbi Zalman Schachter-Shalomi, the granddaddy of Jewish Renewal, opened many new doors for me, showing me how Judaism fit into the broader spectrum of spiritual traditions and how the light of Torah is illumined when seen through the prism of all other forms of knowledge. Reb Zalman's spiritual and intellectual mentoring and guidance have been an invaluable gift in my life.

Under Reb Zalman's influence I have also become what he calls a hyphenated Jew—Jewish and a little something else. As you read this book, you might find that my thinking is a little Hin-Jew, Bu-ish, and Jew-fi all at the same time, for I don't hesitate to borrow stories and spiritual practices from other traditions when they illuminate Jewish teachings. On many occasions my exposure to Hindu mysticism, Buddhist thought and meditation, and Sufism has deepened my understanding of Judaism. Each time I explored a Hebrew word or concept in the language of another spiritual tradition, my understanding of it deepened. Had I not learned about equanimity and emptiness from a Buddhist perspective, I'm not sure I would fully appreciate what the ancient Jewish mystics meant by *hishtavut ha'nefesh* (equanimity) and *ayin* (emptiness or nothingness). Similarly I came to understand the awesome depth of the *Shema*, Judaism's affirmation of God's oneness, through the nondualistic teachings of Hindu mystics like Ramana Maharshi and Meher Baba. Through studying Taoism I came to appreciate Jewish mysticism's penchant for paradox, and by immersing myself in Jungian psychology, I opened myself to the mythic and archetypal dimension of Jewish folklore.

This book is the culmination of my journey over thirty years, as a seeker and wounded healer. In it I attempt to share with you some of the blessings I have extracted by wrestling over and over again with the wisdom of my ancestors.

Acknowledgments

I want to thank and acknowledge my dear husband, Dr. Stephen Goldbart, who believed in me and encouraged me to keep writing this book even when I felt terribly stuck and filled with self-doubt. Thank you for teaching me the meaning of perseverance and for your patience and support during this difficult birthing process. I also want to thank Rabbi Michael Lerner for encouraging me to write and for being a friend and personal inspiration. I am also deeply indebted to my holy teachers, Rabbi Zalman Schachter-Shalomi and Rabbi Shlomo Carlebach (may his memory be a blessing), for illuminating the profound healing wisdom of Torah for me. I am also indebted to Rabbis Gershon Winkler and David Friedman for generously offering me Kabbalah consults when I needed help with source material, and to my best friend, Ilana Schatz, for all her helpful suggestions, emotional support, and patience in reading and rereading ad nauseam successive drafts of my manuscript.

I am deeply grateful to my editor, Eden Steinberg, for skillfully helping me complete this project, as well as Joel Segel, Naomi Lucks Sigal, and Lynn Fynerman, whose editing and feedback during the earlier stages of my work helped shape my thinking.

I also want to acknowledge and thank all my students who have been an inspiration to me over the years. As the rabbis of the Mishneh wrote in the ethical treatise known as *Pirkay Avot* (Ethics of our Fathers), "from my students I have learned the most."

Introduction

More and more in my own work as a healer, I find myself venturing off the beaten track of psychodynamic psychotherapy and talking to my clients about their spiritual journeys. For many years I was reluctant, in my clinical practice, to come out of the closet as a religious person. Though I would often hear the words of ancient sacred text echoing between the lines of my clients' narratives, in the service of maintaining therapeutic neutrality, I kept these personal musings to myself. Over time, as I gained confidence and perhaps a bit of chutzpah as a clinician, I began selectively sharing spiritual teachings from the Jewish mystical tradition with my clients. Almost invariably, these occasions have led to a deepening of insight, and occasionally they have led to a therapeutic breakthrough. The spiritual perspective offered by Jewish mysticism seems to open up new possibilities for healing.

I also began to realize that by sharing some of the teachings that had inspired my own spiritual awakening and healing, I was enabling my clients to explore their own spiritual development. And as they became more focused on their own spiritual formation, they began to resolve many of the problems with which they had previously struggled.

Each time my work as a therapist crosses over into the spiritual realm and focuses on the quest for meaning and true identity, I find that a subtle shift occurs in my clients. Instead of focusing solely on healing their individual selves, they begin letting go of their identification with those very selves in order to make room for a relationship with spirit. As they shift from being "self-centered" to "God-" or "Spirit-centered," transformational possibilities seem to open up.

This book is about the ways that Jewish spiritual teachings and healing practices can enhance our lives and open up new pathways to wholeness. A good deal of what goes on in spiritual healing is that our notion of who we think we are begins to expand. In a sense we are given new eyes, the ability to see ourselves from God's perspective, as it were; from the vantage point of the infinite. Though we may be able to hold that expanded vision of ourselves only for brief moments at a time, even so, it can have a profound effect on our identity. Instead of being overly identified with our problems and pathologies, we can also begin to appreciate our perfection and purpose. Instead of feeling isolated and alone in our pain, we can begin to experience ourselves as part of a larger whole in which our individual stories and lives reflect the larger story of which all people are a part.

An important part of Jewish spiritual healing involves locating ourselves within Jewish myth and metaphor. Jewish mystics of old understood that the stories contained in the Bible and ancient legends were not meant to be taken merely as historical accounts of what happened to our ancestors but also as mythic renderings of what each one of us undergoes as we embark on the healing journey of awakening. For the Hasidic masters, the entire cast of biblical characters lives within each of us, representing dimensions of the soul. A popular refrain in Hasidic literature—"so, too, in each person"— endowed biblical myth with both personal and archetypal meaning.

As a psychotherapist who has spent the past thirty years immersed in the study of Jewish myth and metaphor, I have learned that when we go beyond our personal predicaments and locate ourselves within the larger story, we open doors to the sacred dimension, and our lives become pregnant with meaning, living embodiments of Torah. We come to experience our lives as resonant with a much greater matrix of meaning, in which any transition we undergo, whether it be a death, divorce, illness, or disability, may initiate us into the larger mysteries of life.

As we find reflections of our individual lives in sacred myth, we tend to feel less alone in our suffering. We no longer see our personal struggles as simply personal; instead, we see them as mirroring a sacred process that occurs in all levels of creation, at all times. And by locating ourselves within the crucible of the great myth, we are guided on our journey of transformation by the archetypal forces embedded within the myth. Carl Jung once said that modern people's tendency to "pathologize" stems from the fact that we have forgotten how to mythologize. The gods live on in us as symptoms, he says, rather than as living archetypes. In Jewish spiritual healing we re-learn the sacred art of mythologizing. We learn to embody and live our sacred stories; as Elie Wiesel once said: "People become the stories they hear and the stories they tell."

For the past three and a half millennia, the Jewish people have engaged in an intimate love relationship with the Torah, or scriptures. As with an earthly lover, we have both discovered and transcended ourselves through our relationship to sacred text. The Torah has been the repository of the deepest projections of our soul, and like a Rorschach ink blot, it has in turn revealed the deepest secrets of our souls to us. As God is said to have looked into the Torah to learn how to create the world, Jews have used the Torah in order to know themselves and to awaken and find a pathway back to God.

The ancient sages taught that every story, word, letter, or nuance of Torah can be simultaneously understood on many different levels. They referred to this multiplicity of meanings by the Hebrew acronym PRDS (pronounced "pardes"), which implies an orchard: "P" (*peh*) stands for the *pshat,* or literal meaning of a text; "R" (*resh*) stands for *remez,* the symbolic meaning that is hinted at; "D" (*dalet*) stands for the *drash,* or those meanings that can be extracted through deeper analysis of language and word associations or through the imaginative process of the unconscious; and "S" (*samech*) stands for *sod,* the secret, mystical understanding of the text.

By immersing ourselves in the *pardes* of Torah, we tap into the primordial light of *paradise,* which, as the rabbis say, was hidden away within the words and letters of Torah. When we view our lives through the lens of Torah, we tap into a realm of unfathomable depth. And through the infinitude of meanings that emerge as we engage in the study of Torah, we continually renew our lives. The rabbis referred to this creative process of mining and excavating the underlying meaning of a sacred text as *midrash,* a term frequently used in this book. The midrash also includes the many ancient legends and creative interpretations of Torah that were transmitted orally from generation to generation until they were eventually written down in anthology form. While most midrashim (plural of *midrash*) are drash-level interpretations that attempt to fill in the gaps in a narrative or explain unusual linguistic expressions, many hint at the most sublime mysteries, the sod, or secret meaning, of a text. The earliest Jewish mystical teachings came down in the form of midrash.

This book also draws extensively on the mystical teachings of Hasidism. In Hasidic thought, biblical and kabbalistic myth came to be understood as stories about healing, and so Torah study was transformed into a sacred narrative therapy of sorts. Hasidism popularized the Kabbalah's notion that *all* of life is in need of healing and fixing, not just those who are ill. It affirmed the Kabbalah's deeply optimistic view that however broken and fragmented things may seem, all of life is in fact evolving toward a state of wholeness and that we humans have an active role and responsibility in furthering this evolutionary healing process. Each of us, taught the Hasidic masters, has the power to become a holy fixer and healer.

Jewish mysticism teaches that we participate in this sacred work of healing in two ways: through our acts of *tikkun olam,* healing and fixing the world, and through *tikkun ha'nefesh,* healing and perfecting our own individual souls. These two expressions of the work of tikkun are actually deeply connected, for it is not possible to perfect one's own soul without also becoming deeply committed to the work of healing the planet, and since each individual person is a microcosm of the world, every act of tikkun ha'nefesh is of great, if not cosmic, importance.

This book is about the myths, metaphors, and spiritual practices that have inspired Jewish mystics in this work of soul-making, or tikkun ha'nefesh, and how we can adapt these stories and practices to our own healing journeys. The ideas contained in this book are the synthesis of my work as a therapist for the past twenty years and as a Jewish educator for the past thirty years. Some of the material is derived from classes and workshops I teach on Jewish mysticism, meditation, and healing, and some of it is from my application of Jewish teachings to my work as a therapist.

In my work as a healer, Jewish mysticism and psychology flow as two currents in a single stream, creating a synergistic healing power. Though I find myself using one or the other lens more extensively at different times with different people, one without the other has always seemed insufficient to explain the mysteries that are our lives. This book is an exploration of this synergy, showing how our lives and our healing journeys are illuminated through immersion in sacred story and spiritual practice.

Part 1 begins with an exploration of the Kabbalah's myth of the shattered vessels as a healing metaphor. This myth, created by Rabbi Isaac Luria in the aftermath of the cataclysmic expulsion of the Jews from Spain in the fifteenth century, speaks to the inevitability of brokenness and shatteredness in life. It teaches us that imperfection and impermanence are simply woven into the fabric of creation. This central myth of the Kabbalah shows us how we can restore a sense of coherence to our lives, even when things seem most broken.

Using the symbol of the shattered vessels as a healing metaphor, this section also explores many of the classic types of situations for which people typically seek therapy. These include healing a broken heart, transition, loss, depression, and illness. Each chapter includes examples of sacred rituals and spiritual practices that can be used for dealing effectively with these kinds of life passages. Finally, part 1 examines the role of love and loss in spiritual awakening—how we are led to God's doorstep when our hearts break open.

Part 2 explores how identity is enlarged and transformed through spiritual awareness and how we heal and birth the larger self. Chapter 4 begins by examining the paradoxical nature of the self in Jewish thought, contrasting it with Western psychology's more narrowly focused definition of the self. According to Jewish thought, we must balance the polarities of self (ego) and no-self (egolessness) in order to be whole. This chapter also discusses the importance of humility in enabling us to balance these polarities and heal the narcissistically split self.

In chapter 5, the biblical myth of the Exodus is viewed as a healing metaphor for the process of change and self-liberation. Each of the stages of the Exodus journey from slavery to liberation teaches us important lessons about the nature of psychological and spiritual unfolding. Chapters 6 through 8 take an in-depth look at Jewish mysticism's understanding of *teshuvah,* or repentance. This section begins with an exploration of the role of spiritual awakening in healing (chapter 6), followed by a discussion of the parallels between the traditional steps of teshuvah and the stages of psychotherapeutic healing (chapter 7). Chapter 7 explores teshuvah as an alchemical process that enables us not only to heal the mistakes of the past but also to transform our vulnerabilities into strengths and our character deficits into virtues. This chapter also highlights the importance of forgiveness and self-acceptance in healing. In chapter 8, the redemptive dimension of repentance is explored through the archetypal image of the Messiah as wounded healer. Through the myth of messianic redemption, Judaism teaches us how we may discover our own unique path to enlightenment through whatever personal adversity or difficulties we face in our lives. Chapter 9 concludes part 2 with a discussion of the role of compassion in healing, focusing on the Hasidic healing practice of bestowing blessing by consciously focusing on the good in oneself and others. This chapter also takes an in-depth look at the High Holy Days as a healing paradigm, showing how the holiday cycle initiates a spiritual attitude adjustment—moving us from a "seat" of judgment to one of divine love and compassion.

Part 3 explores the themes of wholeness and integration in the Jewish mystical tradition. Chapter 10 begins with an exploration of the role of paradox in healing, showing how the path to wholeness ultimately lies in embracing and integrating the contradictory and often fragmented aspects of our being. Chapter 11 follows with an exploration of nondualism in Jewish thought, showing how a nondualistic understanding of life can help us deal with life's many difficult challenges, such as illness and depression. This chapter also explores how nondualism supports the development of higher-level coping mechanisms such as the psychological capacity for integration, which enables us to simultaneously hold good and bad feelings about ourselves and others and accept the mix of good and evil in all things.

Using the Kabbalah's model of the four worlds, chapter 12 explores how we become whole by integrating the physical, emotional, cognitive, and spiritual dimensions of our being. This chapter also includes some practical exercises for enhancing self-integration.

While a broken heart may launch us on the healing journey, the goal of healing is the ability to live wholeheartedly and mindfully, from the depth of our true being. And so in the final chapter (chapter 13) I explore the theme of wholeheartedness, how by giving our selves fully to life without holding back, we can transform our lives into sacred narratives—living embodiments of Torah.

In order to bring the teachings down to earth and make them more accessible, I have included meditations and practices at the end of every chapter that can be used for developing a personal spiritual healing practice. Along with Hasidic stories, poetry, and teachings from other mystical traditions, including Sufism and Buddhism, I have also woven stories from my own life and the lives of my clients and students into the narrative. In doing so, I am trying to demonstrate the intimate reciprocity that exists between sacred myth and each of our lives and healing journeys. Though all case material is based on real people, identifying characteristics have been changed to preserve their anonymity.

The Jewish sources I draw on include the Bible, Talmud, Midrash, and Kabbalah. My favorite sources on healing come from Hasidism, the movement of Jewish spiritual revival that swept through eastern Europe in the eighteenth century. Hasidism took the esoteric, mystical concepts of the Kabbalah, and by applying them to everyday life, rendered them emotionally and psychologically accessible. For instance, Hasidism took the Kabbalah's creation myth and translated it into a map of the human soul, using the Kabbalah's model of divine unfolding as a guide to human development. Similarly, in Hasidic thought, the stories of the Torah and its entire cast of characters are seen as existing within each of us, so that when we study biblical myth, we come to know ourselves.

Many of the Hasidic masters were themselves known to be great psychic and spiritual healers. The Ba'al Shem Tov (1698–1760), founder of the Hasidic movement, was adept in both herbal medicine and shamanistic healing techniques. Stories abound of his clairvoyant and healing powers, including his ability to heal souls through story-telling, prayer, and the mystical power of love. The Ba'al Shem Tov, or Besht, as he is often called for short, brought about a spiritual revolution among the masses of Eastern Europe's Jews. Emphasizing the importance of love, joy, simple faith, and mystical devotion in serving God, his teachings, and those of his many disciples, offered an appealing alternative to the stringent, disciplined path of the traditional yeshiva world, where Talmudic *pilpul* (legalistic debate) and adherence to religious law were the focus of religious life.

Another innovation of Hasidism was its emphasis on the unique relationship between the rebbe (spiritual master) and his Hasidim, or disciples. The rebbe was seen as possessing a *neshama klalit,* a collective soul, much like the avatar in Hindu mysticism. The rebbe acted as an *axis mundi,* a bridge between heaven and earth, for his followers; through his soul connection with the rebbe, the Hasid gained access to the root of his own soul within the divine.

In addition to being the unifying focal point of the community, many of the Hasidic masters conducted one-on-one counseling sessions with their followers. Though these sessions were primarily opportunities for followers to receive spiritual, emotional, and moral direction from the rebbe, on many occasions they would result in the spontaneous remission of the illness or the resolution of the worldly problem for which the disciple sought the rebbe's counsel and blessing. Among a certain sect of Hasidim known as Chabad or Lubavitch, these intimate meetings with the rebbe, known as *yechidus,* became somewhat institutionalized. In a sense they came to serve a parallel role to that of the therapy encounter in secular society. Interestingly, the word *yechidus* comes from the same Hebrew root as *yichud,* or unity, suggesting that through his union with the rebbe, a Hasid could tap into the divine unity that is ultimately the true source of all healing. Rabbi Zalman Schachter-Shalomi's *Spiritual Intimacy: A Study of Counseling in Hasidism* describes the healing power of the yechidus encounter in exceptional depth and detail. This scholarly work deserves attention from all those interested in Jewish spiritual healing practices.

Sacred Therapy was not written just for healers and patients with diagnosable illnesses. Rather, it is meant to be a guide, based on Jewish mystical teachings, for anyone engaged in the psycho-spiritual quest for wholeness and healing. When I speak about healing throughout this book, I am not referring to the kind of healing our doctors typically talk about when we are sick—namely, the recovery from symptoms. Instead, my focus is more on how we might actually be healed *by,* or in spite of, whatever illnesses and difficulties we face in our lives. Though recovery is a welcome part of any healing, it is possible to be healed in spite of the persistence and even the worsening of one's physical symptoms, for even when a healing of body is not possible, one can always find a healing of soul.

If my unapologetic use of the word *God* in this book pushes buttons for you, try replacing it with another name you are more comfortable with, like "higher power," "spirit," "Infinite One," or "All Being," whichever works for you. Judaism has many names for the divine, each one reflecting a particular aspect of divinity. As you read this book, keep in mind that the God you were most likely raised to believe in, or not believe in, is not the God I am referring to. The Kabbalah's understanding of the divine, which is the one I espouse, is essentially nondualistic. It is similar to the Advaitic tradition of Hindu mysticism. According to the Kabbalah, God is all that is— nothing exists outside of the divine. The kabbalists often referred to God as the Ein Sof (infinite, limitless, endless) or Or Ein Sof (light of the infinite, limitless, endless). As you read this book, try to stay open to your own felt experience of the divine and to come up with your own names and images to describe it. But keep in mind that while Judaism uses many different names and words to describe God, including ayin, which implies divine nothingness or emptiness, God is ultimately beyond anything we could imagine or describe with any single word or image.

Though the blending of Jewish spiritual teachings into my work as a therapist began as my own idiosyncratic attempt to integrate disparate parts of my being, it has grown into a conscious method of healing. I know that I am not alone in this kind of work. Many other therapists with backgrounds in Buddhism, Sufism, and Christianity have begun to look at ways to blend the wisdom of their spiritual traditions into their work. I believe that this trend is part of a larger rapprochement that is going on between psychology and spirituality. It signals a return to what healing originally was in ancient times, as the Greek word *therapeia* (from which the English word *therapy* derives) connotes—doing the work of the gods. It is my hope that by restoring the sacred dimension to our work as healers, we can offer our clients a more holistic and comprehensive approach to healing.

HEBREW WORDPLAY
The Sacred Language of Healing

Many of the ideas in this book draw on the ancient Jewish practice of wordplay, a linguistic tool used by Jewish scholars and mystics to communicate esoteric ideas. Hebrew was considered a magical language; in fact, it was known as *lashon ha'kodesh,* a language of the sacred. There is an ancient belief that heaven and earth and all things therein were created through the letters of the Hebrew alphabet. The *aleph-bet,* as they are known, were seen as the primordial creative power with which God spoke/sang the world into being, as suggested in Psalms 33:6 ("By the word of God the heavens were made/by the breath of His mouth, all their hosts"). The magical incantation abracadabra, which may very well be a variation on the Hebrew-Aramaic expression *ibra k'dibra,* or "I create through my speech," hints at the creative and magical power of words in Jewish thought.

Every Hebrew word has a two- or three-letter root, and words that share the same root are thematically related. Sometimes their connection is immediately apparent, and sometimes one must search beneath the surface to find the deeper levels of connection. By looking deeply into the multiple meanings of Hebrew words, one often discovers profound and esoteric truths. For example, the Hebrew word for health or healing—*le'havri*—shares the same root (*bet-resh-aleph*) as the Hebrew word for creation—*beriah.* When we ponder the possible connection between creation and healing, a simple mystical truth emerges—namely, that all healing involves a process of renewal, of being created anew. When we live our lives with the possibility of renewal and re-creation, we open ourselves to healing on many levels.

Perhaps it is because of the deep connection between creation and healing that healing rites among many tribal people include a recitation of the tribe's cosmogonic myth, their sacred account of life's origins. This practice is based on the belief that by bringing the ill person back to the beginning of time, a time when all things were whole, we might facilitate healing. And so we begin our exploration of Jewish spiritual healing paths and practices with an exploration of the Kabbalah's creation myth, the myth of the shattered vessels. This creation-healing myth contains many potent symbols and metaphors for the healing journey and for times of personal transition. Like many mystical paradoxes, the Kabbalah's creation myth teaches that the path to wholeness and healing often begins with brokenness.

THE BLESSING FOR TORAH STUDY

Before engaging in Torah study, Jews traditionally recite several blessings. These blessings are intended to focus personal intention, or *kavannah,* so that one's Torah study becomes a mitzvah, a sacred rite in which we align our minds with the divine mind. The traditional blessings, which have been incorporated into the daily prayer service, express the longing that the words of Torah we study should be "sweet" in our mouths and that we should come to know God's name or essence through immersion in sacred text. One of the blessings, which is composed in the present tense, affirms the ongoing nature of divine revelation, that Torah is continually being revealed to us as we immerse ourselves in sacred study. My kavannah, or intention, in writing this book is to pass on the sweetness I have discovered in the words of the Torah. What follows is a free-form English rendition of the traditional blessings, should you wish to recite them before reading on.

Blessed are You, Infinite One, our God whose presence fills creation and who makes us holy (and connects us) by means of the *mitzvot* (good deeds/spiritual practices). You have enjoined us to

engage in words of Torah. Please, Infinite One, our God and the
God of our Ancestors, make the words of Your Torah sweet in our
mouths and in the mouths of the Your people, the house of Israel, so
that we and our descendants and the descendants of Your people, the
house of Israel, will all know Your name (essence) and be engaged in
the study of Torah for its most pure sake. Blessed are You who im-
part the wisdom of Torah to Your people, Israel. Blessed are You,
Infinite One, our God whose presence fills creation and who has chosen us to receive the Torah, a revelation of truth. Blessed are You
who continually give over the Torah.

PART ONE

Becoming a Vessel of Light
Kabbalistic Cosmology and Healing

Spirit entering into form, breaks off from itself, breaks itself, breaks itself into pieces, is broken. Wherever we see spirit, there is something broken.

Here the heart is broken, here the spirit enters. The prayers of a broken heart call the spirit in, inevitably heal, are therefore whole.

When great hearts break, we take the pieces into ourselves. Then everything is singing.

—Deena Metzger, "On Prayer"

I

Broken Hearts and Shattered Vessels

Nothing is more whole than a broken heart.
—*Rabbi Menachem Mendel of Kotzk*

In the course of our lives, each of us will inevitably have our hearts broken more than once. We will all experience times when our lives, as we have known them, are suddenly shattered by the intrusion of fate or disappointment. These "shatterings" can have many faces: a divorce or separation, the unexpected death of a loved one, a sudden job or financial loss, a personal betrayal, an acute illness, or the onset of a chronic disabling condition. We may become the victims of a natural catastrophe or social upheavals that forever alter our lives. In recent times many of us have had to cope with the shocking new reality posed by the threat of terrorism, namely the loss of our sense of personal safety and security, and the loss of an innocence we once possessed. We are all a little brokenhearted these days.

Yet at those very times when it seems as though our whole world is crashing in on us, we may be the beneficiary of one of those personal epiphanies that change the course of the rest of our lives. Though our hearts may be broken and our lives awash in chaos, we may sense a newfound inner strength and resilience that have been born out of our difficulties. Many survivors of trauma tell about the ways that they feel forever changed for the better by their ordeals. Having brushed up against mortal danger, they describe feeling a heightened appreciation for life itself and profound gratitude for the love and support they received from others.

Perhaps this was what the nineteenth-century Hasidic master Rabbi Menachem Mendel of Kotzk meant when he said that there is nothing more whole than a broken heart. Like many Jewish mystics who spoke about life and healing in paradoxical terms, the Kotzker Rebbe, as Rabbi Menachem Mendel was known, understood that things are not always what they appear to be. In fact, many things first manifest as their opposite. What appears to be bad may ultimately turn out good; illness may, at times, be the path to our deepest healing, and brokenness is sometimes the only way back to wholeness. Just when things seem to be falling apart or ending, new life is often generated, and just when we think we have it all together, things often fall apart. From the mystical perspective, reality is always both broken and perfect all at once.

When I meditate on what the Kotzker may have meant by the wholeness of a broken heart, I flash back on times in my life when the pain of loss struck so deep that my heart simply broke open. At those most difficult times, instead of feeling all alone in my pain, which is often my pattern, I felt deeply, empathically connected to everyone and everything around me. It was as though the walls that ordinarily separate me from others had been brought down by my heart's shattering. And as those walls came down, a universal love, a love for all sentient beings, came to rest in the place that once knew only a limited love. "The heart must break to become *large*," writes Andrew Harvey, for "when the heart is broken open, then God can put the whole universe in it."[1]

One such time for me was twenty-five years ago, when I was living in Jerusalem. I had immersed myself in the world of pious Jews and mystics, and I was teaching Judaism to American college students who were studying abroad. Eight years into my spiritual quest, I went through a personal crisis that shattered my youthful dreams and drastically changed the direction of my life.

I had married young, as is the custom in the religious world, only to discover that I had made a terrible mistake. My husband, who presented himself as a scholar and mystic and who came from a family steeped in the study of Kabbalah, turned out to be unstable and fanatic, and after the birth of our daughter it became painfully clear to me that I would have to leave the marriage. I was devastated and felt ashamed to have made such a big mistake, and to make matters worse, my ex-husband refused to grant me a *get,* or religious divorce, threatening to leave me hanging as an *agunah,* a woman who, according to Orthodox law, is not allowed to remarry.

During the months following our separation I went through a dark night of the soul as I wrestled with a loss of faith. I felt depressed and lonely, overwhelmed with responsibility as a new mother, and spiritually unmoored. I knew that a certain stage of my life was coming to an end, as the old forms I had embraced to express my spiritual longings no longer seemed to fit, but I was not yet able to articulate a new vision.

The painful ending of my marriage, a marriage that had been blessed by one of the most esteemed kabbalists living in Jerusalem at the time as "a match made in heaven," shattered my religious naivete. I felt spiritually confused and disillusioned, and it seemed as though a thick wall stood between me and the God with whom I once had felt so intimate.

One Shabbat afternoon, when I was feeling particularly sorry for myself, I took a walk in the Jerusalem forest at dusk. I sat down under a tree, closed my eyes, and started to cry. As I found myself begging God for help and guidance through this dark time in my life, my heart finally broke open in prayer. In this state of communion, my bitterness began to lift and was replaced by a sense of sweetness. A comforting presence encompassed me as I sensed, once more, my connection to the source of all being.

Before I knew it, night had fallen, and there I was in the middle of the forest. I could hardly see two feet in front of me. It was a moonless night, and the nearest lights were quite a distance away. I realized that it was going to be a one-step-at-a-time trek back to the road. As I took the first step, I noticed that my range of vision suddenly extended another two feet ahead of me. Another step, another two feet . . .

As I made my way very slowly back up the trail, I had a mini-epiphany. Through each step of my journey home in darkness, it was as though God were whispering to me: "Just take it slow . . . one step at a time . . . you only need to see one step ahead of you in order to take the next step . . . you will find your way back to wholeness . . . your heart is broken right now . . . the path is unclear, but don't hide in shame . . . let your brokenness be the path you walk. . . ." By the time I reached the top of the trail, I realized that my prayer had already been answered.

After that night-trek, my depression began to lift, and my eyes no longer burned with tears of anger and shame. Instead of snapping shut in pain, my heart had finally broken open, enabling me once again to feel a sense of connection with God and everyone around me. Looking back on that night, I sense I had encountered the face of the divine that King David refers to as "the healer of shattered hearts" (Psalms 147:3). The journey ahead of me was long, with a lot of twists and turns on the way, but after that night I knew I was on my way home. A new chapter was opening in my life in which I would discover my path as a healer. That one-step-at-a-time walk in the dark became an important lesson in how to navigate my way through life's dark and often confusing times. On many occasions, I have drawn courage from it.

LIGHT OUT OF DARKNESS

The Jewish mystical tradition is replete with metaphors of how spiritual awakening begins with learning how to navigate our way through the dark times. "Night" is a recurrent symbol in Jewish myth, signifying the fertile and transformative power of the un-known—the hidden face of the divine in this world.

For Jews, time always begins at night. This is true both literally and figuratively. On the Jewish calendar, each new day begins with nightfall rather than daybreak, and the Biblical account of creation repeatedly stresses that "there was evening and there was morning." Before there could be light, darkness had to be created, and so all of creation emerges out of a state of primordial darkness and emptiness:

"And darkness was on the face of the deep. And a wind from God moved over the waters. And God said Let there be light" (Genesis 1:2).

The fact that darkness is the womb from which all life emerges is understood by the Kabbalah to have deep spiritual significance. It implies an understanding that creation, in all its forms, emerges out of its opposite, the state of emptiness. All life moves in cycles from darkness into light, from contraction into expansion, brokenness into wholeness. In the symbolism of the Kabbalah, the darkness of night is associated with the fragmented state known as exile—the state of being disconnected and dislocated from one's true place. The history of the Jewish people, like creation itself, begins in what the thirteenth-century kabbalist text known as the Zohar refers to as the dark night of exile in Egypt. It was out of this first encounter with exile that the Israelite nation was born and the light of Torah, the revelation of Spirit, emerged out of the darkness. "There is no greater light," says the Zohar, "than that light which emerges out of the greatest darkness."[2]

Just as creation emerges out of a state of primordial darkness and emptiness, in our own lives, we find that it is most often the dark night of the soul, the existential crisis of meaning and faith, an illness or traumatic loss, that awakens us and ultimately compels us to grow and birth new dimensions of ourselves. We all have stories of difficult times that propelled us to grow and manifest new dimensions of our soul. For many of us, it is precisely at those times when things fall apart that we feel compelled to embark on a healing journey. Though we often embark on the journey kicking and fighting with our destinies, we may later come to recognize that the dark times were what fertilized the soil of our souls to prepare the way for new growth.

Rabbi Nachman of Breslov (1772–1810), the great-grandson of the famed Ba'al Shem Tov (1698–1760), was a master spiritual guide for the nighttime encounter with the divine. In fact, he used to advise his followers to go out into the night to commune with God. This meditative practice, known as *hitbodedut,* or holy aloneness, involves simply talking to God in one's own words, as one might talk to a good friend. The idea is to bring one's feelings of brokenheartedness to the

divine ear. Though hitbodedut can be practiced anywhere and any-
time, Rebbe Nachman specifically recommended that people go out
of their habitual environments and talk to God in a forest or meadow
at night, far away from the buzz of human activity. From my practice
of hitbodedut meditation over the past thirty years, I have learned
that no matter what is going on in my outer life, in those moments
when I experience true communion with the divine, as I did on that
dark night in the forest, I feel a sense of sweetness and deep inner
peace. Paradoxically, in holy aloneness, we no longer feel so alone.

Rebbe Nachman, who himself battled episodes of depression and
melancholy his entire life, knew firsthand that there is a big difference between depression and brokenheartedness. Depression, he
taught, was an expression of anger at and disconnection from God.
Brokenheartedness, in contrast, said Rabbi Nachman, is free of anger
and blame.[3] It is rooted in the humble awareness that all beings experience sorrow and pain. A broken heart is simply a sign of our deep
humanity. And as we bring our sorrow to God's doorstep, we join
the broken and the whole; our broken heart becomes the point of
connection to the All, and to all others who hurt.

In a midrash attributed to the third-century Palestinian Talmudist
Rabbi Alexandri, God is described as the seeker of shattered hearts:
"When a man uses a broken vessel he is ashamed of it, but not so
God. All the instruments of His service are broken vessels, as it is
said: 'The Lord is close to the brokenhearted' (Psalms 34:19); or 'Who
heals the brokenhearted' (Psalms 147:3)."[4]

A similar image of the divine appears in the following midrash,
quoted in the thirteenth-century anthology *Midrash Ha'Gadol:* "A
man of flesh and blood, if he has a vessel, so long as the vessel is
whole he is happy with it; broken he does not wish it. But not so the
Holy One, blessed be He. So long as the vessel is whole, he does not
wish to see it; broken he wishes it. And what is the favorite vessel of
the Holy One, blessed be He? The heart of man. If the Holy One,
blessed be He, sees a proud heart he does not wish it; as it is said:
'Every one that is proud in heart is an abomination to the Lord.'
(Proverbs 16:5) Broken, he said: This is mine; as it is said: 'The Lord
is nigh unto them that are of a broken heart' (Psalms 34:19)."[5]

The broken heart that is whole/holy in God's eyes, according to the midrash, exists in those who are humble. What does humility have to do with it? A healthy dose of humility enables us to experience brokenness or sorrow in a non-self-centered way. When we lack humility, we tend to experience our pain as *our* pain, and we tend to wear it as a badge of privilege with which we separate ourselves from others. We may even feel a need to compete with others whose suffering pales in comparison with our own. But when we do this, we end up feeling very lonely.

Similarly, if we are ashamed and afraid of our pain, we may feel a need to hide and to isolate ourselves from others when we are hurting. Ultimately, how we hold our feelings of brokenness determines our felt experience. If we can find a way to hold and embrace our pain gently, recognizing that brokenness is simply part of the human condition—in a sense, nothing special—then we may begin to feel empathically connected to all other beings. This is the broken heart that makes us whole.

While helping to organize a fund-raiser for victims of terror in the Holy Land, I spoke with a couple who had lost their daughter in a terrorist attack. Instead of becoming bitter and angry as a result of their terrible loss, they had founded an organization to help other victims of terror and their family members deal with the trauma of loss and injury. Their own experience of heartbreak compelled them to reach out to others (Jews and Arabs alike) who were dealing with the unimaginable pain of losing a child or loved one to terror. They both described how, as a result of their loss, their capacity to love and empathize with others had deepened beyond anything they could previously have imagined. In reaching out and connecting with others in pain, they felt they were doing the only thing they could possibly do to redeem and assuage their own pain.

After the bombing of the World Trade Center we saw this same phenomenon operate on a mass scale, as the brokenhearted citizens of New York came together with volunteers from across the country to help in the rescue effort and the aftermath of the crisis. In an essay entitled "Voices from Ground Zero," Courtney V. Cowart describes the deep altruism and compassion that were unleashed at Ground

Zero. "Whether you're a policeman or an ironworker," Cowart writes, "a commodities trader or construction worker, missionary or sanitation worker, fireman or rocker, in the pit of enormous need at Ground Zero everyone seems to be discovering we're all more generous, less fearful, more accepting, less judgmental, more compassionate, both more vulnerable and yet somehow stronger than we ever, ever thought we could be."[6]

Jewish spiritual healing is essentially about breaking out of the narrow prison of our own personal heartbreak to enter the heavenly palace of compassion and connection. It is about how the human heart can be broken *open,* so that the veils that keep us separate from one another and from our connection with the divine can be removed.

The truth is, it's all about connection. Whether we bare our souls before the divine or our personal pain becomes a point of connection with others, when we feel part of a greater whole, we experience a sense of joy and well-being. When we feel disconnected from ourselves and others and separate from the Whole—what in religious terms we refer to as "God"—we suffer. The Hebrew word for oneness—*echad*—comes from the same root as the word for joy—*chedva*. We experience joy when we feel a sense of oneness and connectedness. This is the central aim of all Jewish spiritual healing—to restore a sense of unity, joy, and connectedness in a world in which brokenness seems inevitable.

CRISIS AND TRANSFORMATION

When we are in crisis, we often feel as though we were being compelled by life to grow and change, sometimes against our will. I remember feeling as though I were being pushed out of the comfortable womb of the Orthodox Jewish world when my first marriage ended. It was not until several years later, after I moved back to the United States and began studying psychology, that I understood how the shattering of my dreams at that time in my life provided the cosmic nudge I needed in order to go beyond the confines of the Orthodox world. As my world fell apart, new dimensions of my being began to emerge, and I was launched on the next stage of my spiritual development.

While undergoing a personal crisis can catapult us to new levels of consciousness, sometimes the emergence of new aspects of our being or our attainment of higher levels of awareness can lead to a breakdown of old life structures. As we become more fully who we are meant to be, we may have to let go of relationships that hold us back, or we might find that our work is no longer congruent with who we are becoming. To be true to ourselves, we may have to let go of a seemingly successful identity or lucrative career. These times of transition can be quite challenging to our sense of security as the ground upon which we have stood is replaced by a vast unknown.

Jewish mystics of old were acutely aware that in those very moments when things feel most broken and hopeless, healing, or *tikkun,* becomes possible. This theme weaves itself in and out of many of Judaism's central myths and spiritual practices. This essential optimism is at the very core of the Jewish mystical tradition, which sees every person as a participant in the healing and fixing of this broken world.

In Jewish history there has always been a deep correlation between crisis and transformation. The repeated experience of exile, in particular, became a major catalyst in the evolution of Jewish consciousness. Every time the Jews packed their bags and hit the road, they opened a new chapter in the spiritual legacy known as Torah. Never was this link more strongly forged than in the time of Rabbi Isaac Luria (1534–1572), when in the wake of the greatest catastrophe Jews had known for a thousand years, Luria articulated a new way of understanding the world that would redefine our relationship to the divine for centuries to come.

For most Americans, the year 1492 instantly recalls Columbus's journey to the New World. But for Jews, 1492 also marks the end of the legendary Golden Era of Spanish Jewry. That year, after centuries of feeling relatively secure in their Spanish homeland, the Jews of Spain were given an edict by King Ferdinand and Queen Isabella demanding that they either convert to Catholicism or face death or expulsion. Though thousands converted under duress, approximately a hundred thousand Jews packed their belongings on their backs and went into exile.

The Jews of Spain were shocked and devastated by Ferdinand and Isabella's harsh decree. Jews had been living in Spain since the time of the Roman Empire (300 c.e.), when exiles from the Holy Land made their way there in search of a new home. Life was not always easy for the Jews of Spain, especially when Spain was under Catholic rule. But beginning in the ninth century, when Spain was conquered by Muslim rulers, the Jews experienced several hundred years of relative freedom and acceptance, during which they were free to participate in interfaith spiritual and cultural dialogue as well as business and professional life. During this time Spanish Jews became philosophers, courtiers, physicians, poets, and financiers. Some were deeply involved in politics and court intrigue. It was a time when the Kabbalah flowered, and Jewish mystics were free to exchange ideas with their Muslim and Christian counterparts.

All this began to change in the fourteenth century, when the Catholic Church resumed its relentless persecution and oppression of non-Christians. Yet despite frequent massacres and forced conversions, right up until the final edict of expulsion was delivered, Spanish Jews never considered the possibility that they would be homeless and stateless once more.

As Spanish Jews wandered east and west in search of a safe haven, some settled in the Holy Land. Just as Spanish and Portuguese explorers set out to chart the terrain of the New World in the fifteenth and sixteenth centuries, these Spanish Jewish exiles set out to explore the divine landscape and the vast terrain of the human soul. Under the leadership of Rabbi Isaac Luria, also known as the Ari Ha'Kadosh, the Holy Lion, a tight circle of mystics living in the Galilean city of Safed inspired a spiritual renaissance that would deeply influence Jewish theology for centuries to come.

In an attempt to recontextualize and find spiritual meaning in the archetypal Jewish experience of homelessness and wandering, Rabbi Isaac Luria turned to the healing art of myth-making. Luria's teachings, which focused on the theme of divine unfolding, viewed the Jewish experience of dislocation as a mirror image of the divine exile.

Just as the Jews were scattered in exile among the nations, so too was the light of the infinite, the Or Ein Sof, fragmented and scattered in this world of multiplicity. Thus, if the Jewish people feel homeless in the world, it's no great wonder, for how could one feel otherwise in a world in which God, too, lives in a state of exile, in all the multitude of finite forms. Furthermore, their wandering in exile had a divine purpose—namely, to gather up the divine sparks that had been scattered throughout creation.

In his mythic cosmology, Luria provided his generation with a new matrix of meaning, one that transformed their immediate experience of dislocation into a meaningful, divinely ordained experience. Embedded within its symbolism were many important healing metaphors. As we explore the myth in greater depth, its healing message, which is every bit as relevant today as it was in the sixteenth century, will become clear.

DIVINE SPARKS AND SHATTERED VESSELS

Gathering the Sparks

Long before the sun cast a shadow
before the Word was spoken
that brought the heavens
and the earth
into being
a flame emerged
from a single
unseen
point
and from the center of this flame
sparks of light sprang forth
concealed in shells
that set sail everywhere
above
and below
like a fleet of ships

each carrying its cargo
of light.

Somehow
no one knows why
the frail vessels broke open
split asunder
and all the sparks were scattered
like sand
like seeds
like stars.

That is why we were created—
to search for the sparks
no matter where they have been
hidden
and as each one is revealed
to be consumed
in our own fire
and reborn
out of our own
ashes.

Someday
when the sparks have been gathered
the vessels will be
restored
and the fleet will set sail
across another ocean
of space
and the Word
will be spoken again.

—Howard Schwartz

Creation, according to Lurianic myth, began with a cosmic catastrophe—a shattering that resulted from an imbalance between the

divine emanation of light and the finite vessels created to receive and house that light. In a sense, God made a big mistake in the big bang. And as a result of that cataclysm, nothing in this world is quite in its rightful place.

According to Luria, creation involved three distinct stages: *tzimtzum* (withdrawal), *shevira* (shattering), and *tikkun* (restoration/healing). As you read my description of these stages, keep in mind that they were meant not to be taken as a literal, scientific account of creation but as a metaphor for archetypal processes that occur throughout creation, both in the natural world and in human emotional and spiritual development.

Light and vessels are kabbalistic metaphors for divine essence and embodied forms. The vessels of creation, or *keilim*, as they are called in Hebrew, were created in order to provide a container for the light of the infinite, the Or Ein Sof. Everything in this world was created in order to house the divine, but since the divine is infinite, no finite vessel can ever fully contain its light. This is by design, it seems; the vessels of creation are flawed and inadequate. Yet in order to reveal itself in an embodied universe, the infinite had to find a way to inhabit the finite. This is one of the paradoxes inherent in creation that Luria attempted to address in his myth of divine unfolding.

Tzimtzum

Creation, according to Luria, began with the formation of a primordial vacuum—a space within which the finite realm might come into being. Through a process known as tzimtzum, the Ein Sof is said to have withdrawn itself, creating a womblike empty space in the very heart-center of God's infinite being. Describing this process, Rabbi Hayim Vital, Luria's most illustrious disciple, writes: "When it arose in the simple Divine will to emanate a creation . . . God withdrew Himself to the sides, in the center of His light, leaving an empty space. In this space exist all the worlds."[7]

Without this tzimtzum, there would have been no room for anything finite or separate to exist, for all would have been obliterated by the immense light of the infinite. Another way of looking at this is that the infinite could only reveal itself through some measure of concealment. (The Hebrew word for "world"—*olam*—comes from the Hebrew root *ne'elam,* which connotes hiddenness.) Paradoxically, the world's existence as a seemingly separate and independent entity depends upon some degree of divine hiding.

A useful metaphor for the role of tzimtzum in creation comes from the parent-child relationship. Tzimtzum begins during pregnancy, when the mother makes room inside herself for her baby to develop into a separate, autonomous being. After the child is born and as it continues to mature, parents must provide a different kind of space—a "psychic space"—in which the child will develop its autonomous self. For instance, when a child is learning to take its first steps, a parent must step back and allow room for the child to stumble and fall on its own. If the parent is too helpful, the child will never learn to walk on its own. A good parent knows how to balance love with some measure of tzimtzum, or limitation on the expression of that love that takes into account the child's needs for space, autonomy, and limits. This kind of restraint on the part of a parent is ultimately also an expression of love, though it may not be immediately apparent.

So, too, when God withdrew the light of the infinite, this withdrawal was also an act of love, for it created the space for the world's existence. Yet paradoxically, the same withdrawal that enables existence and creates the possibility of human autonomy and free choice also creates the possibility for evil to exist. For in the apparent eclipse of the divine, there is room for human autonomy to become so extreme that we forget our connection to the source of all life. An exaggerated sense of separation/autonomy is, according to the Kabbalah, the root of all evil and suffering.

Shevira

Into the primordial vacuum, the infinite, or Ein Sof, then emanated a single ray of light that was to be contained by a set of vessels created simultaneously to receive the divine light. However, this primordial light was so powerful that it shattered some of these original vessels. Considering that the universe is located at the heart-center of

God's infinite being, you might say that God's very heart was broken as the world came into existence!

Luria suggests that the original vessels, or *sephirot,* were vulnerable to shattering because they were disconnected from each other. While they each received the effulgence of divine light, they had no means of communicating and sharing their light with one another. Because of their isolation they were unable to form a whole strong enough to withstand the powerful revelation. It was this state of intersephirotic disconnection that led to the fragmentation or cosmic catastrophe known as *shevirat ha'keilim*—the shattering of the vessels.

Some see the shattering of the vessels as a metaphor for the birth process, the shattering being a symbol of the moment when the mother's waters break. In order for new life to come forth, the unity with mother must be shattered. Just as creation begins with a shattering, the soul begins its journey of awakening at birth with a shattering of primal unities, both with birth mother and with God. So, too, with each new threshold we cross in life: something is always lost. Life is continually pulsating between a force that creates form and a force that destroys it, between chaos and order. Nothing is created without also shattering some preexisting order, just as the undivided oneness of God that existed prior to creation had to be sacrificed in order for the world of multiplicity to come into being. The kabbalists often used the image of a seed that must decompose underground before it can give birth to new life as a metaphor for the shattering of the vessels. This image appears in the writings of the sixteenth-century Italian kabbalist Rabbi Menahem Azariah of Fano: "The supernal vacuum is like a field, in which are sown ten points of light. Just as each grain of seed grows according to its fertile power, so does each of these points. And just as a seed cannot grow to perfection as long as it maintains its original form—growth coming only through decomposition—so these points could not become perfect configurations as long as they maintained their original form but only by shattering."[8]

Tikkun

Following the shattering, most of the light of the infinite is said to have returned to its source; however, some sparks fell along with the broken shards of vessels and became trapped in the material world, where they await redemption. Until all these fallen sparks of divinity are restored to their source, the world is said to be in a broken state, needing tikkun, or repair. Each of us, according to Luria, has a role in the task of healing and mending the world, or tikkun olam. Our job is to redeem and elevate the fallen, exiled sparks of divinity by finding and extracting the good that exists in all things, including evil. We do this through the mindful performance of the mitzvot, or divine commandments, and by living our lives in holiness, and by acting justly and righteously. This work of tikkun, or healing/restoration, according to the Kabbalah, is the very purpose of all existence.

These three stages of creation—tzimtzum, shevira, and tikkun—are not just a one-time occurrence but part of the ongoing process of creation. Since God continually brings forth creation—*yesh mi'ayin,* something out of nothing—then the cycle of tzimtzum-shevira-tikkun is one that goes on throughout creation at all times in all levels of existence. It is part of the very molecular structure of the cosmos.

This is precisely how the Hasidic masters viewed the shattering of the vessels. They understood the myth as an archetypal story about all life. All things and all beings that are born into being pass through these three gates. At every transition point in the life cycle, when one stage of life ends and another begins, we inevitably pass through this death-rebirth cycle of creation, dissolution, and re-creation.

The shattering of the vessels is, in a sense, the Kabbalah's unique idiom for talking about what the Buddhists refer to as life's essential impermanence. As soon as something is created, its dissolution is already at hand. The vessels of creation, the finite forms created to house the infinite, are always imperfect and impermanent. They must inevitably shatter to make room for the next manifestation of divine unfolding. The light of the infinite simply cannot be contained and limited by any finite form, and so by shattering, the vessels of creation continually allow more light to be revealed. And just when things seem most broken and shattered, that is when healing or tikkun begins.

Everything in this world including ourselves, our intimate relationships with friends and family, all life on earth, according to Luria, is essentially a shattered vessel, splintered into many pieces. The work of tikkun olam, or universal repair, is to join the shattered pieces of the whole back together, so that the unique sparks of light and truth may shine forth from each part.

So whether we focus on integrating the disparate parts of our individual being—what psychoanalysis aims to accomplish by making the unconscious conscious—or whether we work on transcending our sense of separateness from one another, we are participating in this work of tikkun. When each detail or fragment of creation is allowed to reveal its unique attributes within the framework of a unified whole, the very purpose of creation is fulfilled. The light of the Infinite One finds a dwelling place in the lower realms in the infinite variation of creation. All people, in their very uniqueness, are holy vessels for the light of the infinite; and creation, in all its multiplicity, reveals the many faces of the Divine One.

The healing work of tikkun ultimately involves fine-tuning the delicate balance between light and vessel. If the light of the Ein Sof is the energy that unites all life and the vessel is that which makes us unique, then the balancing of light and vessel is about living harmoniously with the polarities of oneness and separateness, infinite and finite, spirit and matter, chaos and order. Our job is to transform ourselves and all creation into a vessel that is spacious and transparent enough to contain the light and love of the infinite.

The Shattered Vessels

A Myth for Our Times

The myth of the shattered vessels seems particularly relevant in our times, when so many people on the planet are experiencing a profound sense of dislocation. Today it's not just Jewish people who feel rootless and dislocated. Countless communities and ethnic groups from around the world have been forced to flee their homelands as a result of war, famine, economic hardship, and persecution. Family members frequently live separated from one another by continents and cultures. If you walk through the streets of practically any big city in the world, you will be struck by the colorful mixes of ethnic groups and neighborhoods. In America today, it feels as though we are rapidly becoming a nation of exiles, much as Israel has, for the past fifty or so years, been home to an ingathering of exiles from nearly every corner of the world. One can only hope that this great mixing of cultures will lead to a time when the One will be recognized in the many. And as each group brings its special customs, languages, music, spices, and what the kabbalists would call "holy sparks" from their countries of origin, the shattered fragments of the original divine vessels will be reconfigured.

But beyond the realm of geographical exile, so many of us today experience a sense of psychological exile. Our lives feel fragmented, frenetically paced, and out of touch with our deepest values and truths, and we feel disconnected from our spiritual and emotional center. In a sense, the holy sparks of our own souls are in exile.

How can we begin to gather up and reintegrate our own fragmented parts? And how can we create a greater sense of wholeness, meaning, and coherence in our personal and communal lives, even when they feel broken and fragmented? These are some of the questions that will be addressed in the next two chapters as we continue to examine Luria's creation-healing myth and other wisdom teachings from the Kabbalah.

Daily Spiritual Practice

The *Tallit,* or Prayer Shawl

Having a daily spiritual practice can help us become more aligned with Spirit. One that I find particularly helpful is to begin each day with personal prayer and meditation while wrapped in a tallit, or prayer shawl. The tallit is a symbol both of divine protection and of divine light. When we wrap ourselves in a tallit, we remind ourselves that we, too, are beings of light, part of the Or Ein Sof, the light of the infinite that fills all creation. The tallit can help us concentrate, block out outside distractions, and focus our awareness inward.

The tallit is an aid to remembrance of God-consciousness. Many different mystical meanings have been associated with the ritual fringes, or *tzitzit,* that hang from the four corners of the tallit. One teaching suggests that the eight strands that hang from each corner of the tallit symbolize the presence of the infinite in this finite world, the number eight (drawn sideways) being a symbol of infinity (∞). Just as the fringes extend beyond the garment, the tzitzit point us beyond the finite borders of the garment to that which is beyond. The Hebrew word *tzitzit* itself suggests vision—*leha'tzitz* means to catch a glimpse or to peek. Wrapped in the tallit, we seek to catch a glimpse of that which is beyond our ordinary finite vision.

Before putting on the tallit, we traditionally recite a blessing, along with passages from Psalms 104 and 36, which speak of God as being robed in light and a source of protection. When we pray or meditate wrapped in a tallit, we are reminded that we are essentially beings of light, and we feel surrounded and protected by the light and love of the Infinite One.

Here is the traditional blessing, along with some passages from these psalms:

> Bless the Lord, O my soul. Lord my God, You are
> very great; You are robed in glory and majesty. You
> wrap yourself in a garment of light; You spread out
> the heavens like a curtain. . . .
> You are a Source of Blessing, Infinite One, whose
> presence fills creation. You have made us holy with
> the mitzvot by enjoining us to enwrap ourselves in
> the fringed garment.
>
> How precious is Your loving-kindness, O God.
> Humankind can take refuge under your protective
> wings. . . . In Your light we see light.

MEDITATION

Becoming a Vessel of Light

Take a few minutes to relax and become centered by paying attention to your breath. Notice any tensions, tightness, or holdings in your body. As you deepen into a state of relaxation, allow yourself to breathe effortlessly. With each in-breath imagine you are breathing in the divine out-breath, and with each out-breath imagine you are sending your breath back to its source in the divine.

Now imagine that a river of white light flows from the heavens down to the crown of your head, where it enters your body and begins to fill you with light, filling every organ and indeed every cell of your body with radiance and warmth, bringing healing energy to your entire body and your entire being. As this light fills you, see yourself as a radiant and luminous being of light. Now imagine you are also surrounded by light in all directions, so that you are both filled with light and surrounded by light.

Let yourself bask in the light of the infinite, the Or Ein Sof, and feel your body becoming lighter and lighter as you rest in the radiance of God's loving presence.

(Optional for healing.) Now let yourself also become a channel for healing, allowing yourself to both receive and send healing energy out into the universe. You may wish to picture a person or persons to whom you wish to send healing energy. As you hold them in your mind and heart, share your light with them. Send them healing energy through the light emanating from your hands and fingertips. Let yourself both receive and send blessings for a complete healing (*"refuat ha'nefesh urefuat ha'guf "*—a healing of body and soul).

As you bring this meditation to a close, become aware once more of your breath and the boundaries of your body, the gentle rise and fall of your chest, your presence in the room where you are sitting. Then gently open your eyes . . .

The Unbroken

There is a brokenness
out of which comes the unbroken,
a shatteredness out of which blooms the unshatterable.
There is a sorrow
beyond all grief which leads to joy
and a fragility
out of whose depths emerges strength.

There is a hollow space
too vast for words
through which we pass with each loss,
out of whose darkness we are sanctioned into being.

There is a cry deeper than all sound
whose serrated edges cut the heart
as we break open
to the place inside
which is unbreakable
and whole,
while learning to sing.

—RASHANI

The Broken Tablets
of Sinai
Embracing Imperfection

We should find perfect existence through imperfect
existence.
—*Suzuki Roshi*

Everything that we are in a positive sense is by virtue
of some limitation. And this being limited, this being
crippled, is what is called destiny, life. That which is
missing in life, that which oppresses us, forms the
fabric of life and maintains us within it.
—*Emily Dickinson*

Rebbe Nachman of Breslov was a master
storyteller. Though many of his tales appear to be fabulous fairy tales,
they are, in fact, mystical parables alluding to the secrets of the Kabbalah. In the following tale known as "The Menorah of Defects,"
Rebbe Nachman offers an interesting interpretation of the myth of
the shattered vessels.

A young boy went off into the world and returned after many
years to his father's house after becoming a master artisan, specializ-
ing in the crafting of ritual candelabra, or menorahs. Claiming to be
the most skilled menorah maker in all the land, he asked his father
to invite all the other artisans in town to come and view his prize
menorah. The father did this, and to his surprise, the town's artisans

were not entirely pleased with what they saw in the menorah; in fact, each of them found fault with it. But when asked what they found unpleasing about the menorah, they each found something different in it that bothered them. They simply could not agree on what its defect was. In fact, what one person found defective in it another found to be its most beautiful feature!

The father turned to his son and asked for an explanation, at which point the son replied, "By this have I shown my great skill. For I have revealed to each one his own defect, since each of these defects was actually in the one who perceived it. It was these defects that I incorporated into my creation, for I made this menorah only from defects. Now I will begin its restoration."[1]

In this tale, the menorah is a symbol of creation—its seven branches corresponding to the seven days and seven divine emanations, the original vessels through which creation came into being. In portraying the menorah as made of defects, Rebbe Nachman is suggesting that the shattering of the vessels was not so much an "accident" but part of God's creative process. The broken shards were the necessary raw materials from which this world of multiplicity was fashioned. Shevira was an inevitable outcome of creating an embodied universe, as error is an inevitable part of living. The tale also suggests that God created a flawed universe in order to give every creature a role in its restoration. This world, like the menorah made of defects, was created with a basic faultiness, so that perfection might be reached through imperfection, or as the Zohar suggests, that light might be revealed through darkness. Each of us was created with some deficit or character flaw we need to fix in ourselves—our own inner chamber of darkness. Through the work of tikkun ha'nefesh (soul-healing/character refinement) we illuminate the "dark" and uninhabitable places within our souls so that our defects ultimately become the cracks or openings through which our inner light can shine forth into this world. And by seeking out the holy sparks, or goodness, that exists in all things—in all times, in all places, and in every person—we participate in the collective work of tikkun, or restoration, enabling the broken, imperfect vessels of creation to reveal the light of the infinite.

Rebbe Nachman's parable of the menorah maker adds another dimension to the Lurianic myth of creation—namely, that we were created in order to be a lamp for the divine. The seven-branched menorah, the Kabbalah's symbol of the tree of life, represents God's gift of existence to us. We are all part of God's menorah. All creation exists in order to receive the light of the infinite and shine it back to its source.

But first we must reckon with the fact that the world, ourselves included, is constructed with defects—that imperfection is part of the very fabric of creation. And if God can make a big mistake that ultimately gives rise to the possibility of tikkun, or healing and redemption, then perhaps we, too, can find ways to be holy "fixers" in this imperfect life of ours. As Rebbe Nachman of Breslov used to say to his Hasidim: "Know that whatever you break, you can fix."

The Broken Tablets

The broken tablets were also carried in an ark.
In so far as they represented everything shattered
everything lost, they were the law of broken things,
the leaf torn from the stem in a storm, a cheek touched
in fondness once but now the name forgotten.
How they must have rumbled, clattered on the way
even carried so carefully through the waste land,
how they must have rattled around until the pieces
broke into pieces, the edges softened
crumbling, dust collected at the bottom of the ark
ghosts of old letters, old laws. In so far
as a law broken is still remembered
these laws were obeyed. And in so far as memory
preserves the pattern of broken things
these bits of stone were preserved
through many journeys and ruined days
even, they say, into the promised land.

—Rodger Kamenetz

Healing and mending the broken and shattered pieces of reality is a theme that repeats itself over and over again in Jewish lore, much like a musical refrain played successively by different instruments in an orchestra, each one lending its unique interpretation to the melody. Variations on the theme appear in biblical, midrashic, and kabbalistic myth, as well as in Jewish ritual and custom.

Luria's myth of the shattered vessels is actually an echo of an earlier biblical myth—the myth of the broken tablets of Sinai, the original tablets of the law that Moses shattered at the scene of the golden calf. In this myth about failed beginnings and second chances, we learn about the power of forgiveness and the wisdom that can be gained as we learn from our initial failures.

Fifty days after leaving Egypt, while encamped at the foot of Mount Sinai, the entire Israelite nation, a nation of newly freed slaves, was graced with a collective spiritual awakening. According to legend, at the break of dawn on the fiftieth day following the Exodus, a deep stillness and silence descended on Mount Sinai. This silence was unlike any other the people had ever experienced. In its wake the entire Israelite nation collectively perceived the essential oneness and interconnectedness of all being. Encamped at the foot of the mountain, say the rabbis, "as one person with one heart,"[2] they simultaneously heard and saw the voice of the divine as it clothed itself in the words of the Decalogue. At this moment, according to the midrash, "No bird chirped, no fowl fluttered, no ox lowed, the angels did not fly, the Seraphim did not utter the Kedusha [sanctification prayer], the sea did not roar, the creatures did not speak; the universe was silent and mute. And the voice came forth 'I am the Infinite (YHVH), your God.'"[3]

The revelation at Mount Sinai marked the climax of the Exodus and, according to legend, was its very purpose, for Israel was redeemed from Egypt in order to receive the Torah and bear witness to God's oneness and presence within creation. Everything that occurred until that moment, including the exile and enslavement as well as the miraculous redemption, was simply preparation for the revelation of the divine word, or *dibbur,* at Sinai.

But just as the primordial light revealed at creation shattered the vessels created to contain it, the revelation at Mount Sinai proved to be a moment of divine illumination too intense for its earthly recipients. According to legend, the Israelites heard only the silent Hebrew letter *aleph* of the initial divine utterance—*Anochi* (I am)—before their souls left their bodies. In essence, they died, or you might say their physical vessels shattered when they heard/saw the word of God! This death, the legend tells us, was temporary, for a host of angels immediately descended from the heavens to resuscitate the Israelites by sprinkling a dew of redemption upon them. In the words of an ancient midrash:

> When the word of God went forth from the mouth of the Holy One of Blessing . . . sparks and lightning went forth . . . and when Israel heard the word spoken from the mouth of the Holy One of Blessing, they ran and retreated a distance of twelve miles and their souls left them, as it says [in the Song of Songs] "my soul departed with his utterance. . . ." What did the Holy One of Blessing do? He brought down the dew of redemption with which the dead will be revived in the messianic future.[4]

In its uniquely metaphoric style, this midrash is teaching us about the nature of spiritual awakenings, which are often first experienced as a death or mortal blow to the ego, as the modern-day mystic Andrew Harvey describes in his autobiographical account of his own spiritual awakening. "There is a violent beauty," Harvey writes, "in revelation that the soul loves but the ego fears as death."[5] It is a death, however, that also brings life, for as one dies to a sense of oneself as separate, one enters into proper alignment with the totality that is God. In mystical terms, this is paradoxically when true healing occurs.[6] At moments of spiritual awakening, we realize we are not only who we thought we were—an individual consciousness or separate self who lives within the boundaries we call "I"—but also part of an ineffable unity. For the Israelites, the revelation at Mount Sinai was such a transformative moment of awakening.

But being spiritual novices, the Israelites were unprepared for the intensity of the vision with which they were graced, and as a result they were unable to hold on to it or integrate its significance. They were like a person who sees beyond the illusion of separation under the influence of a psychedelic drug but is unable to incorporate that vision into ordinary life after the effects of the drug have worn off. In fact, the Israelites were left feeling confused and terrified by what they perceived. So when Moses tarried on the mountaintop, they panicked and sought reassurance in one of the familiar, concrete, man-made idols of their past, the golden calf. The nameless, formless, infinite God of being and becoming that spoke to them out of the emptiness or no-thingness of the desert was simply too frightening to grasp. When Moses then returned at the end of forty days, he found the people worshiping the golden calf, and instinctively (perhaps also impulsively) he threw down the tablets of the law that he had received, shattering them to bits.

But something amazing happened after Moses broke the tablets. According to legend, the Israelites proceeded to gather up the broken pieces. Realizing their mistake and what they had lost, they collected the fragmented remains of their mystical vision, and they began to mourn their loss and repent their folly. In fact, they spent the next eighty days in a process of repentance that would ultimately earn them divine forgiveness. On what was to become the first Yom Kippur, or Day of Atonement, the Israelites were given a second set of tablets and a second chance, as described in the biblical narrative following the story of the golden calf: "YHVH said to Moses: 'Carve two tablets of stone like the first, and I will inscribe upon the tablets the words that had been on the tablets that you shattered'" (Exodus 34:1). According to legend, the Israelites carried the two sets of tablets—the broken and the whole—around with them in an ark for the rest of their desert journey. Both sets of tablets were taken into the Promised Land, say the rabbis, where they were kept side by side until they were eventually placed in the holy temple in Jerusalem.

So what does it mean that the Torah was given not once but twice? What was different about these two revelations? And what spiritual lessons can we learn from the fact that the Israelites gathered up and carried the broken tablets with them on their journey?

The myth of the two tablets suggests that mistakes and even failures are a natural, inevitable part of development. In fact, failure is often a gateway through which we must pass in order to receive our greatest gifts. It was only after Israel's greatest single act of folly—namely, worshiping the golden calf—that they were able to truly receive and hold on to the gift of Torah, or spiritual illumination. Sometimes we learn to appreciate life's gifts only after we have lost them. If, however, we are lucky enough to be given a second chance, with the wisdom we have acquired through our experience of failure, we learn how to cherish and hold on to what we are given.

The first tablets of Sinai did not endure, say certain biblical commentators, because the Israelites had not developed sufficiently strong inner vessels to hold on to their powerful light. The first revelation at Sinai, given as a gift of divine grace, was simply not sustainable. Ultimately, the Israelites had to do the inner work of repentance to strengthen their own immature vessels. This inner work, referred to in the Kabbalah as *itoruta dile'tata,* arousal from below, enabled them to earn, through their own efforts, what was initially given as a gift of divine grace, what the rabbis call *itoruta dile'eila,* an arousal from above.

A contemporary parallel can be drawn from the fact that people cannot make constructive use of insights and early memories retrieved in therapy unless they have adequate internal psychic structure. Without the necessary psychological capacities, momentary insights are often forgotten or misunderstood. In fact, when the ego is not strong enough to bear certain psychic contents, their availability to memory can be more harmful than useful.

The two revelations at Sinai can also be seen as symbolizing the inevitable stages we go through in our spiritual development. The first tablets, like the initial visions we have for our lives, frequently shatter, especially when they are based on naively idealistic assumptions. Our first marriages or first careers may fail to live up to their initial promise. We may join communities or follow spiritual teachers and paths that disappoint or even betray us. Our very conceptions of

God and our assumptions about the meaning of faith may shatter as we bump up against the morally complex and often contradictory aspects of the real world. Yet if we learn from our mistakes and find ways to pick up the broken pieces of shattered dreams, we can go on to re-create our lives out of the rubble of our initial failures. And ultimately, we become wiser and more complex as our youthful ideals are replaced by more realistic and sustainable ones.

As we move through the life cycle, we will continually embody and disembody life structures. We will shed old skins and grow new ones. The first "vessels," or "life structures," we embody, by necessity, must shatter in order to make room for the continual growth of the self.

If the two sets of tablets represent developmental stages we go through in our spiritual and emotional development, the first tablets correspond to our youthful dreams and ideals. Not having been modified by "reality," they are often not sustainable precisely because of their purity and idealism. The second tablets represent our more mature visions and dreams, which perhaps are not as lofty as our youthful visions and dreams but are more viable. The myth of the broken tablets teaches us that it is important to hold on to the beauty and essence of dreams we once held dear, for our initial visions contain the seed of our purest essence. Gathering up the broken pieces suggests that we must salvage the essential elements of our youthful dreams and ideals and carry them forward on our journeys so that we can find a way to realize them in a more grounded fashion. For ultimately the whole and the broken live side by side in us all, as our broken dreams and shattered visions exist alongside our actual lives.

In addition to representing the stages we go through in spiritual development, the myth of the two tablets also serves as a paradigm for the stages we go through in our intimate love relationships. Like the first "big bang" of Sinai, first awakenings of love, human or divine, are often so powerful that they knock us off our feet. In the magical intoxication of new love, our usual boundaries and defenses are temporarily taken down, and we experience an expanded sense of self. But as time passes, we begin to take the "miracle" of love for granted. This is typically when our needs for autonomy reassert themselves, along with our age-old defense mechanisms. Our early "romantic idealizations" of our partner are dislodged by reality and ideally are replaced by more integrated and realistic images of him or her. No longer seen as quite so perfect, partners then have to work at creating an enduring relationship that takes each other's strengths and weaknesses into account.

In spiritual practice as in romantic love, our motivation is often strongest during the initial honeymoon phase. But over time, the excitement and "high" generated by our spiritual awakening tend to dim, and boredom and habit tend to set in. The initial magic we may have experienced tends to pass. This is when the real challenge begins and we have to work at sustaining our commitment to a spiritual practice.

As the first stage of romantic love must inevitably yield to a more integrated and grounded relationship, our spiritual development begins to deepen when we commit ourselves to the difficult work of the everyday—of listening for the hidden voice of the divine in all the mundane aspects of everyday living. What we first get as a gift of divine grace must later be earned through the hard daily work of committed practice.

The first big bang of Sinai, in all its grandeur, could not endure. Though far less dramatic than the first revelation, it was the second revelation that endured. Like Elijah's vision at the same mountain centuries later (I Kings 19:17), the second tablets were revealed through the more modest "still, small voice" of the divine rather than the deafening and blinding blasts of thunder and lightning—the *kolay kolot* (the mother of all voices) that characterized the first revelation. "Nothing is more beautiful than modesty,"[7] says the midrash about the second revelation, for, ultimately, it was the second revelation that inscribed itself not just upon the tablets but also upon the hearts of the Israelites.

Embracing Imperfection

The shattered vessels and broken tablets clearly echo one another. Both stories teach us about the role of failure and forgiveness in our lives. As a therapist, I became particularly fascinated with these two myths when I hit midlife. Both in my personal life and in my clinical work I found that they illuminated a key issue my clients, students, and I were dealing with—namely, coming to terms with imperfection.

In my personal life I was struggling to make peace with the long-term ramifications of my own youthful folly. The mistake I had made in my first marriage at age twenty-one came back to haunt me in midlife when my grown daughter, Miriam, with whom I am very close, returned to Jerusalem, her birthplace, to live. Though I shouldn't have been so surprised by her decision to live in Israel, given all the encouragement I had given her over the years to embrace Jewish values and spend time in the Holy Land, still, I felt totally unprepared for the heartbreak I was experiencing. I just couldn't accept that our lives would go on at a distance and we would not be able to intimately share in each other's joys and sorrows.

There was, however, a strangely comforting element of cosmic irony in my daughter's return to Jerusalem. Just as I had left my mother heartbroken when I went to Israel at the age of seventeen, my daughter, who was not much older than I had been when I left home, was leaving me to find her own unique spiritual path. If ever I was convinced that God has a sense of humor, it was when these proverbial tables turned. Adding to the irony of the situation, Miriam also fell under the spell of the religious world in Jerusalem, as I had done some twenty years prior.

Cosmic irony aside, when Miriam left, I felt as though my life would never be whole again. Even though I was blessed in so many areas of my life, I now felt like a shattered vessel myself, and I realized that in order to find peace of mind I was going to have to make peace with imperfection.

What helped me most in coming to terms with my own predicament was just knowing I was not alone in my experience. As I meditated with my students and sat with my "broken piece," I came to understand that each of us has something in ourselves or in our lives that is incomplete or broken. I don't know anyone for whom this is not true on some level. One friend of mine has a wonderful marriage and satisfying work but is childless. Another friend has three wonderful children but suffers from multiple health problems. A colleague of mine recently achieved professional fame beyond her wildest dreams, yet she is single and lonely, while another colleague has a wonderful relationship yet continually has to deal with the debilitating effects of a car accident she had in her late teens. The list goes on.

These kinds of problems are inescapable. And over time, the broken pieces and shattered dreams we carry around with us only increase. And we just have to let go of our need for things to be perfect; otherwise we are going to suffer additional pain on top of whatever difficulties we are already experiencing. Perfectionism compounds our problems because instead of just dealing with the painful effects of what is missing or broken in our lives, it also causes us to suffer from our own inability to accept the imperfectness of things.

In my work as a therapist, I have been struck by just how many people are plagued with perfectionism. All too often I find myself sounding like a broken record, telling my clients that they would be a lot happier if they could just let go of their need for things to be perfect. This concept seems so simple, yet it eludes so many of us. Most perfectionists don't even realize that they are afflicted by this condition, for it can be masked by an array of symptoms, including depression, anxiety, procrastination, and excessive defensiveness, as well as underachievement and overachievement. While some perfectionists become chronic overachievers, never satisfied with themselves no matter how much they achieve, others become underachievers, paralyzed by their own unrealistic expectations of themselves. Instead of compromising their ideals, they prefer to spend their lives hiding out in a self-protective cocoon, never really testing their capabilities. And then there are procrastinators, who somehow strike a compromise with perfection. Since their "very best" is unattainable, procrastination serves to limit their unrealistic, grandiose expectations of themselves. By waiting till the last moment to do things, they can let themselves off the hook for not doing their "very best," since time inevitably runs out on them. Unfortunately, procrastinators never give themselves an opportunity to achieve their full potential because procrastination undermines their best efforts.

The tendency toward perfectionism seems to come from several sources. To begin with, parents can unwittingly instill perfectionism in their children by constantly placing unrealistic expectations on them, or by being excessively critical and not praising them enough. In the absence of sufficient love and praise, children often grow up thinking that they need to be "great" or "special" to receive love and approval. And when such children's best efforts are still not met with love or praise, they often conclude that they simply have not yet reached the necessary level of perfection. As their sought-after "ideal self" continues to elude them like an ever-receding, unattainable horizon, perfectionism sets in.

Perfectionism is also reinforced by our pop culture. The media and movie industry, for instance, constantly bombard us with unrealistic images of how we ought to look or how life ideally ought to be. We also are fed unrealistic images of romantic love by Hollywood's superficial portrayal of fairy-tale relationships that hardly ever go beyond the first stage of love. Rarely are we shown the nitty-gritty ups and downs and complexities of long-term relationships, and so we have no map to guide us through the real-life struggles we inevitably face in love. Real life is hardly ever as perfect as it is in the movies or media. And the sooner we learn to make peace with imperfection, the happier we are going to be.

THE MIDLIFE JOURNEY OF HEALING

In addition to not living up to our own unrealistic images of ourselves, throughout our lives each of us will inevitably have to mourn the loss of those possibilities and promises that we simply chose not to actualize. Every decision we make in our lives means that we must let go of certain other options and potentialities that we may have held on to dearly in our youth.

These feelings of loss often become particularly pronounced at midlife, when we acutely feel the finiteness of our time on earth. Thus, to successfully navigate the midlife passage, we have to come to terms with the losses that resulted from each important choice we made earlier in life. Midlife is a time when we must revise our old ideals and move on to re-create ourselves. We must reclaim parts we have lost, while at the same time mourn what is over. It is a time to accept that we cannot possibly, in one lifetime, do or be it all.

For example, those of us who chose to have children when we were young may have limited our choices in other areas of life, while those of us who chose not to have children may have had tremendous freedom to develop ourselves as individuals, yet at midlife we may come to regret or mourn the absence of children in our lives. Midlife is a time when we must accept the long-term consequences of choices we made earlier in our lives. We may have to come to terms with the lasting effects of a divorce or make peace with the imperfection of being a single parent or part of a blended family. We may have to accept being childless, or finally decide to adopt a child on our own.

Many of the people I work with in therapy are struggling to make peace with the fact that their lives have turned out far different from what they had always imagined for themselves. Their real lives don't match up with the idealized images they still carry inside them from childhood and early adulthood. Unfortunately, those who cling to their idealized images from the past and refuse to mourn their loss often remain emotionally and spiritually frozen, their ideals intact but their lives far from ideal. They remain more committed to their fantasies about life than to their actual lives. In contrast, those people who are able to mourn the loss of their unrealized dreams are more equipped to pick up the pieces and renew themselves at midlife. They then can go on to thrive in the second half of life.

John, for instance, had dreamed of being a singer-songwriter throughout his adolescence and early college years, but when he decided to go to medical school upon finishing college, he abandoned his artistic dreams. Throughout the years, John tried to keep up with his guitar playing, but music clearly took a back seat in his life. His medical career simply demanded too much of his time and attention for him to stay focused on his music.

When John came to see me, he was going through somewhat of a midlife crisis. Though he wasn't clinically depressed, he was having sad feelings about many of the decisions he had made earlier in life. He was particularly regretful that music was no longer an important part of his life. He felt as though an important aspect of his core being was dying. It wasn't that he wanted to give up practicing medicine; he simply was unhappy about having sacrificed such an important part of himself in order to become a doctor.

In our work together I spoke with John about the myth of the broken tablets and how we inevitably have to sacrifice aspects of our youthful ideals and visions as we make important life choices. Viewing his situation through the lens of this myth opened up a new way of thinking about the developmental tasks he was now facing in midlife. When I suggested that he could gather up more of the broken pieces of his youthful dreams, John felt encouraged to create more time and space in his life for music. Though he might never become the professional musician he had once dreamed of being, he realized he could enjoy his musical talents more than he had been doing. This compromise, though imperfect, enabled John to make peace with the important choices he had made in his life while preserving aspects of his youthful dreams.

In contrast to John, many people I know prefer to do nothing about a problem rather than accept an imperfect solution or compromise. If something can't be done just right, they simply won't attempt to do it. I know many perfectionists, for example, who choose to live in complete chaos rather than straighten their homes partially or imperfectly. Their harsh inner critics simply won't allow them to do a less than perfect job at anything. Ironically, some of the messiest people I know are closet perfectionists.

Like John, Sandy also came to see me with a midlife reckoning; however, she was much more depressed than John about the compromises that life was demanding of her. On the surface, it seemed as though Sandy had everything that most people dream of. She was married and had two children and a successful career as a schoolteacher, yet she was unhappy with almost every area of her life. What her problem boiled down to was a struggle to come to terms with the ways her current life did not match up with the fantasies and idealized images she had of herself while growing up.

Sandy was the daughter of wealthy and highly successful parents. She had been groomed throughout her privileged childhood, adolescence, and young adulthood to work hard, succeed, and be financially comfortable. She had indeed been highly successful throughout her school years, graduating at the top of her class and going on to complete a master's degree in education. So long as she had been able to devote herself completely to her work and studies, Sandy felt happy and successful.

Things began to change, however, when Sandy married and had children. Balancing career and family, she found that she was unable to progress in her career as rapidly as she had hoped. One of her children had special needs and demanded a great deal of Sandy's time and attention. Instead of forgiving and accepting herself for needing to slow her career goals down, Sandy became angry and frustrated and felt unable to make peace with the compromises she had to make. As she realized that she could no longer be at the top of her field and at the same time be the good parent she aspired to be, Sandy gradually became depressed. Her husband, whom she loved very much, also did not live up to her grand expectations. Though he worked very hard in his job as a teacher, he was unable to provide the kind of financial security that she had grown accustomed to in her youth. Having to live within a tight budget was not something Sandy was prepared for. As the years passed, nothing felt good enough for Sandy. Though from the perspective of others around her, Sandy had everything, she was unhappy with herself, her home, her husband, and her life. Her need for perfection was destroying her.

In therapy, I repeatedly spoke to Sandy about how she was spoiling her life by always comparing it to some imagined "ideal." Finally, using the Kabbalah's metaphor of the shattered vessels, I tried to help her accept the notion that imperfection is built into the very fabric of creation. When I described the myth of the shattered vessels, something began to click for her. The myth seemed to touch her deeply, opening up the possibility of living more gracefully with life's imperfectness. As Sandy's fortieth birthday was approaching, we began planning a birthday ritual together that would be based on the imagery of the shattered vessels. The kavannah, or intention, of the ritual would be letting go of perfection.

The ritual, which Sandy planned to enact the week before her fortieth birthday, involved writing down on a scroll all her childhood hopes and dreams for how she imagined her life was going to be. She would then place the scroll in a beautiful ceramic vase that she had owned for many years and deeply treasured, bring these objects to therapy, read what she had written, and then smash the vase and burn the scroll.

Sandy spent a few weeks working on the scroll in preparation for the ritual. When she finally brought it in, we spent some time first talking about her childhood hopes and dreams. Then, as Sandy smashed the ceramic vase and burned the scroll, she was overcome by a tremendous wave of grief. Through the ritual she was finally able to face her grief over the way life had turned out for her. Smashing the vase, something she had been deeply attached to for a long time, became a powerful symbol of letting go of the past and allowing life to bring change. In grieving over her lost hopes and dreams, Sandy began to feel more ready to accept her real, though imperfect, life. She even decided to take the broken pieces of the vase home with her in order to make them into a mosaic that she could use as a reminder, whenever she needed reminding, of the wisdom of the shattered vessels.

Sandy will probably continue to struggle with perfectionism all her life. Therapeutic rituals are no panacea, and certainly no substitute for long-term work on oneself. Yet they do have the power to awaken us to new insights, and long after their enactment they continue to leave an imprint on our psyches, reminding us of moments of profound realization.

HEALING RITUAL 1
The Shattered Vessels

As a therapist and as a Jewish educator, I have experimented with different ways of using the myth of the shattered vessels as the basis

for therapeutic rituals and other creative processes, both with individual people and with groups. Ritual can be a powerful means of getting in touch with the deeper meaning of myths and symbols—of
going beyond the words and ideas to the very experience of the myth.
It is not easy to do this with kabbalistic myth, however, without running the risk of trivializing something that is deeply esoteric and
mysterious. The ritual described below is not meant in any way to
diminish the profound meaning of the myth of the shattered vessels.
It simply is an example of how we can personalize myth in a way
that is deeply healing.

The ritual I am about to describe took place as part of a workshop
I taught on Jewish meditation and healing. It used the myth of the
shattered vessels to help the class members come to terms with and
heal what was "shattered" or broken in their lives. As you read this
section, you might think about ways to devise a ritual of your own,
either by yourself or with friends and family.

In planning this group ritual, I felt very much like a wounded
healer. I knew that everyone in the group had some primal wound
that they were there to heal, and I sensed that my own experience of
loss was enabling me to craft a ritual that was about something larger
than any one of our stories yet spoke to each of us in a personal way.

The ritual began with a group meditation on the moment before
creation—the time before time—when all things were one and
whole. After a period of silent meditation we came into a standing
prayer circle, and for several minutes we chanted together the Hebrew word *echad,* which means *one.* Then, as a group, we smashed a
large earthenware pot that was wrapped in a cloth. We then opened
up the cloth and each of us picked up a broken piece, sat down, and
meditated once more, this time on that part of our lives that felt
broken or fragmented. People were guided to use their fragment of
the earthenware pot to focus on their sense of brokenness or woundedness. They were instructed to hold it with compassion and forgiveness, knowing that brokenness is just a part of life, something we all
share, part of the very fabric of existence.

After this time spent in silence, participants were given an opportunity to share with one another what they had experienced during

the second meditation. A great number of the participants found that enacting the myth enabled them to access its healing power. Several described feeling that "somehow, being wounded seemed to be less of a problem—part of the nature of things." One woman described feeling that "it was easier to embrace my pain with forgiveness and compassion knowing that we are all in it together. We are all just broken pieces of the whole."

Participants were encouraged to put their broken piece of pottery in a special place of honor in their home, such as a personal altar, or to use it in a piece of artwork such as a mosaic. I carry my broken piece around with me in my guitar case, where it serves as a frequent reminder to me to be compassionate with myself in relation to my own imperfections.

HEALING RITUAL 2

Reassembling the Broken Pieces

In preparing to lead a Jewish meditation and spirituality retreat in preparation for Yom Kippur, I devised the following ritual as a way to connect with the archetypal healing power of atonement (at-one-ment!). Using the mythic imagery of the broken and whole tablets, the ritual provided a hands-on experience of how we heal by bringing the "broken pieces" back into relationship with the whole.

In preparation for the ritual I spent weeks collecting hundreds of pieces of mosaic tiles, miniature mirrors, stones, polished glass, and jewels. I have to admit I became a bit obsessed preparing for this ritual—wherever I went, I found myself looking for broken shards! On Saturday night, following *havdallah,* the closing ritual of the Sabbath, we gathered as a group around a large slab of clay shaped in the form of the tablets from Sinai. With drummers playing gentle rhythms in the background, participants, in groups of four, silently took turns embedding the broken pieces of mirror, polished glass, and mosaic tile into the clay. The kavannah, or spiritual intention, for the ritual was to reassemble the broken pieces of our lives and begin to reintegrate the exiled and rejected parts of ourselves back into the totality of our being.

In addition to the powerful sense of group cohesion that we experienced in the process of enacting this ritual, we created a striking piece of art. Working together and building on one another's creativity added to the profound sense of self-integration that we each were experiencing. At the end, the tablets held all of our imperfections and broken hearts together in one beautiful piece. We each left that weekend feeling less lonely, knowing that our private pain is a reflection of our common humanity and our commonality with divinity itself.

3

THE WISDOM OF AYIN (NOTHINGNESS)

Transitions and Spiritual Awakening

Before a thing is transformed into something else, it
must come to the level of Nothingness.
—*Maggid of Mezerich*

Only a heart that has burned empty is capable of love.
—*Irina Tweedie*

From the moment of our conception to the
instant of our death, the ever-flowing current of life leads us through
an unending series of changes.[1] One could say that the very essence
of life is change or transition. But change, even when it's for the
better, is not always welcome or easy to cope with. We may yearn for
a change in our lives, yet when it comes, we often panic and wish we
could return to the way things were.

Part of the challenge of change is that with every major life transition we inevitably pass through a time of darkness and unknowing—a liminal, or in-between, space where we no longer are who we
used to be yet haven't become who we are becoming. At the same
time that we must face our fear of the unknown, we must also mourn
what has been lost. These in-between times, when we hover between
the old life we are leaving behind and the new one we have yet to

birth, can be frightening and stressful, particularly for people who lack a spiritual reference point for dealing with uncertainty. As anyone who has ever undergone a major life transition knows, they are times of extreme vulnerability, in which we are stripped down to our bare and purest essence. Transitions can be so terrifying that people often prefer to stay stuck in stifling, unhealthy situations rather than make needed changes in their lives and thus be forced to face the terror of the unknown.

Most ancient cultures honored the in-between time as sacred. They marked transitions as a time of retreat from the outer world of "doing" in order to return to the womb of "becoming." By providing sacred time-out for life passages, ancient societies supported their members through these stressful and vulnerable times. Unfortunately, modern society hardly recognizes, let alone provides for, our needs when we are in transition. We are often expected to return to school and function in the external world of work despite whatever inner or outer transition we are undergoing. And if we want to mark an important change in our lives, we typically have to improvise and create our own personal rituals without the support of the community.

Over the years, I have noticed that, with almost uncanny regularity, people who fail to take time out for important transitions become sick or accidentally injure themselves and thus are forced despite themselves to retreat from their ordinary lives. Sickness or injury ends up providing them with an alternative sort of "rite of passage." A client of mine, for instance, spent the two months prior to his fiftieth birthday flat on his back after injuring himself in a tennis match. Injuring himself on the eve of his fiftieth birthday forced him to contemplate the meaning of this important marker of aging with very few distractions. Another person, a friend, badly sprained her ankle the day after signing her divorce papers. With no hiking, biking, or yoga on the agenda for a few months, she slowed down enough from her usual frenetic pace to process the finality of this important ending in her life.

The Jewish mystical tradition contains many rituals, symbols, and spiritual practices that can support those going through a life transition. The myth of the shattered vessels is itself a guide or map of

sorts for transition. Luria's three stages of creation—tzimtzum, shevira, and tikkun—mirror the three stages we inevitably go through as
we evolve from each stage of life to the next. Using Luria's cosmology
myth as a guide to the stages of transition places our individual experience of "becoming" in a larger mythic context. Thus, our personal
struggles no longer seem merely personal; instead we see them as
mirroring sacred processes that occur at all times and all levels of
creation. Through our personal experience of transition, then, we
may come to understand the very mysteries of creation.

Just as creation began with an act of divine withdrawal, or tzimtzum, all classic rites of passage begin with a retreat or withdrawal
from ordinary life. Initiates undergoing a life passage typically move
to a sacred initiation hut, somewhere removed from ordinary tribal
life. Through such a withdrawal, one can begin to disidentify with
one's old life and allow the old self to die. During this time of tzimtzum, we create the emptiness, or womb-of-becoming, within which
new dimensions of the self can emerge.

In classic rites of passage, initiates, after withdrawing from ordinary life, then symbolically enact the death of the old self that they
are undergoing. This might include being buried in the ground for a
period of time or being ritually painted, maimed, or tattooed. These
death and dismemberment rituals let the psyche digest the fact that
change is occurring, that the old self is dying in order to make room
for the new self to emerge. This stage of transition corresponds to
the "shattering of the vessels," or shevira, stage.

That stage is the one where most of us get stuck. We can't allow
ourselves to let go of our old identities before we have a sense of
what comes next. We are afraid to face the unknown abyss that's an
inevitable part of the in-between time of transitions. However, when
we avoid the "void," we may end up feeling empty and depressed or
develop an array of troubling symptoms that result from being stuck.
Ultimately, these symptoms serve a healing purpose, for they give us
the push we need to overcome our inner resistance to change.

The last stage of a rite of passage involves reincorporation; the
initiate reenters the tribe as a new person with a new identity. Corresponding to tikkun, this phase typically includes rituals of rebirth.

For instance, the initiate might immerse herself in a body of water and then emerge from it to symbolize her emergence from the maternal womb of becoming; or he might be given a new name to signify that he has become a brand new person. Following the disintegrative phase of transition, in which one's old self dies, this stage of a transition involves reintegration and new beginnings. It is a time for trying on one's new identity, with its new roles and behaviors.

Using Luria's creation myth as a guide for transitions can be helpful in another way: it allows us to "name" our experience when we face the stress and uncertainty of transition. This can be tremendously reassuring. Knowing we are on a journey that has distinct stages and knowing where we are on the journey can help us find our balance when the very ground on which we have stood is shifting. For instance, knowing we are in the shevira stage of transition may make it easier to accept the feelings of disorientation and grief that frequently accompany this stage of "endings." If we feel a sense of vertigo and dread as our old life structures dissolve, we can be reassured that this stage of shevira or disintegration will be followed by tikkun—a time of healing and reintegration.

THE TRANSFORMATIVE POWER OF AYIN

Meditation can also be very helpful in dealing with the stress and uncertainty of transitions. In taking us past our usual, limited consciousness, meditation teaches us to become comfortable with uncertainty. In deep meditation we encounter a state of "unknowing" that is much like the in-between state we pass through during times of transition.

In kabbalistic meditation this in-between state is often referred to as ayin, or nothing. Ayin is the divine nothingness out of which the world is continually re-created. It is the backdrop and source of all creation—the ground of all being. Much like the Buddhist notion of *bardo,* ayin is neither "this" nor "that" but exists in the open space between things. Ayin can be accessed in those moments of in-betweenness in meditation, between one thought and the next or in the pause between breaths, when we allow ourselves to dissolve into the infinite luminosity of the divine.

Ayin meditation can be particularly helpful during times of transition, for ayin itself is the experience of extreme liminality; indeed, it is often identified by the Kabbalah as the moment in-between being one thing and becoming another. All deeper healing and transformation, according to the Kabbalah, require a surrender to the ayin. As the eighteenth-century Hasidic master Rabbi Dov Baer, also known as the Maggid (preacher) of Mezerich pointed out, "Nothing can be transformed from one thing to another unless it first loses its original identity. Thus, for example, before an egg can become a chicken, it must cease completely to be an egg. Each thing must be nullified before it can become something else. It must be brought to the level of ayin (divine nothingness). Only then can it become something else. And this is how all miracles involving a change in the laws of nature come about. Each thing must first be elevated to the emanation known as ayin, nothingness. Influence then comes from that emanation to produce the miracle."[2]

The Hasidic masters understood that to grow and evolve spiritually and be able to embody the infinite, one must *become* ayin, for only by allowing one's separate sense of self to temporarily dissolve can one become a vessel for the divine nothingness. Thus the Maggid of Mezerich advised his disciples, "Think of yourself as ayin and forget yourself totally. Then you can transcend time, rising to the world of thought, where all is equal: life and death, ocean and dry land. This is not the case when you are attached to the material nature of the world. If you think of yourself as *yesh,* as something, God cannot be clothed in you, for God is infinite, and no vessel can contain God—unless you think of yourself as ayin."[3]

Jewish shamanistic healing practices involve accessing the transformative power of ayin. By meditating on ayin one can return to the time before time, the undifferentiated oneness out of which the multiplicity of creation continually emerges. In this state one can draw down new life and healing energy, as the eighteenth- and nineteenth-century Hasidic master Rabbi Levi Yitzhak of Berditchev, writes:

"When man nullifies his ego completely and attaches his thoughts to ayin, then a new sustenance can flow into all worlds. . . . A person must be so in awe of God that his ego is totally nullified. Only then can he attach himself to ayin. [Divine] sustenance, filled with all goodness, then flows to all worlds."[4]

Levi Yitzhak goes so far as to suggest that matter itself can be transformed alchemically as it passes through the divine crucible of ayin: "When a person gazes at an object, he elevates it into his thought. If his thought is then attached to the [realm of] supernal Thought, he can elevate it [the object] to the [realm of] supernal Thought. From there it can be elevated to the level of nothingness [ayin], where the object becomes absolute nothingness. This person can then lower it once more to the level of Thought, which is some-thingness [*yesh*]. At the end of all levels, he can transform it into gold."[5]

It is only through the dissolution of self, or what is known in Hebrew as *bittul ha'yesh*,[6] that one can heal into an expanded sense of self. Paradoxically, new life is generated through the self-tzimtzum or self-negation of the ayin state.

In surrendering to ayin through spiritual practices such as prayer and meditation, we re-create the primordial womb from which we can be born anew. As the Maggid of Mezerich said, "Ayin is the source of all things, and when one brings anything to its source, one can transform it."[7]

Transitions have the potential to renew and heal us precisely because they put us in touch with the transformative power of the ayin state. The symbolic encounter with death or nonbeing through immersion in ayin gives us access to our full being and thus enables us to become more fully ourselves. Every time we shed an old skin, we are renewed, and with each death of an old self, new capacities can be activated in us.

Transitions also have the power to awaken us to the luminous dimension of existence—the spirit realm. Rabbi Ya'acov Leiner of Izbitz, also known by his Torah commentary as the Beis Ya'acov, spoke about how times of transition are especially conducive to spiritual awakening, expanding our consciousness of the divine. The Beis

Ya'acov then adds, "At the very moment that He brings about a change in time [season], God reveals more of Himself. . . . And so it is with every moment that arises and passes, a great revelation [of Godliness] occurs."[8] For this reason, many Jewish holy days fall during those moments in the yearly cycle when change is in the air. Two of the major pilgrimage holidays—Passover and Sukkot—for example, fall on the spring and fall equinoxes, respectively. On Passover one senses the awakening of nature. As spring emerges out of the bonds of winter and new life is breaking out all around us, Jews reenact the ancestral journey from slavery to freedom. On Sukkot, the last warm days of Indian summer give way to the cool winds and changing colors of autumn. Sitting in the outdoor sukkah, exposed to the elements, one can readily sense the powerful wake-up call that the fall winds of change bring.

Similarly, daily prayer times are fixed to the rising and setting of the sun, the changes from dark to light and back. We may be creatures of habit, but when we perceive change in the world around us, we remember the divine hand moving all reality. Change and transition have the power to awaken us from our habitual slumber. This is why the ancient pilgrimage holidays—Passover, Shavuot, and Sukkot—were times of *aliyah la'regel,* ascent by foot to the Temple in Jerusalem. This ascent (*aliyah*) was both literal and spiritual, for the Hebrew word for foot (*regel*) also implies habit (*hergel*). So an aliyah la'regel suggests the uplifting of that which is "habitual" to a level of conscious action.

MICHAEL'S STORY

Michael, a student of mine who was facing an important life transition, found Jewish mystical teachings on ayin and transformation particularly helpful. In a spiritual guidance session Michael revealed to me that he was going through an identity crisis vis-à-vis his work life. He had been a social worker and had founded a small nonprofit agency where he had worked for over twenty-five years. Though he felt proud of what he had accomplished over the years, he wasn't feeling passionate about his work anymore; in fact, he was actually bored with it. Michael sensed it was time to let go of his professional identity, but he was afraid to do so without having any idea of what he might do next in his life.

Michael was feeling extra pressure to make a decision because the agency he founded was at a turning point, and it needed strong leadership to take it to the next level. Though he felt unprepared to meet this challenge, Michael was being forced to make a decision. He had to either recommit himself to his work or turn the agency over to someone who was prepared to do what was needed. Michael had to make a decision rapidly because if he remained paralyzed by inaction, there was a chance the agency would fall apart.

As we explored his dilemma together, I asked Michael if an image came to mind that captured his current feeling of being stuck. His immediate response was: "It feels as though I am carrying around a dead corpse! Holding on to my old self is like carrying around dead weight that drags me down. No wonder I feel so depressed."

I suggested that perhaps it was time to bury his old self and allow himself to take a break from work altogether. Instead of holding on to a sense of "self-importance" by clinging to a professional identity he no longer wanted, Michael could put his knowledge of Jewish mysticism into practice by being "nobody" in particular for a while— in other words, by embodying ayin. Michael understood what I meant when I made this suggestion, and in response he came up with the idea of taking a sabbatical as a way to renew himself before he figured out what came next.

As Michael began to fantasize about this possibility, he became excited. For years, he had longed to be able to travel and have more time for meditation, reading, and his secret passion, photography. The idea of having time for these interests, as well as simply slowing down the action, was extremely appealing. Michael even began to wonder if he might just find the inspiration to take the next step in his life by turning one or more of these personal passions into a new career.

In our next follow-up session, Michael excitedly announced to me that he had taken steps to turn his position as director of the agency over to his assistant and that he was making plans to go on a personal pilgrimage to holy sites in Israel and India. He intended to travel off-season so that he would not have to plan everything in advance. This in itself was a radical concept for Michael, who prided himself on being an extremely responsible and plan-full person. It felt important to him to enter into this unknown phase of his life not knowing exactly what might come next. Allowing life to unfold one day at a time would be a symbolic act of faith and trust for Michael. Having faith in life and trusting in the future are spiritual qualities that did not come easily to Michael. He recognized, however, that they were going to be indispensable as he continued on his journey.

Despite his trepidation about letting go of his work life, Michael was truly feeling exhilarated by the possibilities that lay ahead. Leaving the familiar turf on which he had stood for the past twenty-five years was no small matter. But using Luria's cosmology myth as a guide for the journey enabled Michael to feel more grounded. By framing his situation in sacred, mythic terms, Michael was more able to accept the mixed feelings that were arising. Michael intuitively understood that by letting go of his job and taking a sabbatical, he was entering a tzimtzum phase in his life. He saw his pilgrimage as a means of withdrawing from the outer world of work to attend to his inner self. He also realized that by shedding his external identity, he was making room for new dimensions of his inner being to emerge. And as he took his first steps into the unknown with faith and trust, Michael felt certain he would discover many new spiritual capacities as he continued on his journey.

As Michael learned from his experience, transitions give us a chance to live in intimate connection with the source of creation—the divine nothingness out of which all creation continually emerges. We simply have to be willing to let ourselves go, again and again, to rest in "not-knowing" in order to be reborn and re-created anew throughout our lives.

Love, Loss, and Spiritual Awakening

While all transitions provide an access point to the sacred realm, the experience of losing a loved one can be a particularly powerful trigger for spiritual awakening. When someone we love disappears, we immediately develop a relationship with the invisible realm. And as we continue to feel connected to someone who is not in the finite world, our connection to the infinite, the God realm, is potentially activated.

In a strange way, our primal wound of separateness often begins to heal when later losses or shatterings awaken in us the desire to be whole once more. Loss, for instance, has a way of nudging us to pay attention to the soul's lovesickness—its longing for reconnection with the divine. Paradoxically, the pain of loss and separation, because it stimulates the yearning for ultimate connection with God, can bring about a deeper healing of our sense of aloneness and separateness. For this reason, loss was frequently the gateway to spiritual awakening for the ancient mystics.

According to legend, the famous thirteenth-century Sufi poet Rumi achieved his profound spiritual awakening after the disappearance and death of his beloved and inspiring teacher-friend Shams. So long as Shams was alive and present, Rumi's love was focused intently and exclusively on him, to the chagrin of Rumi's jealous students. After Shams's disappearance, or as some say, his death at the hands of Rumi's jealous disciples, Rumi went through a period of profound heartbreak and mourning. In his grief, however, his heart didn't just break. It broke open, and thereafter his love knew no boundaries. He began to find the presence of the Beloved One everywhere and in everything. Through the loss of his mortal beloved, then, Rumi's whole being opened up, and his heartbreak was transformed into the music and poetry of mystic love and longing.

Loss seems to have played a significant role in the lives of many great Hasidic masters as well. Many were orphans or had lost a parent at a young age, including the famed Ba'al Shem Tov, whose mother died in childbirth and whose father passed away when he was five. Like all children who suffer early losses, young Israel must have struggled to overcome feelings of abandonment and loneliness—perhaps even depression. As a child, he used to go out alone into the forest to commune with the divine. There, in his aloneness, he formed a deep bond of attachment with God called *devekut*—or union with the divine. Through devekut, the Ba'al Shem Tov was able to transcend his own wound of abandonment and to feel connected to *all* beings and *all* creation. In healing his own broken heart by cleaving to the ever-present love and unity of the divine, he blazed a spiritual pathway for others to follow.

When I look back on my life, it is clear that my own spiritual quest was initiated by a wounding, though at the time I embarked on my journey, I was not yet aware of this. As children of Holocaust survivors, my brother and I grew up in a home in which the unspeakable pain and loss that my parents had endured in the war were an ever-present, though invisible, force in our lives. We felt acutely the presence of the absent. Named after our parents' lost relatives, my brother and I were classic second-generation children of survivors, raised with our parents' unrealistic, unspoken, and unconscious expectations that we could replace those who had perished and fill up the emptiness that our parents felt. Adding to this legacy of loss, my father died unexpectedly on Yom Kippur when I was eleven, leaving me in a state of emotional shock and grief that lasted for years. But despite the ways that my father's death hurt me, it compelled me to wrestle with questions of ultimate meaning at a young age.

Losing my father so suddenly in childhood also taught me a lot about how the human heart can either shut down in response to the pain of loss or completely open up. When we lose someone we love, we tend to close our hearts down in self-protection. We may even unconsciously vow to ourselves never to be vulnerable or love again. But in doing so, we inevitably hurt ourselves because we also shut love out. The truth is, love and loss are inextricably bound together. We cannot love without risking heartbreak. And, ultimately, in love's service, we must be willing to be shattered many times.

In my own healing journey, it was not until many years later, when my first marriage ended and my heart was broken in a big way once more, that I was able to access my childhood grief and finally heal those old wounds. The protective walls I had unconsciously erected around myself at the time of my father's death were finally brought down when my hopes and dreams were shattered once more. As is often the case, traumatic events have a way of opening up all our old wounds. But in doing so, they offer us an opportunity finally to heal.

In his spiritual autobiography, mystic-philosopher Andrew Harvey describes how his own spiritual awakening to divine love resulted from a wound of abandonment he experienced as a young child, when his mother sent him off to boarding school, far from home: "Her abandonment of me at six-and-a-half . . . opened a wound that no other love, until the love this book describes, and no success of world happiness, could heal. This abandonment was, I see now, a blessing. It baptized me in despair; those so baptized have no choice but to look for a final truth and its final healing, or die of inner famine."[9]

Harvey's spiritual quest brought him from Oxford University, where he was a professor, back to India, his childhood home. There he came into intimate contact with a powerful spiritual being named Mother Meera, who according to Harvey and her many disciples, was the embodiment of the Divine Mother. Harvey describes the connection between his early childhood wounding and his spiritual experiences with the Divine Mother two decades later:

> India gave me a mother, then took her away. Years later, I found in India another Mother in another dimension, and the love I had believed lost returned. Without that first wound I would not have needed love so much or been prepared to risk everything in its search. . . . From the deepest wound of my life grew its miraculous possibility."[10]

The experience of loss, of course, is not limited just to the loss of a loved one. As we move through our lives we continually deal with loss, since nothing is permanent. Everything and everyone we try to hold on to eventually slips through our fingertips. We have control over so little. The one thing we *can* do is stay openhearted and not shut down in self-protection when our hearts are broken.

Rabbi Isaac of Acco, a thirteenth- and fourteenth-century kabbalist who lived in Palestine, once told a parable about a rather crude man who, through the experience of unrequited love and longing, became a wise sage and healer. According to the tale, the man was smitten by the beauty of a princess who passed him by in the street one day. In his crude way he said to her something to the effect of "would that I could have my way with you." The princess responded, "That will only happen in the graveyard," implying that his vile fantasy would never come true in her lifetime. But the man did not understand that the princess was brushing him off, and instead went to the graveyard and waited for her, thinking she would come that night. When she failed to appear, he simply became more steadfast in his longing and desire, and he continued to await her eventual visit to the graveyard. After many days and nights in this state of single-minded longing, coupled with his continual encounter with death and impermanence in the graveyard, the man saw through the transitory and limited aspect of his sexual longing and eventually was transformed. As he buried his heart's desire, his longing shifted instead to the source of all desire and all love, the Beloved One.[11]

While the loss of a love object can trigger the longing for ultimate connection with God, the experience of love itself can also engender self-transcendence. When we open our hearts in love to another person, we go beyond the boundaries of our local self. Experiencing ourselves as connected with another being, we open the door to a connection with all beings and all things. As we awaken to this higher love, we die to a sense of ourselves as separate and apart from anyone or anything. This is why Hillel, the famous first-century Talmudic sage, said that the entire Torah could be summed up by the single mitzvah "And you shall love your neighbor as yourself" (Leviticus 19:18). By truly loving others as ourselves—as though they were actually a part of us—we begin to understand the oneness and interconnectedness of all being.

An ancient midrash makes this same argument by pointing out how the first and last letters of the Torah—*bet* and *lamed*—combine to spell the Hebrew words *bal* (nothingness/ayin) and *lev* (heart):

Why did the Holy Blessed One create the world with [the Hebrew letter] *bet* as in *Bereishit* (in the beginning), [the first

letter of Torah]; and end the Torah with [the Hebrew let-
ter] *lamed* in the word *Yisrael?* When you connect them
together you will come up with *bal* (nothing), and when
you turn them around you have *lev* (heart). Thus did the
Holy Blessed One say to Israel: "My children, if you embody these two attributes, humility and heart, I will consider it as though you have fulfilled the entire Torah from
bet through *lamed* (from beginning to end)."[12]

The idea behind this midrash is that the entire Torah from beginning to end is about having an open heart and humbly embracing the
fact that we are never truly separate or apart from anything or anyone
(bal). *Bal,* which literally means "without," suggests that we are without (*bli*) any separate existence of our own. It is another way of saying
that we are essentially ayin—part of the essential oneness of all being.

The mystics teach us that having an open heart and knowing that
we are not separate go hand in hand. We come to discover the sweetness of an open heart only when we are able to go beyond ourselves;
and, conversely, when we transcend our separateness, our hearts
open. And to the extent that we see ourselves as ayin, we become a
vessel within which the infinite (in all its many forms) can dwell. So
long as we are too filled with ourselves, there is simply no room for
the other—human or divine.

Rabbi Nachman of Breslov taught that by seeing ourselves as ayin,
we create the space within us to become, like God, the heart-space of
the world: "When a person has heart, he is no longer restricted by
'space' (*makom*). On the contrary, he becomes the space within which
the world exists. . . . This is because Godliness resides in the heart as
it says (Psalms 73) 'God is the stronghold of my heart.' "[13] Just as God
became the space (makom) within which the world came into being
through tzimtzum, our own self-tzimtzum (self-transcendence) opens
up a space where we can hold others in our hearts and give them the
gift of existence. According to Rabbi Nachman, this is the work of
the tzaddik (righteous, realized being), who, like God, becomes "the
place" where all beings can rest and find their true existence. With

an open heart, then, we become like the tzaddik and the Divine One, the place within which all beings find a space to grow in love.[14]

Being an effective therapist or healer involves a good measure of personal tzimtzum, for in order to give people the space to grow and open up to their true being and potential, one must contain many of one's own personal feelings, agendas, and reactions. Skillful listening involves a tzimtzum of one's own narcissism and reactivity as well as a willingness to let go of all preconceived notions and concepts about others. In the heart that is empty of self and the mind that is vacant of limiting thoughts and agendas, people can heal into their wholeness. Having a meditative practice can help therapists develop these abilities.

THE BROKEN-GLASS RITUAL

The intimate connection between love and loss is poignantly symbolized in the ancient ritual of breaking a glass at the climax of the Jewish wedding ceremony. To the cries of *"mazel tov!"* newly married couples stomp on a wine goblet, shattering it to bits. Underlying this ancient, joyous rite is a mysterious reminder of brokenness and loss. The rabbis say that this custom is meant to evoke the memory of the destruction of the Temple in Jerusalem by the Roman Empire in 70 C.E. It is one of several rites that are considered to be in memory of this tragic event, considered to be the most cataclysmic in all Jewish history. Through this ancient rite, the expression of grief and loss are paradoxically evoked and welcomed at the moment of greatest joy and union.

The destruction of the Temple can be understood both literally and symbolically. In its most literal sense, the loss of the Temple is significant because it marked the end of an era of Jewish sovereignty and the beginning of the long exile in which the Jewish people would be scattered to the four corners of the earth in their homeless wanderings.

On the symbolic level, the destruction of the Temple is an archetypal symbol of the incompleteness and brokenness that exist in this world. When the Temple in Jerusalem stood, according to Jewish myth, heaven and earth were said to be linked; the male and female energies of the universe danced in harmony, and the finite and the infinite realms of existence were united. The Temple's destruction (much like the shattering of the vessels) symbolizes just the opposite—a world in exile from its source, in which all the parts and polarities stand in isolation or opposition to one another. Though every marriage reflects the *hieros gamos* (cosmic union) and the Temple's rebuilding, every marriage on a certain level also recapitulates its destruction; for no matter how perfect a relationship may be, alienation and incompleteness are part of the package. In the Jewish collective unconscious, wholeness and brokenness, like love and loss, always exist side by side.

For those of us who choose to marry, our wedding day may be one of the happiest moments of our lives, marking the culmination of years of longing and dreaming. Yet, as the broken-glass ritual hints, something is also lost and shattered when we commit ourselves to one partner for the rest of our life. When we partner, we must let go of all the other possible lives we might have lived had we not made this choice. Marriage also entails the sacrifice of our singularity as well as the sacrifice of all other potential loves we might have known. Despite all the ways that our lives are enhanced by partnership, there are also compromises we will have to make in marriage that will limit our autonomy and freedom of choice.

From my own experience of marriage and from my experience counseling many brides and grooms, there is a deep healing wisdom in the broken-glass ritual. Brides and grooms often feel confused when sad feelings arise around the time of their weddings because they think that they should only be happy at such times. The ritual allows them to acknowledge and express the mix of contradictory emotions that can arise even in the most open, joyous, and loving moment in their lives. There is no escaping the fact that a wedding entails an "ending" as well as a "new beginning," which the broken-glass ritual aptly captures.

But perhaps there is another dimension to the broken-glass ritual. In moments of intense love and connection, we may also revisit old wounds of loss and separation, a point that was borne out by my work with Sarah, a thirty-year-old schoolteacher.

SARAH'S STORY

Love as a Rendezvous with the Past

Sarah came to see me in a state of confusion after she and her boyfriend, Richard, had become engaged. Though she thought she loved him, she was perplexed by the intense sadness that she seemed to be feeling since they had begun to talk about deepening their commitment to one another. Instead of simply feeling joyous about finally finding a partner she could trust and count on, Sarah was also feeling anxiety and grief. It made no sense to her at all. She also found herself withdrawing emotionally from Richard, particularly after they would spend a day or so apart. When they reconnected, Sarah noticed she had trouble opening up. She began to wonder if she was making a mistake by committing to this relationship.

As Sarah and I explored the possible sources of her sad feelings, she began to realize that her parents' divorce when she was a child was having a belated effect on her. Sarah's parents had divorced when she was five years old, and her father had slowly faded out of her life during the ensuing years. Though she had few conscious memories from that time in her life, it seemed that Sarah's childhood grief over the loss of her father—along with other forgotten feelings of shame, anger, and mistrust—was surfacing now that she was truly opening her heart up to another man.

For Sarah, as for all of us, falling in love became a rendezvous with the past, bringing up all the old ghosts of love lost. But it also provided her with a unique opportunity to heal the hidden wounds of her childhood, wounds she otherwise did not have access to. In order to heal, however, Sarah needed to learn how to keep her heart open with Richard, even when she felt hurt or disappointed by him. In childhood she had emotionally shut down in order to stop her unbearable heartbreak. Now, as an adult, she found that her heart automatically shut down when she felt the least bit threatened. Her emotional defense system was in extreme overdrive. But as Sarah learned to compassionately hold her childhood feelings of grief as they surfaced, she found that she could stay more present to her loving feelings. In being able to distinguish between the unbearable pain of the past and the minor slights and disappointments she was experiencing in the present, she managed to take control of her overly self-protective reactions.

Even for those of us who never experienced the traumatic loss of a loved one, deep feelings of love and openheartedness can trigger feelings of grief. This grief is not always so specific as Sarah's. Sometimes, it is simply the sadness we feel about having been previously shut down. Letting love into our hearts reminds us of all the time that we blocked love out or felt unlovable. Paradoxically, we often feel the prior loss or absence of love in our life precisely when we let love in. Likewise, powerful feelings of grief can surface when we open our hearts up to God or simply to the experience of self-love in meditation or prayer. When I lead meditation and prayer groups, I notice that group members often begin to cry. I see these tears as tears of teshuvah—of a soul coming home to its true source. In a moment of intense connection to God, one feels the loss or grief of having been so far away from one's heart for so long.

Unrequited Love as a Gateway to Spiritual Awakening

The inextricable bond between love and loss is beautifully expressed in the biblical account of Jacob's love-at-first-sight encounter with Rachel at the well, from Genesis 29:10–11. "And it came to pass," the passage reads, "when Jacob saw Rachel the daughter of Laban his mother's brother, and the flock of Laban his mother's brother, that Jacob stepped near, and rolled the stone from the well's mouth, and gave drink to the flock. . . . And Jacob kissed Rachel, and lifted up his voice, and wept."

Rashi, the famous twelfth-century medieval commentator, wondering why Jacob cries, answers with the following midrash: "because he foresaw by the Holy Spirit that she would not be buried with him in the cave of Machpelah."[15] Before I attempt to explain the meaning of this enigmatic midrash, let's take a deeper look at this biblical love story.

At the very instant that Jacob sees Rachel, he feels Herculean powers streaming through him, and he is able to single-handedly lift a huge stone off the opening of the well—a stone that, according to scriptures, typically took a large group of men to move. The experience of falling in love, according to this biblical narrative, empowers Jacob and enables him to go beyond his ordinary limits. But after his initial feat of heroism in removing the stone, Jacob feels exposed and vulnerable, and he begins to weep as he senses the heartbreak he will have to endure because of his newfound capacity to love. That stone that Jacob removes from the well, I would suggest, symbolizes the "heart of stone" that typically blocks off the soft and vulnerable side of us. In order to love we must gain access to this soft inner core by removing the unfeeling (invulnerable) protective shields we ordinarily wear.

Though he longs to spend his whole life in the bliss of union with Rachel, his beloved, Jacob prophetically intuits in those very first moments of love that they will be tragically separated, for Rachel will die prematurely in childbirth and be buried apart from him, as it says in Genesis 35:17–20: "And in her difficulty giving birth, the midwife said to her: 'Do not fear for you have borne a son.' And as her soul departed—for she died—she called his name *Ben-oni* (son of my sorrow); and his father called him Benjamin. And Rachel died and was buried on the way to Efrata, at Bethlehem."

The tragedy of Rachel's premature death and her burial apart from Jacob and away from the ancestral burial-ground have profound symbolic meaning in the midrashic and mystical imagination. The cave of Machpelah in Hebron was the site where Jacob's parents (Isaac and Rebecca) and grandparents (Abraham and Sarah) were buried in pairs. The very name Machpelah, in Hebrew, suggests pairing or coupling, from the root *chaf-peh-lamed*, which means double. While Abraham and Isaac spent most of their lives with their beloved partners and were laid to rest with them as well, Jacob would not have this privilege. Instead, his life would be marked by traumatic separations (from his son Joseph as well as Rachel) and many years in exile from his land, first to Padam Aram (twenty-two years) and then to Egypt, where he spends the rest of his life until he dies. While "the lives of each of the patriarchs and matriarchs are said to be a sign for the fate that would befall their descendents," Jacob's life, was seen as foreshadowing the two-thousand-year-long exile that the Jewish people would endure following the destruction of the second Temple.[16] Jacob's tragic separation from Rachel, his beloved, symbolizes the sense of estrangement and displacement that the Israelite nation would experience during these years of homelessness and wandering away from their homeland. Rachel is, in fact, buried alone on the very path the Israelites would cross on their way into exile after the destruction of the Temple. There, in Efrata, her spirit hovers at her grave site, where she is said to have mourned and comforted her children on their way into exile. The first Temple prophet of doom, Jeremiah, alludes to Rachel's tears when he prophesies the future redemption: "Thus says YHVH: A voice of bitter weeping is heard on the hill. Rachel is mourning for her children. She refuses to be consoled over her children who are no longer there. Thus says YHVH: Hold back your voice from crying and your eyes from tears, for there is a reward for your (righteous) deeds. Thus says YHVH: (Your children) will return from the land of their enemy" (Jeremiah 31:14–16).

Jacob's intuition that he would be tragically separated from his beloved also hints at a deeper, metaphysical issue. In a sense, his relationship with Rachel is a symbol of all love in this world, requited or unrequited. Just as Jacob's relationship with Rachel is short-lived, all moments of perfect love and union are fleeting. No matter how wonderful a relationship may be, all love is vulnerable to loss, whether through death or abandonment or through the various contingencies that cause disconnection. In this fragmented and broken world in which the holy Temple is in ruins, true love may be whole for but a moment; then it is often snatched away, preserved only in the protected space of myth and memory.

Shattered vessels, broken hearts, the collected fragments of the tablets, and the broken wedding glass all point to the same truth: Everything in this world partakes of the original shatteredness of creation. Yet from this fragmented, imperfect, and broken state, all creation begins its journey of return to a state of wholeness and connectedness. We all will suffer loss, for to be born means that we inevitably suffer the pain of separation. Our very existence and sense of self-hood are constructed on the illusion that we are separate. But from this sense of aloneness and loss is born the yearning to come home to the source of all being, to a loving connection with God and all other incarnate beings.

AYIN MEDITATION

The Maggid of Mezerich taught that when we pray or meditate, we should think of our souls as part of the Divine Presence, and instead of praying for ourselves as separate and apart from God, we should pray for the needs of the Divine Presence. When we see ourselves as included in divinity, "like a raindrop in the sea,"[17] the divine sustenance more readily flows down to us.

In ayin meditation, we attempt to experience ourselves as included in God; we allow our sense of separateness and distinctness to dissolve temporarily so that we can rest on the ground of our true being. Many teachers consider ayin meditation to be an advanced form of meditation, appropriate only for those who are emotionally and spiritually prepared. If you are new to meditation, you may want to skip this practice and come back to it when you feel ready.

If you do choose to practice ayin meditation, start by finding a place where you can sit and meditate undisturbed. Once you have sat down there, take a few minutes to rest comfortably and begin to pay attention to your body and your breath. As you attend to your breath, you may notice the different parts of the breath—the in-breath, the out-breath, and the pause between breaths. You may also notice your thoughts as they arise, one after another, and as you attend to your breath, perhaps those thoughts will begin to space themselves out so that you begin to notice a gap or pause between thoughts. . . .

Now imagine, if you can, that you can enter into the pause between breaths or the gap between thoughts; in that space you can begin to experience ayin, the divine emptiness that is the backdrop of all creation.

Now come back to your body and notice that your body is made up of the same cosmic stardust from which all creation was made.

Everything that is out there is also within you. As you come to realize this, the boundaries between inside and outside begin to dissolve, and you can begin to experience the unity of all being within the divine. Let your soul dissolve into the Divine Presence like a raindrop falling into the sea or a wave breaking at the shore, and allow yourself to rest in ayin for as long as you are comfortable.

When you wish to return to your ordinary awareness, become aware, once more, of your breath; notice the boundaries of your body and your breath. Begin to notice where your body touches the surfaces beneath and around you. Become aware of your presence in space and time. You may wish to stroke or massage yourself in order to reconnect with your body's boundaries before you gently open your eyes.

Mikveh
A Sacred Ritual of Transition

In working with people undergoing transition, I have found that rituals can promote healing. By speaking in the language of the unconscious—namely, through symbolic enactment—and by shifting our focus from "linear time" to "sacred time," rituals put us in touch with the possibility of continual healing and renewal.

Water rituals, in particular, offer a powerful symbol of renewal and rebirth. Immersion in the *mikveh,* the ritual bath, is the classic Jewish marker of important transitions in the life cycle. In addition to its use in rites of passage such as conversion ceremonies, the mikveh is also used for purification and sanctification. Among pious Hasidim, daily or at least weekly immersion in the mikveh (prior to the Sabbath or holy days) offers a means of attaining spiritual purity.

According to Jewish law, the mikveh must contain at least forty *seah* of water (a seah being an ancient biblical unit of measurement, equal to approximately five gallons), including waters from a live, flowing source, such as an underground stream, or rainwater. A lake, river, or the ocean are also considered suitable for ritual immersion. The traditional measurement of forty seah, according to the late

twentieth-century mystic and scholar Rabbi Aryeh Kaplan, symbolizes the forty days it takes a fetus to form. By entering the waters of
the mikveh, says Kaplan, one symbolically reenters the womb in
order to be born anew.[18] Each of us is born out of the maternal waters
of the womb. All life depends on water. Hence, to immerse oneself
in the waters of the mikveh is to immerse oneself symbolically in the
possibility of change and new growth.

On the other hand, one cannot live indefinitely underwater, so
in a sense, when one immerses oneself fully in the mikveh, this act
symbolizes death as well as rebirth. In entering the mikveh, one temporarily enters into a state of nonbeing, in order to emerge into new
life and renewed being. The mikveh ritual, then, is a way to access
the transformative powers of nonbeing, of the ayin state.

Beyond the classic religious use of the mikveh for transitions and
purification, I have found water rituals to be a powerful therapeutic
tool for all people undergoing transition. I have suggested water rituals for brides and grooms before their weddings (this is actually one
of its traditional uses), following a divorce or separation, after dealing
with death, at the end of chemotherapy or radiation treatments, on
the eve of an especially significant birthday, as a marker of transition
into menopause, and in the aftermath of trauma. I have also suggested the use of the mikveh with victims of sexual abuse and rape,
as part of a therapeutic healing ritual.

Whether used as part of a healing rite or as a marker of transition,
ritual immersion in the mikveh can be an effective way to symbolically mark "endings" and "new beginnings." When combined with
an awareness that as one enters the mikveh one is entering the ayin—
the very womb of becoming—this rite can provide an extremely
powerful meditative, healing experience. For those seeking to incorporate Jewish spiritual practices in their lives, the mikveh is worthy
of special attention.

> Tentatively
> I tip my toe
> into the river of un-knowing
> innocently

I feel for the rhythms
of a transformation's undertowing
wantonly
I open and I open
like a seed that's ripe for sowing
somehow I taste the freedom
and relief
that I don't know who I am
and I don't know where I'm going

—TREASURE MILLER, "RIVER OF UNKNOWING"

PART TWO

Healing and Birthing the Self

Every human being has the freedom to change at any instant.

—Viktor Frankl

4

HEALING THE SPLIT SELF

Humility as a Spiritual Resource

The "I" is a thief in hiding.
—*Rabbi Menachem Mendel of Kotzk*

How can any finite vessel hope to contain the endless
God? Therefore, see yourself as nothing: only one
who is nothing can contain the fullness of the
presence.
—*The Maggid of Mezerich*

Legend has it that Rabbi Simha Bunam of
Pzhysha, one of the early Hasidic masters, used to carry two *kvitel,*
or notes, around with him, one in each pocket, which he would alter-
nately pull out at appropriate moments for meditative focusing. On
one he wrote, "I am dust and ashes" (Genesis 18:27), while on the
other he wrote an excerpt from the extraordinary Talmudic saying
"for my sake was the world created."[1] When Simcha Bunam found
himself in a situation that demanded that he surrender his ego, he
would meditate on the first phrase; and when he wished to express
gratitude and appreciation for the unique blessings that life offers, he
would focus on the second.

Simcha Bunam's practice of carrying these two kvitel around with
him wherever he went captures Jewish mysticism's understanding of

the paradoxical nature of existence. Just as all creation simultaneously exists as form and emptiness—yesh (something) and ayin (nothing)—we live simultaneously in and between two paradoxical realities: We are finite beings bound by time and space (yesh), yet we are connected to and rooted in the infinite (ayin). We are uniquely endowed with gifts and blessings that we must manifest, yet at the same time we are part of the divine nothingness, mere "dust and ashes" in the sense that we have no independent existence apart from the divine. Healing into our wholeness involves learning how to gracefully navigate our lives between these opposite poles of yesh and ayin, form and emptiness. To do so we must learn to balance deep humility with a healthy sense of entitlement. We must be able to celebrate our uniqueness and feel a sense of joy, pride, and gratitude for our gifts and blessings, while also practicing *bittul,* self-surrender.

Whereas most Western psychologies are content simply to help us develop a healthy sense of narcissistic entitlement and ego strength, Judaism insists that bittul is also essential. In fact, according to the mystics of old, not having a sense of bittul is itself a form of insanity, a misappropriation of our God-given powers. Yet, unlike certain Eastern mysticisms that instruct the seeker to transcend this illusory world, Judaism insists that our experiences in this world are of vital importance. Jewish life requires that we become citizens of both the upper and lower worlds, for it is through this finite world, with all its promises and pitfalls, that we open ourselves to the infinite; and it is through our immersion in the infinite that we are able to bring holiness back into our finite lives.

The challenge we face is knowing when to reach into which pocket. There are times when we must assert our will, and there are times to surrender in deep humility to that which is so much larger and more awesome than we are. Many situations demand that we hold on to both kvitel at once, avoiding both the extremes of self-inflation and self-nullification. These are, perhaps, the most challenging times for us, for most of us are already confused about when to assert ourselves and when to surrender. We frequently fail to assert our most important needs when we really should stand up for ourselves, for instance, because we don't think we are important or worthy enough to have our needs met. And we don't know how to back down in situations that demand yielding, because we tend to see surrender and yielding as a sign of weakness rather than as a sign of true strength.

ANIY AND AYIN

The dialectical tension between our need for self-actualization and our need for self-surrender is reflected in the close relationship between the Hebrew words *aniy* and *ayin*. *Aniy*, or "I," the Hebrew word that comes closest to the Freudian concept of ego, shares the same letters as the word *ayin*, only in a different order. While *aniy* is spelled *aleph-nun-yud*, *ayin* is spelled *aleph-yud-nun*. What is the connection? As Kabbalah scholar and author Dr. Daniel Matt once cleverly punned it, the aniy (ego) must be ayinized—brought to recognize divine nothingness (ayin)—in order to be rectified and made whole. In other words, it is only by surrendering itself that the ego finds its rightful place in the scheme of things, as the humble servant of the higher self or soul rather than as its own master.[2] According to Rabbi Shneur Zalman of Liadi, the eighteenth-century founder of Chabad Hasidism, it is through the act of self-surrender that the purpose of creation is fulfilled. "For this," he said, "is the purpose of the creation of worlds from Ayin to Yesh, to reverse it from the aspect of Yesh into the aspect of Ayin."[3]

While God's act of creation brought forth yesh out of ayin (something out of nothing), in spiritual practice we reverse this process. By re-immersing ourselves in the ground of all being through meditation or contemplative prayer, we make our yesh into ayin (something into nothing). This work of self-surrender, or *mesirat nefesh*, as it is called in Hebrew, is the human counterpart of divine tzimtzum. While the Ein Sof, or infinite, contracted itself in order for the finite world to come into being, our job is to complete the cycle through our own self-tzimtzum, by nullifying our separate selves. In doing so, we fulfill the very purpose of creation, which, according to Hasidism, was for the infinite to be revealed through its opposite, the finite. As the ego, in the act of self-tzimtzum, surrenders itself to its source in divine nothingness, it emerges more whole and clear about its true purpose.

Seeing ourselves through the lens of quantum physics can be helpful in understanding the dual nature of the self. Our very bodies, at the subatomic level, appear to be much more empty space than anything else. Though on the gross level we experience ourselves as solid matter (yesh), under the electron microscope we are hardly there (ayin). Knowing this makes it easier for me to imagine that while my existence matters (pun intended), in a less obvious way I hardly even exist.

Applying these teachings to our everyday lives can be challenging, yet when we do, ordinary situations become transformed into opportunities for spiritual development. In intimate relationships, for example, love can easily be hijacked by pride when we take ourselves too seriously. Our prideful egos can make us dig in our heels unnecessarily in an argument, even when it is obvious that winning the argument means losing in the bigger picture of love. My husband and I occasionally get into these stuck places, where both of us feel wronged and dig in our heels, stubbornly awaiting the other's apology. We can get pretty mired in self-righteous muck until one of us is freed from the trap of pride. Sometimes through the simple use of humor, my husband can help me lighten up and take myself a little less seriously. And sometimes I am able to take time out for meditation in order to get perspective. By simply imagining myself dissolving into ayin—like a raindrop falling into the ocean—as the Maggid of Mezerich recommends we do, I find that I can let go of my self-importance and be freed from my attachment to being "right." This kind of self-surrender can be truly liberating, so long as the relationship to which one is surrendering is basically a healthy one and there is some mutuality in the process.

Yet nothing in the West reinforces an orientation toward the ayin, or emptiness. In fact, the very notion of surrender is anathema to the Western mind. Western civilization is based much more on the archetypal myth of heroic conquest. Power, from a Western perspective, is defined in terms of asserting oneself and getting others to surrender, rather than in terms of surrendering one's own will to that of the divine.

We live in a world of overinflated egos and hyperactive superegos, which ruthlessly drive us into constant motion and activity. We fill the airwaves with words and overload our clock time with doing till we hardly remember that we are ayin. But without the ability to balance our individuality and separateness with an awareness of our interconnectedness with all being, our separateness becomes the source of great suffering.

Humility as a Spiritual Resource

For the Hasidic masters, humility was the key quality that enables us to strike a balance between the yesh and ayin aspects of our being. With humility we gain a sense of perspective, so that we neither overestimate nor underestimate our own importance. On the one hand, Jewish mysticism teaches that we matter to God and that there will never be another person who can fulfill our purpose here on earth. As Reb Zusia of Hanipol, one of the disciples of the Maggid of Mezerich, once said to his disciples, "I'm not worried that I'll be asked why I wasn't Moses when I die and enter the heavenly realm, but why I wasn't Zusia." Despite his extreme humility, Reb Zusia still understood that each of us is a precious and unique manifestation of the Divine One, essential to the unfolding of creation. On the other hand, we cannot be whole unless we also understand how to surrender ourselves so that we may experience our unity with all things.

Reb Zusia understood the importance of humility in unlocking not just the gates of self-knowledge but also the gates of divine knowledge. Once, he became engaged in a "chicken or egg" debate with his brother, Reb Elimelech of Hanopil, about the relationship between humility and God-consciousness. Elimelech felt that true humility could be acquired only by contemplating the greatness of the Creator. Standing before the awesome majesty and grandeur of the divine and taking in the great mystery of existence in a state of *yirah* (awe and wonder), one cannot help but be immediately humbled. Zusia, on the other hand, felt that a person must first be humble in order to recognize the greatness of the Creator and stand in God's presence. Since they could not agree, they went to ask their teacher, the Maggid of Mezerich, who was right. In typical rabbinic dialectical style the Maggid responded that both Reb Elimelech and Reb Zusia spoke "words of the living God."[4] But, added the Maggid, "A humble person who contemplates the greatness of the creator stands at a higher rung than one who attains humility as a result of contemplating God's greatness."[5] The Maggid's answer, as we shall see, reveals his special appreciation of the importance of humility in spiritual development.

Whether we need to develop a stronger sense of self or become less self-centered, by cultivating humility we can achieve greater inner balance. Yet in all my years of graduate and postgraduate training in psychology, I have never heard anyone mention the virtue of humility. Humility just isn't part of the lexicon of Western psychology. The longer I practice psychotherapy, however, the more I see authentic humility as one of the most powerful remedies for narcissism and the disorders of the self that afflict so many people.

Humility frees us up to use all our gifts and talents to the best of our abilities by enabling us to accept our limitations and vulnerabilities as well as our strengths. With humility we can enjoy our achievements without unnecessary ego-inflation or -deflation; neither are we full of ourselves nor do we pick ourselves apart. And being humble doesn't mean that we stop trying to better ourselves. We are all works in progress! But it does mean we don't have to be *the* best; we just have to be *our* best.

The truth is, it is not possible to be truly humble unless we accept and love who we are. Ironically, when we don't think highly of ourselves, we tend to think *constantly* about ourselves. In contrast, when we feel more or less okay about who we are, we can more readily put ourselves aside and be present, in the moment, with others. While a lack of humility can be one of the root causes of low self-esteem, low self-esteem can cause us to act haughty or become overly reactive and defensive with others. Out of the need to protect our vulnerable sense of self-worth, we may take everything that happens to us far too personally.

Becoming Ayin

In Jewish mysticism, humility is seen as the only true remedy to narcissistic imbalances, for when we truly stand before God in awe and wonder, we cannot be haughty. The two experiences are mutually exclusive. The Maggid of Mezerich, the legendary leader who galvanized the Hasidic movement after the death of the Ba'al Shem Tov, placed humility at the heart of spiritual development. He taught that to become a channel for the divine, one must become so humble as to become as naught (ayin) in one's own eyes. "How can any finite vessel hope to contain the endless God?" he said. "Therefore, see yourself as nothing: only one who is nothing can contain the fullness of the Presence."[6]

Rabbi Yissachar Baer of Zlatchov, one of the disciples of the Maggid, expanded on his teacher's practice of extreme humility:

> The essence of serving God and of all the mitzvot [commandments] is to attain the state of humility, that is, to understand that all your physical and mental powers and your essential being depend on the divine elements within. You are simply a channel for the divine attributes. You attain this humility through the awe of God's vastness, through realizing that "there is no place empty of it." Then you come to the state of ayin, the state of humility. You have no independent self and are contained in the Creator. This is the meaning of the verse: "Moses hid his face, for he was in awe." Through his experience of awe, Moses attained the hiding of his face, that is, he perceived no independent self. Everything was part of divinity.[7]

For the Maggid and his disciples, the goal of all spiritual practice is to become an instrument of the divine—to see oneself as a hollow *shofar* (ram's horn) that does not contain any sound of its own, only that which is produced when someone blows through it. In the words of the Rabbi Avraham Chaim of Zlatchov, one of the Maggid's disciples,

You must see yourself as ayin. You must realize that you have no merit nor good deeds to your credit. Even though you may fulfill the commandments and do good deeds, you are not the one who is actually doing this. You are only acting through the power that God gives you, and through the intelligence and goodness that He bestows upon you. It is thus written, "Who will come before Me, that I may pay him?" (Job 41:3)

When you pray, you must realize that the Universe of Speech is speaking through you. When you think, you must realize that your thoughts are from the Universe of Thought. You are therefore like a Shofar. A Shofar itself does not contain any sound. It only produces sound when someone blows through it. It is therefore written, "Lift up your voice like a Shofar."[8]

For the divine music of life to be played through us, the ego must step aside; only then can our will be aligned with the divine will. And as the third-century sage Rabbi Gamliel, the son of Rabbi Yehuda, said, "Align your will with the divine will, and God will make your will as His own."[9]

As we evolve spiritually, we realize more and more that our lives are on loan to us from a source beyond and that we are here to serve the divine host, not ourselves, as the mystic poet Rumi suggests in this poem:

> For sixty years I have been forgetful,
> every minute, but not for a second
> has this flowing toward me stopped or slowed.
> I deserve nothing. Today I recognize
> that I am the guest the mystics talk about.
> I play this living music for my host.
> Everything today is for the host."

—RUMI, "THE MUSIC"

This same mystic sensibility is apparent in the following Hasidic story about two disciples of the Maggid of Mezerich: After several years of studying with the Maggid, a certain young man decided he had learned enough, and so he made a decision to return home. On his journey, he passed through the town of Karlin late at night. In Karlin lived Reb Aaron, an old companion from his days at the Maggid's house of study. Though it was almost midnight, the young man saw a light in the window, and so he knocked on Reb Aaron's door. When he heard his friend ask, "Who is it?" he answered simply "I," being so certain that Reb Aaron would recognize his voice. But Reb Aaron was silent and did not respond. The man knocked repeatedly, but his entreaties were ignored. Finally, he cried out in distress: "Aaron, my friend, why won't you open for me?" to which Reb Aaron responded in a somber voice: "Who is it that dares call himself 'I' as befits only God himself!" Upon hearing the rebuke, the disciple instantly recognized his hubris, and without delay he turned around and returned to Mezerich to focus more deeply on the Maggid's teachings.[10]

Rumi told a similar tale about a Sufi master and a seeker, but with a slight twist. In Rumi's tale, the seeker is also sent away because of his lack of spiritual readiness, but after a year of wandering, he returns and knocks once more at the master's door. This time, when asked, "Who is there?" he answers humbly: "It is you, O Beloved," to which the master responds: "Since you are I, enter, O myself; for there is no room in this mansion for two I's."[11]

Spiritual awakening, for the true mystic, demands the relinquishment of all self-importance. Indeed, at the divine table, there is only room for One! Spiritual awakening inspires a profound shift in us from being self-centered to being God-centered. The "I am" of the ego must step aside to allow the eternal "I am" to speak. Advaitic masters, such as the late Indian saint Ramana Maharshi, taught that by meditating over and over again on the question "Who am I?" it is possible to awaken to this expanded identity he called the Self, using a capital *S*. Through this practice, known as self-inquiry meditation, one eventually arrives at the realization that one's own being and all being are essentially one; that nothing exists outside of the one Self. This nondual awareness is the basis of all mystical traditions.

While realized beings like Ramana Maharshi or Moses were said to abide permanently in the nondual state, we are all capable of experiencing moments of awakening to our true nature if we make space in our lives for silence, stillness, and listening. Through the practice of silent meditation and contemplative prayer we can begin to loosen our identification with the small, separate self.

SILENCE AND LISTENING

The role of silence in fostering spiritual awakening is a central theme in biblical narrative, as reflected in the fact that the Torah was revealed in the desert, or *midbar,* a place of silence and emptiness. The desert of the biblical narrative is not just a geographical place but also a metaphor for how we must *be* in order to receive divine revelation, as suggested by the following midrash: "One cannot acquire Torah [wisdom] unless one becomes ownerless/nonattached [*hefker*] like the desert."[12] In silence, the divine call that was heard at Sinai becomes available to each of us, as Rabbi Yehudah Aryeh Leib of Ger teaches: "Hearing requires being empty of everything." And to transcend our current state of spiritual exile we must "forget this world's vanities so that we empty the heart to hear God's word without any disctracting thought."[13]

Judaism offers many spiritual practices that create space for this kind of listening. Sabbath observance, for instance, creates a rhythm in our lives in which there is time for both *doing* and *being*. Capping off the work week with a day for rest and spiritual renewal, the Sabbath offers a powerful rite for balancing our need for assertion and actualization with our need for surrender. A similar balance is brought into the rhythm of each day through daily spiritual practice. Taking time out each day to immerse ourselves in spirit, whether through prayer or meditation, can be deeply healing.

Having a daily spiritual practice of self-surrender can be particularly helpful in dealing with life situations in which we are not entirely in control of our destinies. For instance, when we are ill, spiritual surrender helps us accept the fact that there are powerful forces that move mysteriously through our lives in ways we cannot always comprehend. Spiritual surrender does not mean that we give up our power to heal ourselves. Rather, it implies an attitude of patience and acceptance—acceptance of the universe of its own terms rather than on our terms. Instead of dictating to God how we think things ought to be, it involves a stance of listening and attunement This attunement enables us to perceive how godliness and a sense of meaning may be found in the very place where we stand—no matter how difficult our situation may be. And when we surrender in this fashion to how things are *right now,* we feel a sense of peace and at-one-ment. Out of this state, paradoxically, spontaneous healings frequently emerge.

HUMILITY AS AN ANTIDOTE TO NARCISSISM

Narcissism is somewhat of a buzzword these days in the field of psychology. In the colloquial use of the word we often think of narcissism as a bad thing, as chronic self-centeredness. Like the mythic character Narcissus, who is so taken with himself that he cannot stop focusing on his own image, even for a moment, the narcissist is constantly self-absorbed. He is unable to take in the "other"—be it human or divine.

But narcissism, according to contemporary psychology, is not all bad. Instead it runs along a spectrum from "healthy" to "pathological." A healthy dose of narcissism is necessary in order to enjoy a fulfilling life and feel good about oneself. It is an important ingredient of healthy self-esteem. It becomes pathological when it is not balanced by empathy—the capacity to take in the needs and feelings of others.

Pathological narcissism always involves some identity confusion, an overestimation of one's own importance—an overestimation that typically masks its opposite. While narcissistic individuals may appear self-confident and overly entitled, deep inside they generally feel empty and unworthy. Seeking constant validation/attention from others is an attempt to compensate for these painful feelings. The narcissist's need to feel he is *better than* everybody else protects him from feeling utterly worthless.

Narcissistically wounded people generally suffer from a split self-image. Their unconscious expectations and images of themselves are out of sync with their actual capabilities. Unconsciously, they hold themselves up to unrealistic, grandiose ideals that they are often unable to live up to in the real world. Because they're under constant pressure to prove their worth, their self-esteem levels tend to gyrate wildly. And since they have little emotional middle ground, life often feels to them like a wild roller-coaster ride. While they may appear self-confident or haughty on the surface, deep inside they often feel a sense of inferiority and unworthiness.

Narcissistic wounding tends to occur in children who grow up feeling unloved and insufficiently recognized by their caretakers. Instead of seeing their parents as flawed and limited human beings, these children often grow up blaming themselves, interpreting their parents' lack of love as an indication that they simply weren't worthy of love. In order to compensate for these feelings of unworthiness, they may try to prove their worth by compulsively striving to be great or by seeking constant validation from others. However, no matter how successful they become, narcissistically wounded individuals are never truly able to feel fulfilled and take pleasure in their accomplishments, unless they begin healing their childhood wound, as Joan discovered in our work together.

Joan's Story

Overcoming Overachievement

Jewish teachings on humility became an important tool in helping Joan, a thirty-eight-year-old physician whom I counseled, to heal her split self-image. At the time she began treatment, Joan was at the peak of her success. She had a thriving medical practice, and from a professional standpoint she had achieved more than most of us could dream of. Viewed objectively, Joan was extremely smart, successful, and attractive, yet she seemed unable to derive pleasure from her many accomplishments. She also seemed to have very low self-esteem, as reflected by her habit of making self-deprecating remarks, especially when given a compliment. Much of the time, she felt like an impostor. When she accomplished something noteworthy, she felt that she was fooling everybody and that it was just a matter of time before the world found out how bad and stupid she was.

As we began to explore together the meaning of Joan's self-deprecation, it became apparent that it actually masked an opposite unconscious attitude. She was, in fact, plagued by an intense unconscious grandiosity. Joan continually put herself down because she unconsciously expected herself to be not just good but great; not just pretty but stunning; not just smart but brilliant. Whatever she did, she just didn't measure up. Joan's external show of "humility" actually masked its opposite—a haughty inner voice that continually compared her to some fictitious perfect other.

This haughtiness, it turned out, masked a still deeper feeling of insufficiency. As we explored the source of these feelings, Joan got in touch with early childhood memories of physical and emotional neglect, experiences that caused her to feel unworthy of love. To compensate for these feelings, Joan lived under intense inner pressure to constantly prove her worth. No matter how much she accomplished, however, she never felt okay about herself. In addition to her problems with self-esteem, Joan also could never relax long enough to enjoy her many achievements. Instead, she felt chained to a fast-moving treadmill that threatened to knock her over if she slowed down. In order to keep up with all the expectations she placed on herself, Joan had begun to resort to a variety of drugs to crank herself up during the day, and she often took tranquilizers or sleeping pills to fall asleep at night. As irrational as it may have been, the more Joan accomplished, the more she seemed to feel unconsciously compelled to defeat herself, as though failure might reduce the tension she felt between her despised inner self and her successful outer persona. Though it seemed counterintuitive, when Joan fantasized about being caught using drugs, she felt strangely relieved. Somehow, the idea of failing reassured her that she was, in fact, the unlovable person she deep down believed herself to be.

In our work together I began to point out to Joan when I thought she was being controlled by her grandiose inner voice. I suggested that she was going to have to tame this voice/force in order to free herself from its unreasonable demands. When I first pointed this out to Joan, she was taken a bit by surprise. She didn't see how she could possibly be grandiose when she felt so down on herself all the time. So I asked Joan to paint a picture in her mind's eye of the voice that constantly made her feel inadequate. By inducing a light trance state through relaxation and self-hypnosis, Joan was able to visualize this voice as a mean-looking character that was always looking down its nose at her from some imaginary throne of perfection. Having a visual image of the voice helped her see it as a *dybbuk* of sorts—as a form of possession from which she could free herself. Experiencing haughtiness as an alien presence enabled Joan to reconnect with her authentic inner self, a self that was capable of being both strong and weak, gifted and vulnerable, and sincerely humble.

As our work together deepened, I began sharing Jewish stories and teachings on humility with Joan. No one had ever spoken to Joan about humility. In her medical training she had unwittingly internalized the classic hubris of Western medical education, which is geared toward turning out superhero-like doctors trained to show no vulnerability. As a female physician she felt particularly under pressure to prove herself by never revealing weakness. In becoming a doctor, then, Joan had been forced to continue suppressing her true inner needs and feelings, much as she had done throughout her childhood.

Over the coming months, as Joan began to free herself from her haughty inner voice, she slowly got more in touch with her needs and feelings. This process, which was intensely humbling, was accompanied by a series of dreams in which Joan found herself repeatedly removing facial masks, as though she were peeling off a second skin. When I asked Joan what she thought these dream images meant, she suggested that perhaps they symbolized her shedding of the protective layer she had been wearing from as far back as she could remember, her mask of self-sufficiency and invulnerability. I suggested that the masks in her dreams were like the *klippot,* the shells or husks described in the Kabbalah's myth of the shattered vessels as the external forces of evil that entrap the sparks of divine light. In freeing herself from her own klippot, Joan was reclaiming her original face as a beloved child of the divine, worthy of love just as she was.

In therapy Joan also began to explore ways that she might carve out time in her busy life for Sabbath rest, time for meditation and relaxation or to kick back and do nothing—time, in short, to just be. At first, it was difficult for Joan to stop doing and just relax. Her inner voices taunted her with accusations that she was worthless and lazy whenever she tried to slow down. But over time Joan found that if she responded to the taunts with humility, she could relax. Humbly acknowledging to herself that she simply did not need to *do* or *be* it all gave her a huge measure of relief. Though this may seem rather obvious to some of us, for serious overachievers humility is a truly liberating concept.

MOSES

The Most Humble of Men

In the Torah, Moses is described as the most humble man on the face of the earth. Interestingly, this description comes in Numbers 12:1–3, in the context of the story in which his siblings, Miriam and Aaron, criticize him behind his back: According to the passage, "Miriam and Aaron spoke about Moses regarding the Cushite [black] woman that he had taken, that he had married a woman from Cush. And they said, 'Did the Infinite speak only with Moses? Didn't God also speak within us?' And God heard [these words]. And the man Moses was so very humble; as humble as any man on the face of the earth."

According to the famous medieval biblical commentator Rashi, Miriam's criticism of Moses boiled down to questioning why he had separated himself from his wife to become celibate. Since Miriam and Aaron were also prophets in their own right and they had not taken it upon themselves to be celibate, Miriam questioned Moses' actions. God is angered by Miriam's speaking behind her brother's back, and as a consequence she is smitten with leprosy, as recounted in Numbers 12:4–10:

And God said suddenly to Moses and Aaron and Miriam:
"Go out all three of you to the tent of meeting." And all
three went out. And God descended in the cloud of glory
and stood at the opening of the tent and called Aaron and
Miriam and the two of them went out. And He said: "Listen to my words. If there is a prophet among you, I the
Eternal will speak to him in a dream. My servant Moses is
not so. He is faithful in all my house. With him I speak
mouth to mouth in plain vision, not in riddles. The face
of God he sees. How could you not fear to speak against
my servant Moses?" And the wrath of God glowed against
them and then went away. As the cloud departed from
off the tent, behold Miriam had become leprous, white as
snow.

Without going into the rightness or wrongness of Miriam's questioning of her brother's celibacy, I would like to focus on Moses' extraordinary response and how his response itself testifies to his extreme
humility. Immediately upon learning of Miriam's leprosy, Moses responds by praying "Please God please heal her" (Numbers 12:13).

Typically, when people criticize or slander us behind our backs,
we become hostile, or at least defensive, in response. If we don't actually get angry at them we might at least distance ourselves from them.
The last thing most of us would think to do is pray for them. The
Bible's testimony to Moses' extreme humility is that he doesn't hesitate for a moment to pray for his sister's healing, even though she has
just criticized him. Moses doesn't take offense because he is detached
from his own ego. As a prophet he has become so steeped in God-
consciousness that he no longer is affected by pride, and so he is able
to answer insult with blessing and unfair criticism with the healing
salve of love.[14]

Learning not to take offense when our pride is wounded or when
we are criticized is quite a challenge for most of us. In our self-
preoccupation, we tend to take everything that happens to us far
too personally. When the Kotzker Rebbe said that the "I" is a thief
in hiding, perhaps he was alluding to the way the ego personalizes

Healing the Split Self

everything, taking both credit and blame for whatever comes its way, rightfully or not.

Don't Take It Personally!

The importance of learning not to take things too personally is apparent in the following tale about the nineteenth-century Hasidic master Rabbi David of Lelov.

Once, while on the road, Rabbi Isaac of Vorki and his teacher, Reb David of Lelov stopped in an unfamiliar town. Suddenly a woman approached Reb David and began to beat him, having mistaken him for her estranged husband, who had abandoned her and her children several years earlier. While screaming and hitting Reb David, the woman suddenly realized that the man she was beating was not her husband but a famous Hasidic rebbe who happened to look a lot like her husband. Completely mortified, she immediately began to beg the rebbe's forgiveness, apologizing profusely for her terrible mistake. Instead of getting angry, Reb David responded with words of comfort, saying: "It's okay, don't worry; it wasn't *me* you were hitting." The woman was completely baffled, but she went away feeling as though a heavy burden had been lifted from her soul.

When Reb David said "it wasn't me you were hitting," he was, in fact, teaching the woman a very deep lesson. When we are hurt by another person's actions, our pain is often amplified by the fact that we tend to take personally what was done to us. We experience the pain as though it were intentionally directed at us and as though we must have deserved it. "It wasn't me you were hitting," was the wise rabbi's way of saying he was not identified with the "me" that had been the target of the woman's outrageous, insulting behavior. As an evolved spiritual being, Reb David was not primarily identified with his ego, so he felt no need to defend his honor or pride. When he said "it wasn't *me* you were hitting," perhaps he was also teaching the woman that she need not take her husband's abandonment of her so personally. If she could realize this, perhaps she would be released from her rage and be able to heal the damage that her husband's actions had inflicted on her self-esteem.

When we are identified with the God-self, the unfortunate stuff that happens to us, the stuff we typically have no control over, doesn't define us. Too much of the time, we let the pain of our past and our symptoms define who we think we are. A lot of self-help groups reinforce this attachment to victimhood. We get stuck defining ourselves as "adult children of" this or that circumstance we couldn't control. Jewish mysticism, on the other hand, teaches that the more empty and spiritually transparent we become, the more clearly we can see and experience life from a place of nonreactivity and compassion. When we stop taking it all quite so personally, we can achieve a greater measure of emotional freedom than we might otherwise be capable of. We are free to *respond* to the present moment rather than *react* based on memories from the past.

Not taking things too personally also applies to our successes. When we are called upon to do something great, humility can free us up to meet the challenge. Rabbi Shneur Zalman of Liadi learned this from his wife when, after the Maggid of Mezerich's death, hundreds of disciples flocked to Rabbi Shneur Zalman's home to proclaim him their new spiritual leader. Overwhelmed by the flood of Hasidim and the admiration they showed him, Shneur Zalman wanted to flee. His wise wife, however, calmed him down by reminding him that it was not "him" they were seeking but the Torah he had learned. When Shneur Zalman realized that his newly acquired popularity was not so much about "him" as about transmitting the divine gift of knowledge he had received, he felt free to take on the role of "rebbe."

In doing our work in the world and in serving God, it is important, of course, that humility not disempower us or make us passive. For the notion that everything that occurs is from God can inadvertently support a kind of passive acceptance and surrender to things we ought to confront and change. Indeed, the traditional rabbinic prohibition against studying the Kabbalah before the age of forty may have actually been a safeguard against a kind of premature enlightenment that leads to personal disempowerment.[15]

I know that I paid a price for surrendering too much of my own personal power and will to what I thought at the time was God's will. When I embraced Orthodox Judaism at age seventeen, I let go of some important parts of myself. As a woman in the orthodox world, I was expected to be modest and somewhat "invisible," a support to others rather than a powerful person in my own right. For many years, then, I accepted a role that inhibited my self-expression. At that time I didn't fully understand that my "spiritual surrender" was holding me back in certain areas of my development. It was only when I left Israel and began to study psychology that I realized, in retrospect, that mixed in with my youthful embrace of religious idealism, I had been avoiding taking full existential responsibility for my life.

Finding the right balance of self-empowerment and self-surrender can be quite challenging. When we look to Jewish sources on the subject, there seems to be an imbalance. While there are many teachings on humility and self-surrender in the mystical texts, there are very few teachings on self-assertion and self-empowerment. This imbalance is most likely the result of the long history of oppression that Jews faced in exile, during which they rarely had control over their external circumstances. By surrendering to God's will, Jews obtained at least some measure of internal control.

This isn't to say Hasidic masters never cautioned against excess humility. For example, Rabbi Levi Yitzhak of Berditchev taught his disciples, "You must be humble in all your ways and in all your deeds. You might therefore think that you must also be humble in serving God. Heaven forbid that you say that. You must say, 'When I fulfill God's commandments, my observance is very important to God. He has great delight from my observance.'"[16]

A similar warning is found in the teachings of Rabbi Ya'acov Yosef of Polonoye, one of the disciples and scribes of the Ba'al Shem Tov, who said that "it is possible to be so humble that your very humility keeps you far from God. A humble person may not believe that his own prayer can cause the Presence to flow through all the worlds. But how then can you believe that even angels are nourished by your words. Know the power of your prayer and serve your God in fullness!"[17]

This teaching may sound a bit *chutzpadik* (outrageous), but without a certain measure of holy chutzpah we can't really use our full potential to serve God in the world. As is often the case in Jewish spiritual healing, we are charged with the task of integrating seemingly contradictory qualities. Humility is essential for spiritual development, but we must be able to hold on to its sacred counterpart as well, for with holy chutzpah our humility is fully potentiated, creating a powerful spiritual synergy for divine service.

I learned a lot about the power of holy chutzpah from one of my teachers, the late Rabbi Shlomo Carlebach, with whom I studied over the course of several decades. No matter where Reb Shlomo went, he took his open heart and holy chutzpah with him. On airplanes and in airports, in prisons and in hospitals, on army bases and on the streets of nearly every big city in the world, he made friends with everyone he met, including the homeless, whom he often invited not just into his heart but also his home. Though he rarely spoke about his own troubles, people poured their hearts out to him, seeking comfort and guidance. Reb Shlomo was truly the king of schmaltz, never embarrassed to say the most outrageously loving thing to people he had just met. Everyone he encountered became his beloved, beautiful holy sister or holy brother. He never held back from saying or doing in the moment whatever was in the deepest depths of his loving heart. That takes holy chutzpah.

AYIN MEDITATION 2

Rabbi Pinhas of Koretz taught a meditation in which one visualizes oneself being consumed by a bonfire for the sake of heaven. This practice of self-nullification, which borrows its imagery from the myth of the *Akedah*—the binding of Isaac—and from Jewish martyrology liturgy,[18] allows us to go beyond knowing God intellectually; we do this by experiencing ourselves as completely nullified within God's infinite being. Interestingly, the famous Zen teacher Suzuki Roshi used a similar image to describe wholehearted Zen practice, saying: "When you do something, you should burn yourself completely, like a good bonfire, leaving no trace of yourself."[19]

5

THE MYTH OF THE EXODUS
Birthing the Self

It was not enough to take the Jews out of Egypt. It was necessary to take Egypt out of the Jews.
—Hasidic saying

The real exile of Israel in Egypt was that they learned to endure it.
—Rabbi Hanoch of Alexander

The biblical story of the Exodus, which recounts the Israelites' journey of spiritual homecoming from slavery to freedom, and from exile to redemption, forms the core myth of Jewish spiritual life. Alongside the Kabbalah's myth of the shattered vessels, it is Judaism's other great healing myth.

Observant Jews live and breathe the Exodus every day, as religious life continually revolves around this great myth. A retelling of the Exodus and the crossing of the Red Sea is at the heart of the daily Hebrew prayer liturgy, suggesting that one must remember and relive the journey out of Egypt each day. In what amounts to a refrain, there are more than fifty references to the Exodus in the Torah. Many important spiritual practices, including the Sabbath and holy days, are considered to be a "remembrance of the Exodus from Egypt," or *zecher le'yetziat Mitzrayim.* At the same time that they recall the historic events of the Exodus, these daily, weekly, and annual rites of remembrance also bring to life the story's mythic and archetypal dimensions.

The Exodus myth speaks to many different dimensions of healing. It enjoins us to heal the world's social ills, like oppression and subjugation, while also hinting at the most sublime aspects of both psychological and spiritual healing. Indeed, its healing message on both the micro and macro levels places it among the world's great healing myths. It is in the biblical account of the Exodus that God is revealed as the force of healing in the world, as it says in Exodus 15:26: "If you listen to the voice of YHVH your God, and do that which is truthful in God's eyes and listen to the commandments and keep all the statutes, all the illnesses I placed on Egypt I will not place on you. I am YHVH your healer."

In his book *Jewish Renewal,* Rabbi Michael Lerner, philospher, theologian, and social theorist, points out that through the Exodus God reveals Himself to Moses not just as Creator but also as the healing and transforming force of love that underlies creation—a force that is slowly helping all things evolve from how they "are" to how they "ought to be," showing that the oppression and evil in the world are not inevitable but are conditions that can and must be changed.[1] Embedded in this perspective is the idea that all life, inspired by the divine essence, is continually coming out of Egypt, evolving out of levels and dimensions of enslavement. This is why God is identified in the first of the Ten Commandments not as the "creator of heaven and earth" but as "the Lord Your God who has taken you out of Egypt, out of the house of bondage" (Exodus 20:2). A variation of this message is echoed in both the mystical and psychological interpretations of the Exodus myth, which are the focus of this chapter.

THE EXODUS IN THE MYSTICAL TRADITION

In Jewish mystical teachings, the Exodus is seen not just as a one-time historical event or a story of national liberation but as a myth about the transformation of human consciousness and healing journey of the soul from the narrow confines of the ego to the Promised Land of the spirit. According to the Hasidic masters, the Hebrew word for Egypt, *Mitzrayim,* suggests *meitzarim,* narrow straits, or more colloquially, "a tight place." Jewish mystics saw Mitzrayim not only as a geographical place but as a symbol of constricted consciousness. Israel's exile and suffering in Mitzrayim are emblematic of the different forms of suffering we experience when we lose touch with our true nature and become stuck in narrow and constricted states of consciousness, or when we become enslaved by inflexible roles, behaviors, and mind-sets. Anything that diminishes and restricts our awareness of the true nature of our being is a state of mitzrayim.

According to the Hasidic masters, we continually leave mitzrayim each day of our lives, as we move from the state of consciousness known as small mind, or *katnut d'mochin,* to the state of consciousness known as big mind, or *gadlut d'mochin.* According to Rabbi Shneur Zalman of Liadi, we leave mitzrayim every time we open ourselves to an awareness of God's oneness and experience ourselves as included within God's infinite being. This shift in consciousness is the goal of the daily spiritual practice of reciting the Shema, the prayer that affirms the oneness of all being:

> In every generation and on every day, a person ought to see themselves as though they are leaving Mitzrayim [Egypt] that very day. And the meaning of this is the freeing of the divine soul from the prison of the body, in order to experience the [temporary] dissolution of the separate self [as it is absorbed] into the unity of God's infinite light. [This is made possible] through Torah [study], [the practice of the] mitzvot, and particularly . . . when reciting the *Shema* through which, one accepts and draws upon oneself God's blessed unity when saying: "The Infinite is our God the Infinite is One."[2]

When said with deep kavannah, or focused intentionality, the Shema transports us from the narrow confines of the separate self, our personal mitzrayim, to the expansive awareness of our interconnectedness and interdependence with all being. For Shneur Zalman and other Jewish mystics, this mystical state of unity opens the heart to love. Indeed, the prayer that traditionally follows the Shema opens with the word "*ve'ahavta*"—and you shall love.

It is this mystic love for God and for all being that motivates the Jewish imperative to heal and transform the world. For out of the realization that all beings are one, we come to experience the suffering of others as though it were our own, and we are compelled to act in accordance with that empathic knowledge by struggling to end oppression and human suffering in all its many forms. Thus, mystical awakening, like the one the Israelites experienced at Sinai, leads to social action.

A Myth about Personal Transformation

In addition to its mystical, spiritual meaning, the Exodus can also be understood as a myth about personal change and transformation—the story of how each of us can be freed from the narrow and limiting aspects of our upbringing and early conditioning. Each of us, metaphorically speaking, goes down to Egypt in our early development. The very formation of the ego and its defenses can be seen as a descent into a mitzrayim of sorts for our spirit, which is essentially limitless. To some degree, the narrowing of consciousness that accompanies ego development is inevitable and necessary, for in order to function in the world we have to develop a healthy sense of our own autonomy and will. But that very sense of our separateness becomes a mitzrayim, which we must transcend in order to embrace the fullness of our true being.

The bottom line is that any time we allow a narrow *part* of the self, rather than the *whole* of our being, to become our sole focus, we enter a state of mitzrayim.

The exile of the Israelites in Mitzrayim represents a condition of self-alienation, of not being in one's true place. In exile we become disconnected from our own true nature and inner being; our outer lives slide out of sync with our inner essence. When we are not grounded in our essential being, we don't have access to the vital energies we need in order to be creative, and we are unable to realize our true potential. Deliverance from exile, or redemption, on the other hand, implies a return to one's true self, to one's own inner heart of hearts. When we come home to ourselves we find that our innermost essence may be expressed in our outermost lives.

For most of us, exile begins in childhood, when we learn to hold back the expression of our authentic full being in order to stay safe or maintain the approval of our caretakers. Our prolonged childhood dependence on the support of family and other caretakers, who are not always fully equipped to nurture our emotional and spiritual development, can force us to make such unhealthy adaptations. In order to free ourselves so that we may go forward on our journeys, we must break out of these self-imposed constraints.

Sam's Story

Breaking Free of Childhood Constraints

Sam was a good example of somebody stuck in restrictive childhood patterns. He sought therapy because he had no idea which direction to take in his life. He felt no motivation or passion in his work, and he was personally stuck in his spiritual practice. For the first few months of therapy Sam spoke in a monotone, and our sessions together seemed lifeless. It often seemed as though Sam had rehearsed what he was going to say before coming in to the sessions. The deadness he felt inside himself was being expressed through his emotional flatness.

In what amounted to a breakthrough session, Sam finally got in touch with some authentic feelings. Realizing that he had spent his whole life trying to obtain approval from others, he became visibly upset and angry for the first time in our work together. He realized that he had sought approval so consistently throughout his life as to lose touch with many of his own needs and feelings. Having grown up with a mother who demanded that everyone in the family cater to her emotional needs, Sam adapted by becoming a pleaser. Though his congenial behavior later won him friends and a great deal of approval from others, he felt hollow inside and was unable to experience his own inner vitality and passion. Being so focused on pleasing others, Sam did not know what gave *him* pleasure, and as a result he could not find his direction in life. In effect, Sam had forfeited his true self in order to accommodate and please others.

As Sam articulated this realization in therapy, he finally broke out of the emotional flatness that had characterized our previous work. He expressed intense feelings of anger and resentment toward his mother, for the ways she controlled the family through her neediness and narcissism. Sam and I both knew at the end of that session that he had reached a turning point in his therapy from which there was no going back. He was breaking out of his mitzrayim, his self-imposed narrow range of affect and expression.

In order to get in touch with the fullness of our being we must, like Sam, break out of our own restrictive patterns. We must develop the ability to *respond* consciously to life rather than *react* to things based on our unconscious conditioning. True inner freedom demands that we overcome our childhood limitations; otherwise, we remain slaves, in effect, to our unconscious pharaohs.

In healthy development, consciousness continually evolves. We continually come out of mitzrayim as we transcend the boundaries of our known, limited universe and become more and more fully ourselves. Under optimal conditions, children have an innate capacity to become their own authentic selves—what British child analyst D. W. Winnicott referred to as the capacity to "go on being."[3] However, when a child's development is impeded by excess parental interference, this capacity is impaired. Forced to deal prematurely with the needs of others, such a child will not be able to stay sufficiently centered within his or her own experience. It is then difficult to develop a continuous and integrated sense of being. Like Sam, the child who must deal with a depressed, anxious, or overly narcissistic parent will often develop a false, caretaker self as a means of coping with the stress that he experiences in the primary relationship.

For those of us who, like Sam, were forced to prematurely accommodate to the needs of others, coming out of mitzrayim means leaving behind the false self we assumed as children. This process involves freeing ourselves from excessive concern with obtaining approval from others and instead getting in touch with our own authentic inner being.

For others, coming out of mitzrayim involves letting go of an overly repressive and punitive superego—a judgmental inner voice that inhibits our self-expression and prevents us from fully enjoying our lives. This particular brand of mitzrayim was the focus of Freud's early work in psychoanalytic theory. Coming out of the Victorian era, Freud's patients were frequently victims of an overly repressive upbringing, and so their healing focused on liberation from the overly harsh superego. But we can also become enslaved to our impulses, what Freud referred to as the id, if we allow ourselves to be led only by them. In this case the id, or the impulses, becomes a personal mitzrayim. Likewise any addiction, be it to alcohol, drugs, food, or sex, or any compulsive activity, such as gambling or compulsive shopping, can become a personal mitzrayim as well. In such instances, the substance or activity on which we depend for our sense of well-being becomes our inner pharaoh. Overcoming our reliance on these compulsive and addictive behaviors can free us from a life of restriction and inner enslavement.

For those of us who have reached a more advanced stage of personal development, leaving mitzrayim is about the larger process of self-realization, in which the ego learns to step aside and allow the larger Self or godly soul to become the center of one's being. This kind of spiritual development is generally not possible until we have achieved some measure of freedom from these other forms of self-enslavement.

THE POWER OF "BEING" AND "BECOMING"

The first step toward healing and redemption in the myth of the Exodus involves learning the mystery of the divine name, YHVH. In the very first stage of the liberation journey, God teaches Moses the mystery of this divine name in hopes that by learning God's true name and essence, the Israelites may come to remember their own true names. In Exodus 6:2 God tells Moses, "I am YHVH. And I appeared to Abraham, to Isaac and to Jacob by means of the name El Shadai, but my name YHVH was not made known to them."

What's in a name? The revelation of the name YHVH reflects the emergence of a new spiritual consciousness in which divinity is perceived as the force of freedom, healing, and transformation that lies at the heart of all creation. The awakening of this new awareness of the divine was in fact the intended outcome of the Exodus. How does the name YHVH invoke or touch freedom?

In Jewish mysticism YHVH is understood to be a meditation on infinite beingness. Known as the *shem havayah,* the holy name of "being," YHVH is a composite of the three Hebrew words *hayah* (was), *hoveh* (is), and *yihiyeh* (will be). YHVH, then, represents the experience of the eternal now, wherein the linear time-space continuum is suspended.

YHVH is essentially a meditation on being in the present. It teaches us to let go of the past and future so that we can be in the mystery of the now, for the power to be in the present is what opens the door to true freedom. So long as we are bound to our past, we are not totally free to be or become who we are meant to be. It is only when we can be fully in the now that we can move forward into our future free of the binding attachments of the past.

The Ba'al Shem Tov once said that our biggest slave driver or pharaoh is all our "yesterdays." When we allow our past to define and limit us, we become slaves to a fixed self-image, an idol of sorts. Who we have been is who we think we will always be. To be a slave in mitzrayim is to become so entrenched in one's known, limited identity that one loses touch with the mystery of becoming. Without the power to dream and imagine, we cannot grow.

A future-tense variation of the name YHVH is revealed to Moses in his encounter with God at the burning bush, recounted in Exodus 3:14. There, Moses asks to know God's name, and in response God says to Moses, *"Ehyeh asher Ehyeh,"* or "I shall be what I am becoming." Then, as if to add a nickname or shorthand version of the name, God says: "Thus tell the children of Israel, Ehyeh [I am becoming] has sent me to you."

For Moses and his people, learning the name Ehyeh, or I am becoming, opens the door to what Rabbi Michael Lerner calls "the possibility of possibilities." Just as God is in a process of becoming, continually emerging anew, at any moment in time we too can birth ourselves anew. In learning this variation of the divine name, the Israelites reconnect with the possibility of change, for the Exodus is essentially a myth about the freedom to change. It reveals how we can free ourselves from the chain of causality by stepping off the path of the inevitable and creating the possible.

YHVH is known as the ineffable name, or *shem ha'mefurash*. Traditionally it was pronounced out loud only by the high priest on Yom Kippur, the holiest day of the year, as he entered the innermost chamber, or holy of holies (*kodesh kodashim*), in the Jerusalem temple. We no longer know how to articulate this name of God, and so when we encounter it in the Bible or liturgy, we say either *Hashem,* which means "the name," or *Adonai,* the divine name representing those aspects of the divine that can be apprehended by human faculties.

YHVH's ineffability hints at the unknowability of the divine, for God is ultimately beyond all the names, metaphors, or images that we employ to talk about the great mystery. YHVH's unnameable essence is an initiation into the mystery of not-knowing, or uncertainty, for YHVH is never a static reality but a process of unfolding. By suggesting that we not limit the divine by naming it, Judaism teaches us not to limit ourselves, as the opening lines of the Tao Te Ching suggest:

> The tao that can be told
> is not the eternal Tao.
> The name that can be named
> is not the eternal name.
>
> The unnameable is the eternally real.
> Naming is the origin of all particular things.[4]

If, as the Tao Te Ching suggests, only "the unnameable is the eternally real," to know the secret of God's unnameable essence is to discover our own eternal name; for we, like God, are eternally becoming, and infinitely unknowable.

Thus, to help people come out of their mitzrayim, the greatest gift we can offer them as healers is to create an open space where they can experience their own vast unknowability. By offering people what John Welwood refers to as "unconditional presence," we allow them to reveal the mystery of their becoming[5] This involves suspending our own preconceived notions and theories about them, so that we don't limit their becoming. If we can be comfortable with not-knowing and just allow ourselves to be fully present as witnesses to their emergence, we offer people the space they need in order to discover their own spacious being. In a sense we must come out of our own limited conceptual universe, our own mitzrayim, in order to allow others to emerge out of theirs.

OPENING TO THE INFINITE

Becoming "Eternists"

Another, more esoteric way of understanding the healing power of YHVH is that it enables us to rise above and transcend the workings of time. When we rest in our consciousness of the infinite—in pure infinite beingness—we open ourselves to the realm beyond time and beyond causality. This is important in relation to healing, because the power to heal demands that we free ourselves from the chain of causality. When we truly experience YHVH in deep states of meditation, we are freed from the suffering that arises because we are captives of time and the processes of change that occur in time.[6]

That a connection to the infinite plays a role in healing is one of the most exciting discoveries in contemporary medicine, what the alternative medicine researcher Dr. Larry Dossey has termed Era III medicine. Based on the extensive body of medical research on the therapeutic effects of prayer, science is finally acknowledging what mystics have always believed—that evoking a sacred connection with the infinite, what many call God, can profoundly improve one's health and sense of well-being. In a radical departure from traditional Western medicine, Dossey suggests that in order to offer their patients a complete opportunity for healing, doctors need to become "eternists" in addition to being internists! Thus, the Bible's assertion that YHVH—the Infinite One—is our healer may be understood literally as well as figuratively, and there is scientific data to back it up.[7] As a psychotherapist who has integrated spiritual awareness and practice into my life and work for over thirty years, I find these developments very exciting.

Enabling people to access their infinite nature, or what Jung referred to as the larger Self, is an important step in healing. As we learn to see ourselves through the lens of our eternal being or infinite nature, we can begin to disidentify with our "problems" and "pathologies." And when we do this, a profound inner shift occurs. Instead of being defined by our histories, we begin to feel called by our destinies; instead of being who we have always been, we are freed up to become who we are truly meant to be. At any point in time, we are free to cut our ties with the past and follow instead our destiny—our soul's unfolding into its wholeness and uniqueness.

This process has a parallel in the Exodus myth, in which the Israelites leave the narrow confines of Mitzrayim in order to enter into a relationship with the divine. To do this, they must leave the realm of the known (the conscious self) and enter into the mystery of the unknown (the unconscious), symbolized by the desert. In the silence of the desert, or midbar, they will encounter the unpredictable and powerful forces of the unconscious. On their desert journey they will face all their inner fears and uncertainties. Yet as they face and overcome their terror of the unknown, they will learn to trust, both in God and in the mystery of their own becoming. As they encounter the still, small voice of the divine on their journey of "unknowing," they will discover that they are being guided and supported by the loving embrace of the divine presence.

To be a psychotherapist is to empower people to see beyond their known, limited vision of themselves and restore their sense of hope and faith in themselves, and in life's many possibilities. I often think of my work as a form of spiritual midwifery. My job is to gently encourage and support people as they break out of their self-imposed mitzrayim, or limitations, and give birth to their fullest selves. The Exodus myth, which in many ways can be seen as a metaphor for how we give birth to the self, often guides my work. As I witness the psycho-spiritual unfolding of my clients, I am often struck by the many parallels that exist between their journeys and the ancient journey of our ancestors.

Symbols of Birth in the Exodus Myth

When we view the Exodus myth as a metaphor for how we give birth to the larger self, we find that many of its symbols are suggestive of the birth process. Ancient midrashim likened Israel's existence in Egypt to that of "an embryo in its mother's womb" and the Exodus itself to a delivery. Indeed, as the story of the Exodus unfolds, the Israelites go through all the stages of birth, from conception and gestation to delivery, complete with blood, birth pangs, and all.[8] In the remainder of this chapter we will examine some of these birth/ healing metaphors and explore how they might be used to guide our healing journeys.

Goshen

The Womb

As conception begins with the implantation of a fertilized egg within the walls of the uterus, the story of the Exodus begins when Jacob's descendants go down to Egypt and settle there to escape the famine in the land of Canaan. Goshen, the part of Egypt that Joseph secures for his brethren, was, like the womb, a place of refuge for the Israelites. For many years they live in comfort and security in the land of Goshen, where they grow from a family of seventy into a great nation. As recounted in Exodus 1:7, "The children of Israel were fruitful, and increased abundantly, and multiplied, and waxed exceedingly mighty; and the land was filled with them."

The accelerated growth of the Israelite nation in Goshen suggests the rapid growth of the fetus in the uterus during the early months of gestation. As the fetus reaches full term, however, it no longer has adequate room to move freely about. A state of constriction inevitably arises, which will set in motion the processes that lead to the birth.

As the Israelites become a great multitude, Goshen, the very womb that had nurtured their rapid growth and development, becomes instead a narrow and inhospitable place of confinement, a *meitzar,* or strait. Just as the fetus will die if it does not leave the womb when it is time to be born, the Israelites had to get out of Egypt if they didn't want to stagnate or die as a nation. Indeed, we all must find the strength and courage to leave situations and relationships that no longer provide us with room to grow. Otherwise we stagnate, too.

We may be reluctant, however, to let go of old, familiar situations, particularly those to which we cling out of weakness or insecurity. Our enslavement to unhealthy relationships, jobs, and situations typically does not occur overnight. Instead, it is a condition that most often develops over time. We may make certain compromises we ought not make, or lower our moral bottom line in order to obtain a measure of financial or emotional security, only to find out that we have lost our true power by making these unwise adaptations. The following legend from the *Midrash Tanhuma* describes this kind of gradual relinquishment of power and freedom by recounting how the Israelites were slowly seduced into servitude by their desire to accommodate and assimilate into Egyptian culture. (When Pharaoh first asked for volunteers for his civic building project of the pyramids, most of the Israelites joined in. After doing the work on a volunteer basis alongside Pharaoh, all those who had volunteered were then tricked into continued servitude.)

> Pharoah had already declared that the Egyptians must "outsmart" Israel. So he gathered all the children of Israel and gave them this "pitch:" "Please do me a favor today and give me a hand." Pharaoh took up a rake and a basket and began to make mud bricks. Everyone who saw him did likewise. Israel worked with him enthusiastically all day. When it grew dark, Pharaoh appointed task masters

over them to count up their bricks. "That," he announced,
"will be your daily quota!"[9]

According to this midrash, the Israelites became entrapped by a situation they willingly entered. Essentially, they traded their freedom for social acceptance.

The unfolding of events described by the midrash is not so different from the way that so many of us today become enslaved to lifestyles we find oppressive. Joel and Mary, a dual career couple I counseled, both felt trapped by the fast-track lives they had unwittingly created for themselves and their family. Both of them had jobs in the high-tech world that required exceptionally long work hours, so that they often had very little leisure time and little energy left for one another or for the kids at the end of the day. They knew that they were heading for trouble as a couple if they did not make a change, but they felt trapped by the choices and commitments they had made. Monthly mortgage payments, private school tuition for the kids, and all the other conventional trappings of upper-middle-class life had left them feeling they had little choice but to continue their driven lives. But truthfully, they felt enslaved by a life that did not reflect their true values, nor did it really deliver the promised happiness.

As with so many of us, when Joel and Mary first started down the path of conventional middle-class living, they had no idea that it would lead to such a loss of personal freedom. Now, facing a crisis point in their marriage, they were beginning to rethink their options. In counseling they began to explore how they might resist the powerful negative influence that conventional and corporate life was having on them. As they reclaimed their inner sense of freedom, they began to figure out ways to simplify and reshape their lives to reflect their own true values.

Joel and Mary both felt that their family life would be more harmonious if they could cut back on the number of hours they both spent at work. In order to do this, however, they realized that they would have to figure out ways to reduce their monthly expenses. After looking at simple ways of cutting back unnecessary spending on such things as vacations and fancy automobiles, Joel and Mary decided to explore the possibility of transferring their children from private to public schools. After doing some serious research on the local public schools, they concluded that their children could obtain a perfectly good education without incurring the high costs of private schooling. The savings from these changes alone made a significant enough difference in their monthly expenses that Mary could begin to work half-time. Being able to stay home with the children after school was extremely satisfying to Mary as a parent, and it eliminated additional child-care and private tutoring expenses.

These and other steps Joel and Mary took toward voluntary simplicity helped free them from enslavement to a life that did not reflect their essential values.

RESISTANCE TO CHANGE

In the biblical tale of the Exodus, the process of redemption begins with the courageous acts of people who resist the status quo. By refusing to carry out Pharaoh's cruel decree to murder all the Hebrew boy babies, the Egyptian midwives engage in civil disobedience. The midwives, who symbolize birth and new life, open up the possibility of change by resisting the oppressive order of things. As Exodus 1:15–17 recounts, "The king of Egypt spoke to the Hebrew midwives, the first one's name being Shifra and the second one's name being Puah, saying: 'When you help the Israelite women give birth and you see upon the birthing stools that it is a son, then you must put him to death; but if it is a daughter she may live.' And the midwives feared God and did not do as the King of Egypt spoke to them. And they allowed the babies to live."

Shifra and Puah's rejection of the status quo is followed by another brave act of resistance. Batya, Pharaoh's own daughter, disregards her father's harsh decree as she opens her heart to the cries of a Hebrew infant floating down the Nile. She rescues the child and brings him to the palace to be raised as her adopted son, Moses, who will grow up to become the liberator of the Israelite nation.

What I find most inspiring in these tales is that it is the courageous acts of resistance by *individual people* that bring about the chain of events that will eventually lead to the redemption. Though more than eighty years would go by between Shifra, Puah, and Batya's actions and the Exodus, were it not for these brave acts, there would have been no Moses and no redemption. Instead of giving in to feelings of powerlessness, these women followed their heart and conscience. In doing so, they planted the seeds of a revolution that would change human history forever.

Even today, we can benefit from their example. Sometimes we feel so powerless to effect change in our lives that we don't even bother trying. We passively accept that who we have been is who we will always be. I often hear people in the early phases of therapy express feelings of hopelessness about ever changing. They say things like "That's who I am; I can't change. I've always been this way. I just can't help it." Part of the struggle in therapy is simply convincing people that change is possible. Our feelings of powerlessness can be even more overwhelming when we try to imagine combating the overwhelming forces of evil and oppression in the world around us. The enormity of the challenge typically paralyzes us because we tend to view our individual actions as simply a minuscule drop in the bucket. If we give in to these kinds of feelings of powerlessness and helplessness we won't even bother trying to effect change.

Shifra, Puah, and Batya may not have lived to see the effects that their acts of resistance would have on history, but their descendants would live to tell the tale. As one Talmudic sage, Rabbi Avira, suggests, "It was in the merit of the righteous women of that generation that our ancestors were redeemed from Egypt."[10]

In more recent history, we can also find stories of individual people whose brave actions spurred revolutionary social-change movements. When Rosa Parks refused to move to the back of the bus, she had no idea that her actions would become a powerful symbol of resistance in the civil rights movement. Acting out of her own sense of personal integrity and her willingness to stand up for truth, she set in motion a chain reaction that would influence history for all eternity. Likewise, the brave actions of such individual people as Gandhi, Martin

Luther King, and Vaclav Havel, to name a few, have had a profound effect on the history of entire nations.

SETBACKS

In the Exodus story, as in every liberation movement, the people's initial acts of resistance are met by counterresistance. When Moses first challenges Pharaoh to let the Israelite slaves go free, Pharaoh responds by tightening his grip on them. Thus, it seems as though Moses' initial attempts to help only make matters worse. As Exodus 5:5–8 recounts, "Pharaoh commanded on that very day that the taskmasters of the people and their police say: 'You will not continue to supply the people with straw to make bricks as before; let them go and gather straw for themselves. And the number of bricks which they have been making up till now, you shall impose on them as before; do not reduce it.'"

In psychotherapy, as in the Exodus story, our initial attempts at change are often met with powerful forces of inner as well as outer resistance. Pharaoh's stubborn response mirrors the way our own inner pharaohs (and rigid family systems) act as a counterforce to our fledgling attempts at self-liberation. For every few steps forward we take on the healing journey, we frequently take a step or two backward as the ego attempts to preserve its control over our lives by maintaining the familiar status quo.

Later in the process, as we begin to make deep inner changes, there is often a tug-of-war or showdown between the old self and the newly emergent self. Sometimes the older parts of the self resist change so intensely that we have to endure tremendous stress or hardship before we find the strength to push through. In the Exodus myth, the ten plagues symbolize the kind of painful symptoms that can arise when the ego stubbornly resists change and refuses to listen to the soul's longing to be free. Like Pharaoh, we may insist on clinging to situations, habits, relationships, and patterns that have outlived their usefulness, and as a result we may suffer.

Thus, it shouldn't surprise us that in therapy, setbacks often occur right after a person takes a radical step toward change or following moments of deep insight. Sam, for instance, found himself wanting to retreat from therapy following the session I described previously, in which he gained insight into his lifelong pattern of pleasing others at his own expense. I was looking forward to our next session together when, to my surprise, Sam called to announce that he had decided to take a break from therapy. He just didn't see the point of it all. Instead of taking Sam's retreat from therapy at face value, I saw it as an expression of resistance, a temporary retreat from the frightening threshold he had just crossed. I tried to empathize with how frightened Sam must have been after our last session, in which it had become clear that he was facing a showdown between his old self and his newly emergent self. He confirmed my interpretation when he admitted that he knew that if he continued to deepen in therapy, he would have to make some serious changes in his life and his intimate relationships. These changes were completely terrifying to him. Yet after articulating his fears on the phone with me, Sam decided to come back to therapy and take a deeper look at what was really so frightening about change.

In our next session, I spoke with Sam about the nature of inner change. Using the myth of the Exodus as a metaphor for the process of change, I suggested that his rigid allegiance to the role of "pleaser" was his familiar Mitzrayim. Though he felt oppressed by this role, he clung to it because it kept him safe. Like the Israelites, who longed for freedom yet frequently expressed a longing to return to Egypt after they were freed, Sam both yearned to break out of the role of pleaser and at the same time clung to it for dear life. To begin to feel anger at his mother's self-centeredness was truly threatening to his familiar sense of self and safety. The truth is, so long as he stuck to a narrow range of self-expression that guaranteed him approval and acceptance from others, he did not ever have to think about whether he approved of himself. He never had to face the uncertainty of this unknown and unfamiliar terrain.

Sam knew that the "false self" he had adopted to survive his childhood was clearly no longer serving him. In fact, it was undermining his chances at happiness and success. And though there no longer would have been any real threat to his survival if he were to step out of his characteristic role, still he felt imprisoned by his own inner pharaoh, the voice within that expected him to toe the line. For Sam, letting go of the role of "pleaser" and of his overdependence on approval from others would become his own personal *yetziat mitz-rayim* (liberation from inner constraint). In order to break free, however, Sam would need to become more comfortable with his true needs and feelings. He would have to allow himself to feel *his* pain.

FEELING AND EXPRESSING OUR PAIN

When we become imprisoned by unhealthy situations or stuck in outmoded ways of being, we often grow numb to our own pain. We learn to endure things we ought not accept. As Rabbi Hanoch of Alexander once said, "The real exile of Israel in Egypt was that they learned to endure it." If, for example, we neglect our spiritual well-being for a long time, we may grow numb to our spiritual hunger. Like the anorexic who has lost her appetite for food as a result of starving herself, we can become so disconnected from our deeper selves that we stop hearing the cry of our souls. We then find ourselves adapting to a lifestyle that leaves no time or space for the care of our souls.

In the Exodus myth, redemption becomes possible only when the Israelites reconnect with their tears. They had to cry out from their affliction in order for divine compassion to be awakened to their plight. This happened after the pharaoh died, at which point, according to Exodus 2:23–24, "The children of Israel sighed from their toil and they cried out and their cries rose before God . . . and God listened to their groaning and God remembered His covenant with Abraham, with Isaac and with Jacob. And God saw the children of Israel and God knew [their affliction]."

In our own lives, healing often becomes possible only when we begin to feel and acknowledge our own pain. This is why it may subjectively seem as though things often get worse before they get better. For Sam it meant that in order to heal, he first had to allow himself to feel his own disavowed hurt and anger. He had to be willing to face his true feelings, which were just under the surface of his cheerful outer persona.

Sam began to get in touch with these hurt and angry feelings as childhood memories began to surface in therapy. He recalled how, in childhood, his mother would withdraw from him whenever he became angry at her. In fact, he remembered several times when his mother refused to talk to him for hours because he had lost his temper. These experiences of rejection had left him feeling unbearably lonely and ashamed of his feelings and emotional needs.

In response to these traumas, Sam learned that to stay safe he must attend to the emotional needs of others while ignoring and essentially denying his own inner life. But in therapy he began to realize that this old strategy, which guaranteed his emotional survival in childhood, now threatened his development as an adult. If he was ever going to find his true pathway and passion in life, he would have to let go of the need for constant approval from others. He would have to learn to focus more inwardly on himself and less outwardly on others.

Sam's healing process began with a series of many small breakthroughs in which he progressively reclaimed aspects of his true self. Each time he successfully identified and expressed a true need or feeling, he felt as though he were slowly but surely coming out of his self-imposed mitzrayim. At first he was able to do this only within the safety of the therapy relationship. Over time, however, he began taking risks by speaking his truth with family members and friends. He started with small assertions of personal preference, instead of always deferring to others, and eventually worked up the courage to express important needs and feelings, even when they conflicted with those of others. By learning to speak his truth, Sam got in touch with his essential self and was eventually able to find his calling as a community organizer and social-change advocate in the nonprofit world. By learning to express his own true needs and feelings, Sam was able to become a spokesperson for the needs and feelings of others as well.

EMOTIONAL EXPRESSIVENESS AS REDEMPTIVE

Just as Sam's healing was connected to authentic emotional expressiveness, when we put previously unexpressed feelings into words, we often feel a tremendous sense of release and relief. Accurately expressing a feeling liberates us from the unconscious control that the feeling may have had over us. This, in turn, frees us up to realize our full innate potential and align our outer lives with our innermost truth.

In the Kabbalah, redemption is frequently associated with the power of speech or verbal expressiveness, while exile is characterized by inarticulateness. In exile we become so disconnected from our inner selves that we are unable to express our essential being. While Israel was in exile in Mitzrayim, says the Zohar, "speech [dibbur] was in exile."[11] As slaves, the Israelites were not able to hear the word of God, nor were they free to express themselves. Since no one hears their pain, slaves essentially have no voice.

Ironically, the man who would free the Israelites from their mute state suffered from his own speech impediment. In trying to dissuade God from sending him, of all people, to redeem the Israelites, Moses reminds God that he stutters. In Exodus 4:10, he says, "O my Lord, I am not an eloquent man, neither yesterday nor the day before, nor since You spoke to Your servant: but I am slow (heavy) of speech and of a slow (heavy) tongue." In the *Sefat Emet,* his commentary on the Torah, Rabbi Yehudah Aryeh Leib of Ger suggests that Moses' difficulty with words is not so much a literal speech impediment as a prophetic block. Moses' prophetic channels are blocked by the people's unreadiness to hear what he might have to say. In their oppressed state they are simply too distracted to listen to the divine message Moses sought to deliver.

Through the Exodus, however, the power of speech, the dibbur, is released from exile. Likewise, the Israelites find their voice when they are freed, and at the shores of the Red Sea they open up in ecstatic song and praise of the divine. Moses, too, finds his voice when he becomes a channel for the words of the living God at Mount Sinai.

Echoing the ten divine utterances with which the world was spoken into being, the Ten Commandments, or *asseret hadibrot,* restore to creation the original creative power of the divine word. As it says in Psalm 33, "With God's word the heavens were created." It is interesting to note that the Hebrew word for speech, *dibbur,* has the same root (*dalet-bet-resh*) as the word for desert, or *midbar.* In the silence of the midbar of Sinai, the divine dibbur is heard—a fact that suggests that authentic speech is that which flows from its source in silence.

The spiritual connection between redemption and verbal expressiveness is also hinted at in the Hebrew name for Passover, *Pesach,* which according to the Hasidic masters can be understood as a play on the Hebrew words *peh* and *sach,* meaning "the mouth speaks." On Pesach we are free, both internally and externally, to fully express the innermost yearnings of our soul and the songs of our heart. The Passover Haggadah, which recounts the story of the Exodus, encourages us to tell the story of our liberation with the greatest possible elaboration: The very word *Haggadah,* which means "the telling," suggests that on the night of Passover, when we celebrate our liberation, we must become the narrator of our experience and be able to tell our story as a *sacred* text.

According to this understanding of the Exodus myth, true inner freedom involves the freedom of self-expression, the ability to reveal our deepest truth, for it is through the act of articulation that we break through the walls that separate us from ourselves and each other.

FROM IMPASSE TO BREAKTHROUGH

Dramatic breakthroughs, like the one depicted in the myth of the Exodus, are a lot like the final stages of a birth. As contractions become stronger and stronger and progressively more frequent, their energy and intensity build toward a climax. For anyone who has ever experienced or witnessed the final stages of labor, the power of this natural process is both frightening and awe-inspiring. For the mother, exhaustion and exhilaration combine to create a powerful sense of inevitability. But for the infant, just prior to the moment when the cervix becomes fully dilated, there is an experience of total impasse. Describing the fetus's experience of this moment, Dr. Stanislav Grof, a psychiatrist and researcher in transpersonal psychology, writes: "Uterine contractions encroach on the fetus and cause its total constriction. In this stage the uterine cervix is still closed and the way out is not yet available . . . there appears to be no way out either in space or time."[12]

In the Exodus myth, this stage of the *delivery* (pun intended) from Mitzrayim is reflected in the drama at the shores of the Red Sea. With the Egyptians chasing after them and the sea before them, the Israelites are faced with an impasse. To go forward seems literally impossible, while to go back to Egypt would surely mean death.

In our own lives these moments of impasse occur when we know for certain that we can no longer go back to an old situation, but we have no idea how to move forward. At such moments, biblical legend teaches us not to give in to despair or fear. Instead, we must simply move forward with faith and courage. According to the midrash, one brave person from the tribe of Judah, Nachshon ben Aminadav, had the courage to take the plunge into the unknown.[13] Following his footsteps, the Israelites entered the sea, but it was not until the waters reached up to their nostrils, according to one version of the legend, that the sea split and they made their way to safety on the opposite shore. In its own uniquely metaphoric style, the midrash is suggesting that miracles happen, but often not until we stretch ourselves past our outermost limits. Sometimes the sea does not part until we face the possibility of our own annihilation.

Like the Exodus and the splitting of the sea, moments of emotional and spiritual breakthrough are often magical and miraculous. When we find the courage to take the plunge into the unknown despite all our inner fears and inhibitions, we often find that we are able to overcome all the inner and outer obstacles we previously deemed insurmountable. Help may serendipitously appear from people and places we could never have anticipated. As the scriptures suggest, we may feel as though we are being carried "on wings of eagles" (Exodus 19:4), helped along, as it were, by divine grace. When we overcome our fear and inertia and take a big risk, tremendous powers of soul are released within us that carry us forward on our journeys. I have seen this again and again in my own life and in the lives of my clients. We just have to take those first steps into the abyss before our path becomes clear and the obstacles that stand in our way disappear.

The Healing Power of Imagination

But how do we find the courage to take those first steps that will break through the impasse? An answer to this question can be found in the following midrash, which suggests that before they could take their first steps into the water, the Israelites had to be able to imagine and prophetically visualize how the waters of the Red Sea would part before them. As the *Midrash Mechilta* suggests, this is the power that Moses imparted to them at the shores of the Red Sea when he said, "'Stand firm and you will witness [see] God's salvation' (Exodus 14:13). They [the Israelites] said to him, 'When [will we see]?' He answered 'Today He [God] will give you the holy spirit of prophecy.' Whenever we see the word *yetzivah* [standing firm] in scriptures, it always implies the holy spirit of prophecy."[14]

According to this midrash, the Hebrew expression used by Moses, *hityatzvu,* or stand still, suggests the power of prophetic imagination. On the shores of the Red Sea, Moses gave the Israelites the power to see prophetically into their future, the power to imagine the possible. And in granting them this vision he inspired them to act, and ultimately it was their action that brought about the miracle. The lesson is clear: divine grace is available to us, but only after we take action and do our part.

When I work with people who are feeling paralyzed by the seemingly insurmountable obstacles they are facing, I often ask them to place themselves within the context of the Exodus myth and to visualize themselves as though they were standing on the shores of the Red Sea. I then ask them to imagine what would happen if they took the plunge into the unknown in their own lives. How might their pathway open up if the waters were to part for them, so to speak.

This kind of imaginative process was helpful to Joan when she was facing a huge personal impasse. All within a month's time Joan realized she was facing three enormous life transitions. First, she was given notice at work that her job would be ending soon. Then her partner of twenty years announced that he was leaving her for another woman. As if these two changes were not enough, Joan was also going to have to deal with the practical challenges of finding a new house, since the house she and her husband had lived in would have to be sold in order to divide their assets. Everything in Joan's life was ending all at once. Understandably, she felt overwhelmed and paralyzed, but Joan did not have the luxury of going into paralysis. Though she was typically cautious and slow to make up her mind, she was going to have to act bravely and swiftly and take some uncharacteristic risks if she was going to survive the ordeal.

Joan's situation reminded me of the moment when the ancient Israelites stood at the shores of the Red Sea and realized that they could never go back to how things were. When I made this mythic comparison, Joan found that the biblical imagery spoke directly to her current dilemma. The Israelites' fear of drowning was a perfect metaphor for how she felt. Having been partnered most of her adult life, Joan feared she could not survive on her own. The waters that threatened to overwhelm her were the many unknowns she faced.

Using the legend about Nachshon and how the sea split only after he took the risk of entering into the abyss, I encouraged Joan to fantasize about what miracles might happen for her if she were to face courageously the many unknowns in her life rather than withdraw in fear. I asked Joan to close her eyes and try to imagine what her life might look like if the waters were to part for her. I suggested that she fast-forward her life six months into the future and try to picture it as she would hope it might be. During this exercise Joan got in touch with an image of herself living in a small, quiet cottage, working out of her home. She imagined herself to be calm and competent, unafraid to be alone, and financially self-sufficient.

Joan's vision proved to be somewhat prophetic because within a short time after that therapy session, Joan found a perfect living situation in which she would have the space to start the kind of home business she had dreamed of. How she found her new home was a bit of a miracle in itself, with the housing market being especially difficult where she lived. Finding it felt like an act of divine grace.

In the coming months Joan had to take many, many steps into the abyss. Each time she did, however, the waters continued to part before her. Things were not easy. Without the security of a monthly paycheck and benefits Joan had to persistently work at keeping the faith and believing in herself. Like the ancient Israelites, who at times wished they could return to Egypt, Joan occasionally regretted having chosen the less-secure path. But by persevering and continuing to take the risk of venturing into the unknown, Joan managed to make it on her own within several months' time.

As she looked back on our work together, Joan acknowledged that by placing her personal drama within the context of the ancient myth, she was able to find additional energy and courage to persevere. Using the myth of the Exodus as a guide on her journey of becoming, Joan was able to give birth to many new and powerful dimensions of her being.

EXERCISE

Breaking out of Your Personal Mitzrayim

Each of us must continually break out of our mitzrayim, our sense of personal limitation and constriction, in order to grow into the fullness of our being. To do this we must first be able to identify the ways in which we are limited or constricted. So take a few moments to reflect on the ways that you may feel stuck in your life, whether because of an unhealthy external situation or because of a rigid inner attitude. In what ways do you feel enslaved to a life or to values that do not truly represent your inner essence? Have you traded your personal freedom for security? Are you caught between a rock and a hard place, afraid to move forward yet uncomfortable where you stand right now?

Now, as you relax and close your eyes, try to open yourself up to an image of freedom, movement, and release from this bind. Imagine yourself unstuck, as you might hope to be at some time in the future. See yourself as free to move on to the new, free from the old stuck patterns that hold you hostage. Witness your own becoming.

You may wish to write about the images that came up during this exercise in a journal or share them with a friend or loved one.

6

Teshuvah
Return to Self and Spirit

Great is repentance, for it brings healing to the
world. . . .
Great is repentance, for it brings redemption to the
world.
—*The Talmud, Yoma 86a*

Everything teems with richness, everything aspires to
ascend and be purified. Everything sings, celebrates,
serves, develops, evolves, uplifts, aspires to be arranged
in oneness.
—*Abraham Isaac Kook*

In the popular children's book *The Wizard
of Oz,* Dorothy, a young girl who is ill, has a powerful healing dream
in which she is carried far away from her home in Kansas by a powerful tornado. Throughout the dream she longs to return home, but
before she can find her way back, she must journey to the land of
Oz. Dorothy's journey to Oz, accompanied by her three companions,
the Tin Man, the Scarecrow, and the Cowardly Lion, becomes a
mythic quest for wholeness and healing, in which the four protago-
nists seek to acquire the character trait each of them most needs in
order to be whole. The Tin Man seeks a heart, the Scarecrow, a brain,
and the Cowardly Lion, courage. Though she is not conscious of it
as she sets out on her journey, Dorothy needs to find her own inner

source of power. Whether the author of the Oz legends realized it
or not, the Hebrew word *oz* implies "strength." Dorothy's journey to
Oz is, indeed, an attempt to reclaim her power and inner strength. It
is only when she faces her deepest fears and takes back the power she
has been projecting onto powerful others, like the Wizard of Oz and
the Wicked Witch of the West, that Dorothy is able to reclaim her
own inner strength and find her way home. And as Dorothy and her
companions courageously overcome the many obstacles in their path,
they discover that, in fact, they already have within them the very
power or trait that they thought they lacked.

The spiritual quest for wholeness is a lot like the mythic journey
to Oz. When we first begin to awaken, we realize just how far from
home, or our true selves, we really are. We long to return, but we
don't know the way back. We may begin our journey by following a
spiritual path (the Yellow Brick Road) or seeking out a teacher/rebbe/
guru (the Wizard). On the way we may meet up with fellow seekers.
But eventually, like Dorothy and her companions, we come to realize
that the strength we seek outside ourselves already exists within us.
We only need to turn inward to discover our courage, heart, and
wisdom. By focusing our kavannah, or spiritual intention, then, on
our deep longing to return ("there's no place like home"), we find
our way home.

In Jewish teachings, the pathway home to our true nature is called
teshuvah. Though typically translated as repentance, *teshuvah* actually
comes from the Hebrew root *shav,* to return. The implication is that
we all have within us a reference point for wholeness to which we
can return—a spiritual essence encoded within our souls that enables
us to remember who we really are. Teshuvah is not something one
does once and for all; rather, it is a lifelong journey, a journey of
spiritual homecoming.

Jewish legend teaches that before God created this universe of
multiplicity, God created teshuvah, as a healing force embedded in all
creation that draws all things back to their source in infinite oneness.
Without teshuvah, the rabbis taught, the world could not have endured. It is through teshuvah that we each, in our uniqueness and

separateness, come to remember ourselves as part of the great unity from which all of life emerged. And it is through teshuvah that all levels of existence, down to the most basic of cellular processes, are continually being healed and restored to their original, perfect form. Having been created before all things, teshuvah exists in a realm that reaches beyond the working of linear time.[1]

Jewish mystics of ages past wrote extensively about teshuvah; they understood it to have mystical, ethical, social, biological, alchemical, and psychological implications. Teshuvah, this inborn longing for wholeness, perfection, and unity, lies at the heart of all Jewish healing. In the next few chapters we will explore the different dimensions of teshuvah, beginning in this chapter with how the soul is awakened in teshuvah.

AWAKENING THE SOUL

Jewish mysticism teaches that no matter how ill or spiritually disconnected we have become, within each of us there is a part that always remains pure and unsullied and will call us back to our center. This aspect of the self, known as the *neshama,* or soul, is our direct connection with the divine. When we attune ourselves to its calling, the neshama provides us with the exact guidance we need for our soul's evolution.

When we embark on the healing journey, the challenge is to awaken the inner healing power of the neshama. Spiritual practices such as prayer, meditation, and dreamwork are ways that we can begin to access the soul's guidance. Contact with a realized being, or tzaddik, may also provide a means of awakening the soul and activating a process of teshuvah. I remember often being brought to tears when I spent time in the presence of my teacher, Rabbi Shlomo Carlebach, may his memory be a blessing. His holy teachings and songs of yearning were like a powerful wake-up call, arousing my soul's yearning to return to its source.

In Hasidic literature there are countless tales of *tzaddikim* who had the power to awaken spiritually and heal even the most unenlightened and wicked people. Reb Zusia of Hanipol, for instance, had a particular gift for this form of healing, as well as an unusual form of clairvoyance. Though he could see a person's entire life written on the person's forehead, he had been blessed by his teacher, the Maggid of Mezerich, to see only the good in others. Even if he were witness to an obvious transgression, he would find the spark of goodness in the transgressor. Strangest of all, when he became aware of a person's faults or misdeeds, he would experience them as though they were his own.

In one tale, Reb Zusia spent the night at an inn whose owner had been a sinner for many years—a fact that Reb Zusia read from the innkeeper's forehead as he checked in. Later that night, alone in his room, Reb Zusia began to vicariously experience the innkeeper's past as though it were his own. As he prayed, he cried out, "Zusia, Zusia, you wicked man. What have you done? There is no sin that failed to tempt you and no crime you have not committed, Zusia, foolish, erring man, what will be the end of you?" Then he began to enumerate and confess the sins of the innkeeper, giving time and place in perfect detail, as though they were his own. As he sobbed out loud in deep repentance, the innkeeper, who overheard Zusia's crazy rantings through the doorway, quietly began to awaken and repent, himself. As one storyteller put it, by sharing in the innkeeper's sins, Zusia was also able to share the light of his own holy soul with him.[2]

Intentionally blurring the boundaries between self and other in order to bring healing is a method commonly used by Jewish mystics. Though it clearly defies a certain clinical logic, keep in mind that the tzaddik is not operating on the level of ego and personality. Rather, the tzaddik heals through his ability to harness the healing powers of *yichud* (unification) and *ahavah* (love). By unifying his own being and entering into a state of mystical unity, the tzaddik can then bind his soul with the soul of the person he is attempting to heal, and in doing so, is able to heal and awaken the person. The tzaddik induces healing through his ability to see the latent holiness and divinity of every person—the person's eternal Self—even when the person cannot yet see it in himself. The tzaddik, in effect, sees through God's eyes to the root of each person's soul.

In the Kabbalah, this kind of soul-healing is based on the tzaddik's ability to see the root of a person's soul as it exists within the cosmic soul of Adam Kadmon. According to Jewish legend, Adam Kadmon was a being of light whose essence stretched from one end of the earth to the other, and whose soul contained all the particular souls, both male and female, who were destined to emerge from the primordial oneness. When the tzaddik sees to the root of a person's soul, then, she perceives how that person's soul exists within the primeval thought of Adam Kadmon, as the pure being he was created to be.

The tzaddik's holy visioning has the power to reconnect the individual person with her role in the cosmic scheme of things. Reb Zalman Schachter-Shalomi is underscoring that role when he quotes these words from the famous Israeli author S. Y. Agnon: "A person has three beings. The first being is the way in which a person perceives himself, the second is the way in which a person is seen by others, and the third being is prior to the first, and it is the being by which he was created by Him who created him. If a person merited and did not damage the being which his Creator made him, then that being overwhelms the other two, and then even his shadow inspires grace and beauty."[3] In a similar vein, Schachter-Shalomi also quotes these words from Goethe: "If we take people as they are, we make them worse. If we treat them as if they were what they ought to be, we help them to become what they are capable of becoming."[4]

So many of us grew up feeling deeply unseen for who we truly are. Not only was our true being not mirrored back to us by our parents, teachers, and friends, but we often bought into the destructive, false images that were projected onto us. We came to see ourselves through the distorted vision of others. It's an amazing gift to find a teacher or healer who can affirm our true being and mirror back to us how beautiful and awesome we really are. But in the absence of such mirroring, sometimes a meditative practice can offer a similar kind of healing experience. One of the simple healing meditations I teach people is to see themselves through God's eyes. This practice can be a powerful means of breaking out of the distorted and limited perceptions we have of ourselves.

The truth is, within each of us, there lies a hidden tzaddik and inner guide. In the absence of an outer spiritual master or teacher, the neshama has the power to awaken and guide us. Even when we are completely cut off from the psycho-spiritual dimension of our being, the neshama—that part of us that is already whole—has a way of bringing about situations that will help us awaken and *re-member,* or put the pieces of our selves back together. The neshama is perennially in a state of teshuvah in the sense that it is never apart from its source. We just have to tune in to its call.

This *re-membering* may come about through an image we receive in a dream. For instance, a feeling or part of ourselves we avoid dealing with in waking life may appear in a dream as a menacing or hungry character who demands our attention. Jon, a client of mine who was disconnected from his own deep sadness, repeatedly dreamed about children who, to his dismay, cried inconsolably. Over time, as we worked with his dreams, the images began to change. Though often still very sad, the children in Jon's dreams were now willing to receive comfort and, at times, gifts from him. Eventually, through working with the characters in his dreams, Jon was able to reconnect with his own childhood sorrow.

Working integratively with our dreams enables us to become more fully conscious of who we are and who we might become. Thus, when we pay attention to them, dreams serve an important healing function. Interestingly, the Hebrew word for dream—*chalom*—shares the same Hebrew root as the word *chalim,* which implies healing and is closely related to the word for illness (*machalah*). Sometimes we can heal (*machalim*) the soul's dis-eases (*machalot*) through our dreams (*chalomot*).

There are countless examples of the myriad ways that the neshama helps us become fully conscious of our whole being. Like the voice that is said to emanate continually from Mount Sinai, calling out to humanity to awaken, the neshama is a perennial spring, flowing with exactly the nourishment we need. When we tune in to our neshama, we engage in the ongoing, sacred practice of teshuvah, or return. It is up to us to listen to its messages, however subtle they may be.

Sometimes physical illnesses or other distressing symptoms or life crises become the trigger for re-membering and expanding our sense of self. A man I counseled who had developed a serious and prolonged case of laryngitis got in touch with the fact that he had, for years, been holding back from expressing his deepest feelings. The illness served as a wake-up call to begin expressing his authentic self. For religious Jews, physical healing is always understood to be connected with the work of spiritual realignment, or teshuvah. Judaism asserts that our bodies and souls are deeply connected and that we cannot adequately treat any illness without also addressing matters of the spirit. At times the role of teshuvah in healing is understood to be literal. According to this understanding, by spiritually realigning ourselves we can effect actual physical healing.[5] But more often, and more to the point of this discussion, teshuvah is understood to bring about spiritual healing. Whenever we turn toward the infinite and experience our true essence, we are immediately healed in the spiritual sense, whether or not our physical symptoms persist.

Not only physical illness but also other uncontrollable events in our lives can conspire, as if by divine serendipity, to bring us back in touch with our whole selves. Sometimes an unwitting stranger may convey an important spiritual message to us through something mundane which she communicates, or an unexpected occurrence may awaken forgotten memories. One day, on a walk around his neighborhood, a client of mine was attacked by a pit bull for no apparent reason. The powerful rage he felt after the assault helped him get in touch with a repressed, traumatic childhood memory of having been attacked by a group of older children while walking home from school. The rage he felt toward the dog that attacked him helped him connect with feelings he was previously unable to access in therapy. Incidents like this suggest that when we are open to the flow, our inner and outer lives operate almost in unison to awaken us and restore us to our *sheleimut,* or whole selves.

Divine Whispers and Echoes

The Hasidic masters were so attuned to the voice of the divine that they were often able to hear it speaking to them through ordinary daily encounters. Once Rabbi Levi Yitzhak of Berditchev was visited by a poor shoemaker who went door to door offering to fix people's shoes. Hoping to obtain some work from the rebbe, the shoemaker knocked at Levi Yitzhak's door. When the rebbe greeted him with a smile, he asked, "Dear rebbe, surely you have something that needs fixing?" Upon hearing this, Levi Yitzhak began to weep. He then turned to his wife and remarked, "You see, even the shoemaker can tell that I need to fix myself!"

In a similar vein, the early-nineteenth-century Hasidic master known as the Yid Ha'Kadosh (holy Jew) of Pzhysha was once walking through the countryside with his disciples when he happened upon a Polish peasant whose hay wagon had overturned. When the peasant asked him to help right it, the Yid Ha'Kadosh and his disciples tried several times but did not succeed in turning it back on its wheels. The rebbe said to the peasant, "I'm sorry, but I cannot do it." To this, the peasant responded, "You can, all right, but you don't want to!" Hearing the peasant's rebuke as a message from beyond, the Yid Ha'Kadosh turned to his disciples and said, "You see, we could raise up the fallen sparks of divine light, the Shechinah, and bring the Messiah, but we just don't want to."[6]

Since the second Temple was destroyed and the prophetic era ended, the *bat-kol,* or divine echo, has come to replace prophecy. Not everything that is said to us or that happens around us is necessarily a message from beyond, nor are all our dreams revelatory. But sometimes the universe (or God) speaks to us in the most uncanny ways, so that our inner world is synchronistically mirrored to us in the outer events of our lives. The following tale, which I have heard from several different sources, provides a good example. This version of the tale is based on Martin Buber's *The Way of Man.*

The Treasure Within Us

There once was a poor Jew living in Cracow named Rabbi Eisik the son of Rabbi Yekel. After many years of great poverty, Rabbi Eisik had a dream in which he was told to go to Prague and dig under the bridge leading to the king's palace. There, he was told, he would find a large treasure. At first he ignored the dream, thinking it was

simple wish-fulfillment. But after the dream repeated itself for the third time, Rabbi Eisik set out for Prague.

When he reached the palace, he discovered that the
bridge at its entrance was heavily guarded both day and
night. Afraid to start digging in front of the guards, Rabbi
Eisek simply waited and watched. The captain of the
guards, who had noticed him, finally asked what he was
doing there, and so Rabbi Eisik told him about his dream.
In response the guard began to laugh and said, "And so to
please the dream, you poor fellow wore out your shoes to
come here! As for having faith in dreams, if I had it, I
should have had to get going when a dream once told me
to go to Cracow and dig for treasure under the stove in
the room of a Jew—Eisik son of Yekel—that was the
name! Eisik son of Yekel! I can just imagine what it
would be like, how I should have to try every house over
there, where one half of the Jews are named Eisik and the
other Yekel!"

When Rabbi Eisik heard this, he turned around and
went home and dug under his own stove, and there he
found the treasure that had all along been waiting for
him.[7]

What the treasure was or how it got there is not clear from the
story. However, according to Martin Buber's version of the tale,
Rabbi Simha Bunam of Pzhysha used to tell it to all those students
who flocked to him, to encourage them to look within themselves
rather than outside themselves for truth.

I first read this Hasidic tale at the age of sixteen, when I embarked
on my journey into Jewish spirituality. As I meditate on it now,
after more than three decades of searching, I hear it telling me once
more that ultimately all roads lead us back home to ourselves. We all
have secret treasures buried deep inside our hearts and souls, though
sometimes we have to wander far and wide to discover these inner
treasures. Much too often, we think the true treasure is hidden somewhere far off, and we are in such a hurry to get away from the place

where we stand that we lose our way. The truth is, wherever we stand in our lives, in whatever situation we find ourselves, that very spot is where we should dig. For the divine can be found in each moment and in every situation—the joyous and the sad, the lucky and the seemingly unlucky, the expected and the unexpected. If we stop running from ourselves, trying to be other than who we truly are, we will discover that in all our strengths and all our weaknesses, in our light and in our darkness, in our gifts and in our most wounded selves—there, in the very place where we stand, lies the only treasures to be found.

Teshuvah, the healing journey of return, is about discovering these very treasures—the ones that lie buried within each of us.

HITBODEDUT MEDITATION
Holy Aloneness

Rabbi Nachman of Breslov advised his disciples to make time each day for the practice of "hitbodedut"—holy aloneness, a meditative practice that involves talking to God in our own words.[8] Rabbi Nachman taught that by pouring out our hearts before God and expressing all the pain and longing that we feel, we begin to develop a deep intimacy with God. He recommended practicing hitbodedut at night, away from noise and human activity. If you go out in certain park areas of Jerusalem at night, you often hear Breslov Hasidim crying out to God at the top of their lungs—"*Ribbono shel olom,* Master of the Universe!"

You might want to try some modified version of this practice by spending some quiet time each day in meditation or in nature. Pay attention during these times to the callings of your neshama in the form of dream images, fantasies, and free associations. Also be receptive to what the neshama may be teaching you through any unusual synchronicities that have occurred in your life. Perhaps the universe has been speaking metaphorically to you in some way. God may be whispering in your ear, if only you are quiet enough to hear. In addition to listening, you will also want to speak to God in your own words about whatever is going on in your life. Try not to judge whatever comes up.

Even if you spend only a few minutes a day practicing hitbodedut, you may begin to notice some positive changes in your life.

MEDITATION

Seeing Yourself through God's Eyes

Take a moment to relax by simply paying attention to your breath. As you settle into a steady rhythm of breathing, notice that you may begin to feel more centered and still inside. Take a few moments to just *be* in this relaxed state—fully present.

Now imagine, if you can, what you might look like if you were to see yourself through God's eyes—through eyes that are filled with wisdom and loving-kindness, eyes that see with compassion and do not judge. Try to see yourself as the amazing mystery and pure being that you are.

7

REPENTANCE, PSYCHOTHERAPY, AND HEALING

In the place where repentant sinners stand even the completely righteous cannot stand.
—*The Talmud, Berachot 34b*

Once, while speaking to his disciples about healing and repentance, Rabbi Simha Bunam of Pzhysha remarked, "The mistakes man makes are not his greatest crime. Rather, his greatest crime is that he has the power to do teshuvah—to turn his life around at any moment—yet he does not do so!"

The freedom and power we each have to make positive changes in our lives at any moment in time is central to the practice of both psychotherapy and teshuvah. A skilled psychotherapist is essentially an agent of change. Likewise, the spiritual practice of teshuvah is essentially about exercising our freedom to choose the good.[1] It is based on the radically optimistic belief that despite whatever mistakes we have made in our lives and despite the effects of the painful legacies we have inherited, there is *always* a possibility of healing and redemption.

The key to teshuvah, according to the rabbis, is knowing how to harness this very moment in time—the *now!* When we live in the now, we are always free to change the course of our lives. The evil urge, said the rabbis, often comes to us as a voice reminding us of our past errors in order to discourage us from believing we can change. This voice tries to convince us that the past will always determine the future. And so the rabbis taught that whenever the word *now* (*atah* in Hebrew) appears in scriptures, it alludes to the possibility of teshuvah, or repentance.[2] Through teshuvah we always have the power and freedom to begin anew so that our past need not determine our future. Not only can the pain of the past be healed, but we actually have the power to transform it into a redemptive force in our lives.

The twelfth-century Spanish-Jewish philosopher Moses Maimonides codified the laws and practices of teshuvah. His writings, as well as those of the Hasidic masters, contain many vital teachings about the healing power of teshuvah and forgiveness that are every bit as relevant today as they were in ancient times. Indeed Jewish teachings on teshuvah outline a highly articulated process for the redemptive work of healing the pain and mistakes of the past and for achieving forgiveness. For this reason, the practice of teshuvah, perhaps more so than any other subject in Jewish thought, offers a unique contribution to the field of psychotherapy. Over the years I have found that both in theory and in practice, my work as a therapist has been continually enriched and informed by Judaism's understanding of teshuvah. In particular Jewish teachings on forgiveness and redemptive healing (the idea that the past can be transformed into a force for the good in one's life) have been a useful tool in my clinical work.

Sadly enough, many of the people I encounter in my clinical work live in an unforgiving universe. Indeed, the very notion of forgiveness is a somewhat foreign concept to them. And since they are unable to forgive themselves and others for the pain that's been caused by past mistakes, they remain forever tied to its damaging effects, creating for themselves an enormous psychic burden of guilt, shame, and resentment.

Part of the problem lies in the fact that most modern people lack access to the living spiritual traditions that have provided people with rites of forgiveness or atonement. Without such rites people have no way of ever clearing the karmic slate and beginning anew. To fill this void, I often find it helpful to teach my clients the ancient Jewish practice of teshuvah, with its concrete steps for achieving forgiveness. By learning these steps, many of my clients have been able to experience a newfound sense of freedom from the burdens of the past, and some have been able to transform their pain into a redemptive force of healing in their lives.

In the previous chapter we explored how teshuvah begins as a process of spiritual awakening—the desire to realign one's life with one's true being. In this chapter we will examine how that awakening can be carried forward through the step-by-step practice of teshuvah as outlined by Maimonides. And as we explore Maimonides' steps, we will see that they correspond with the different stages of psychotherapeutic and spiritual healing.[3]

Teshuvah and psychotherapy share similar aims in that they both seek to restore a sense of psychic or spiritual wholeness we once felt but somehow lost. There are, however, several essential differences between the mostly secular aims of psychotherapy and the religious aims of teshuvah. First of all, traditional Judaism is based on a set of ethical and spiritual ideals that provide an *objective* yardstick against which observant Jews have traditionally measured themselves. Teshuvah traditionally involved a return to these collectively held ideals, which are based on the Torah's precepts. In fact, the popular expression *ba'al teshuvah,* which literally means "a master of repentance," is now used to describe someone who has returned to the religious fold and embraced the Torah's way of life.

In contrast, contemporary psychotherapy traditionally seeks to help the individual person achieve a greater reliance on subjective, inner truth and on personally defined values. If spirituality is considered at all in psychotherapy, it is typically in individualistic, subjective terms, rather than as part of a larger, collective framework of meaning. In contrast to psychotherapy, with its more limited aims, which are geared toward individual healing and self-actualization, Judaism has the broader, messianic vision of tikkun olam—the collective healing and transformation of the world. Individual teshuvah is only one aspect of this. The work of the truly pious Jew does not stop with the achievement of personal fulfillment but extends to the collective effort of bringing about world repair and redemption and an end to human suffering.

Rabbi Abraham Isaac Kook, an early-twentieth-century mystic, kabbalist, poet, and philosopher, as well as the first chief rabbi of pre-state Israel, wrote extensively on both the universal-collective and the individual dimensions of teshuvah. Rabbi Kook's mystical sensibilities enabled him to see these two dimensions as parts of a continuum. Kook writes that "the individual and the collective soul, the world soul, the soul of all realms of being cries out like a fierce lioness in anguish for total perfection, for an ideal form of existence. . . . Through the fact that penitence is operative in all worlds, all things are returned and reattached to the realm of divine perfection. . . . General penitence, which involves raising the world to perfection, and particularized penitence, which pertains to the personal life of each individual . . . all constitute one essence . . . an inseparable whole."[4]

Another important distinction between psychotherapy and teshuvah is that they address different domains of life—the psychic as compared with the spiritual and ethical. These two practices also use very different terminology to talk about the root cause of illness and human suffering. For instance, while religious discourse tends to emphasize the role of "sin" in human suffering, psychotherapists generally view unresolved conflict or trauma as its root cause. While religion sees sin as leading to a sense of separation or alienation from God, psychotherapists focus on how people may become cut off from their full potential when they are internally conflicted or nonintegrated.

For many of us, the use of words like *sin* or *evil* in religious literature is not only foreign but also somewhat alienating. Such words imply a judgmental stance, alien to Western psychology's attempts to remain somewhat neutral and nonjudgmental when it comes to "moral" issues. Yet if we can put aside our knee-jerk negative reactions to such terms, we may find that traditional religious thought contains many useful concepts about healing the self. We just have to translate some of the more archaic terminology into contemporary language. Consider for a moment the possibility that *sin* might refer to all actions and attitudes that lead people to become alienated from their most whole and holy self. In other words, the notion that sin is that which separates us from God can be understood as those actions and attitudes that separate us from our own true being. If so, teshuvah can then be understood as the process whereby we *restore* or *return* to our most natural state of inner wholeness and self-integration. As I pointed out in chapter 6, the word *teshuvah* comes from the Hebrew root *shav,* which implies return.

As we continue to explore Jewish teachings and texts about teshuvah I will include some alternative phrases in parentheses that may help to translate or clarify the meaning of ancient religious terminology.

THE STEPS OF TESHUVAH AND THEIR PSYCHOTHERAPEUTIC COUNTERPARTS

The classic formula for teshuvah presented by Maimonides entails a series of steps that in many ways parallels the process of psychotherapy. Teshuvah, like most analytic forms of therapy, always begins with awareness. In order to change, people have to *recognize* what they are doing wrong or how their lives are out of alignment with their deepest values and truths. In Hebrew, this step is known as *haḳarat ha'chet,* which literally means awareness of how one has "missed the mark." When we "sin," we are like a marksman who has missed the intended target. Our energies have been directed in the wrong direction. Hakarat ha'chet is essentially "error recognition"—the ability to notice that one has gone off course.

It may sound simple, but honest awareness is not easily achieved. We all employ numerous defense mechanisms—including denial, repression, and projection—to protect ourselves from facing painful truths about ourselves. Hence, one of the crucial first steps in psychotherapy involves resistance analysis, the understanding and working through of defenses, for it is only when our defenses relax that we can see ourselves clearly.

While awareness opens up the possibility of change, awareness by itself is not sufficient to bring about change. One must also *decide* to change one's behaviors and self-defeating patterns. This step is known as *azivat ha'chet*—the leaving behind of sin (negative patterns). According to Maimonides, our decision to make needed changes in our lives must also be verbally articulated through the act of *vidui,* confession.[5] Vidui potentiates the process of teshuvah and is its defining characteristic. Rabbi Joseph Soloveitchik, one of Judaism's most articulate contemporary teachers on the subject of teshuvah, speaks of the emotional potency of confession, likening its humbling effects to the symbolic sacrificial offering. Confession, he says, demands that we be able to overcome our defensive pride and shame so that we can look ourselves straight in the eye and face our true feelings. In Soloveitchik's words, it "compels man—in a state of terrible torment—to admit facts as they really are, to give clear expression to the truth. . . . Just as the sacrifice is burnt upon the altar so do we burn down, by our act of confession, our well-barricaded complacency, our overblown pride, our artificial existence."[6]

Therapy, in a sense, is a modern-day ritual of confession. By revealing (confessing) our personal pain and secret conflicts, regrets, and longings to a therapist, we face our truth—no matter how painful that may be. Often, we may not even know what we are going to say until the words are uttered. It is in the act of "telling" that our life narratives become coherent stories, and as we reveal our true selves, we begin to achieve insight and clarity.

A major element of vidui, according to Maimonides, is the expression of regret and remorse over one's misdeeds. Unless we allow ourselves to feel and express regret for our past mistakes and for the pain we have brought upon ourselves and others, we will not be motivated to make needed changes in our lives. Interestingly, the Hebrew word for regret/remorse, *charata,* comes from the same three-letter root as *cheret,* a writing tool used for engraving. Feelings of remorse leave a deep impression engraved upon our souls, enabling us to hold on to important realizations.

Many psychotherapists, influenced by the human potential movement's pathologizing of guilt, have bought into the notion that feelings of guilt or remorse are essentially neurotic. They may prematurely urge their clients to just "get over it," when, in fact, feeling a *healthy* measure of guilt and remorse is often a necessary step in the process of healing and self-forgiveness.

Painful feelings of regret and remorse of a slightly different nature often emerge in therapy just as people begin to open up and experience emotional growth. As we begin to heal in therapy and open ourselves to new possibilities, we may come to regret decisions we made in the past—ones we made as a result of fear or crippling emotional inhibitions. As we deepen in our capacity to feel empathy for others, we may recognize how our behavior in past relationships lacked skillfulness or how our actions were downright hurtful. Ironically, as we begin to heal in therapy, our newfound ability to feel more open and loving can bring up painful feelings of grief and regret for a lifetime spent shut down.

In psychotherapy, as in the process of teshuvah, reconnecting with our deepest, truest self inevitably brings up painful feelings of regret and loss. There is a sense of grief over lost time, the days and years of our lives that we spent in vain, disconnected from our innermost selves, unable to realize our full potential. Feeling and expressing this grief is an essential component of healing.

Therapy can in fact fail when people are unable to acknowledge their regret or grief over the past. I remember once working with a woman named Ann who began to realize in our work together that she had wasted many years of her life in self-destructive behaviors. She had been a heavy drinker and, as a result, had alienated almost all of her closest friends. For years, she had been living in extreme isolation and anger. To change her ways, however, meant that she would have to grieve over the years she had lost and admit to herself that she had wasted these years of her life engaged in senseless, self-destructive behavior. Ann struggled back and forth with this choice. As I witnessed her inner process, I saw firsthand how defensive pride can prevent a person from taking the steps she knows she must take in order to heal. As self-defeating as it might seem, Ann's stubborn pride prevented her from admitting the senselessness of her past errors. And by not mourning her past, Ann was unable to move on to forgive herself. Just when she seemed close to having a breakthrough,

Ann started drinking again and prematurely terminated therapy, undermining her efforts at change.

By contrast, the courage to mourn the past became a crucial step in saving the marriage of Jenny and Robert. After over twenty-five years of marriage, Jenny and Robert came to see me for couples counseling. Their youngest child had just left home for college, and they were facing the terrifying possibility that they might split up. Neither of them had been happy in the marriage for years, yet they had stayed together because of the kids. As we explored what had happened to contribute to their alienation from one another, it became clear that both of them had colluded to avoid intimacy and emotional connection. They had held their grievances inside themselves and not communicated their needs and feelings to one another. It had been years since either of them had been able to say the words "I love you" to the other.

During the course of weekly therapy I helped Jenny and Robert become emotionally reacquainted with each other. As they began to reconnect with their tender feelings for each other, Jenny was overwhelmed by feelings of grief and regret. She was, in fact, grieving for all the years they had wasted, unnecessarily, in anger and resentment. Jenny felt deep regret that she and Robert had not sought out therapy many years ago, when they first fell out of love with each other. "If only I had known then what I know now" was a phrase she used repeatedly. It felt important to honor Jenny's feelings of grief and regret for those lost and irretrievable years. However, I also stressed the fact that by forgiving themselves and one another, Jenny and Robert could move on to salvage their marriage and make the most of their remaining years.

Finding the courage to mourn the past frees us up to move on and change.[7] For many people this means relinquishing the defensive fantasy that the past can somehow be undone. Paradoxically, it is only when we accept the painful reality that the past is over and cannot ever be undone that we are free to reclaim our lives and make the most of our remaining years. As we work through our grief over time irretrievably lost, we are released from the grip of the past. Though mourning and regret are an important stage in the healing process, ultimately this stage must be followed by work on self-forgiveness and acceptance for healing to be complete.

While regret and mourning relate to the past, the next step of teshuvah is oriented toward the future. This step, known as *hachlata le'atid* (future resolve), involves the resolution to change our behavior in the future. Hachlata le'atid involves projecting oneself into the future and imagining doing things differently from the way one has done them before. Specifically, it involves developing the intention never again to repeat the destructive patterns of the past. This resolve will ultimately be tested when we find ourselves in a situation parallel to the one in which we previously had erred. When we resist repeating our mistakes in such a situation, then and only then is repentance complete, according to Maimonides. In fact, when fate presents us with a parallel situation, it is viewed as a grace from God because only when we confront such a situation successfully can we be sure that our repentance is complete.

As in teshuvah, repetition is also an important theme in psychotherapy. Freud's notion of the repetition compulsion, the tendency we all have to repeat unresolved dynamics from the past in the present, is a familiar theme in all psychotherapies. Therapists can aid their clients in overcoming destructive, repetitious patterns by examining how old patterns are being reenacted in all their relationships, including the therapy relationship. Through transference analysis, the working through in the here-and-now of emotions whose origins are in the past, clients can begin to replace destructive old patterns with new understandings and behaviors. Like Maimonides, who believed that repetitions are an opportunity to achieve "complete repentance," therapists can usefully adopt the notion that repetitions are golden opportunities for healing and resolution rather than neurotic reenactments of the past. In fact, the repetition of the past in the present may be a natural way that we attempt to master the past by creating opportunities in the present to finally resolve old conflicts. This is exactly what Maimonides seems to be suggesting when he says that the true challenge of repetitions is to refrain from repeating one's past patterns.

In relation to deeds that involve harm to others, Maimonides adds another step to the teshuvah process—that of making amends. This includes the offering of restitution (when applicable), apologizing and asking for forgiveness, and publicly confessing one's mistakes. Though complete restitution is not always possible, one is required to do whatever one can possibly do to make amends toward all those wronged by one's actions.

If these teachings were applied today, they would probably have a radical impact on our society. Can you imagine, for example, if public apology and confession were considered an acceptable and virtuous act? What implications would such a new ethic have on the penal system, the media, and public leaders and officials? What if politicians and CEOs were encouraged to confess and apologize for their mistakes rather than being told to hide or lie about them for fear of being destroyed? How about criminals? What if teshuvah became part of the rehabilitation process in prisons? These are, in fact, some of the ideas that a progressive think tank headed by Dr. Amitai Etzioni of George Washington University is suggesting, in an attempt to apply the spiritual and ethical teachings of teshuvah to civic culture. The book *Civic Repentance,* edited by Etzioni, discusses how the principles of repentance might be applied to politics, civil rights, psychotherapy, and racial reconciliation and in the work of restorative justice for offenders and convicts.[8]

While twelve-step recovery programs routinely emphasize the importance of making amends, traditional psychotherapy typically misses out on this important step of healing. Clinical training simply does not prepare most therapists to think about the therapeutic role of "restitution." Nevertheless, I find that certain clients' healing is accelerated when I encourage them to seek forgiveness and make amends to loved ones they have intentionally or unintentionally hurt. When they offer to make amends or provide restitution, they are relieved of their burden of guilt, and they develop a greater sense of moral accountability for their actions. In work with former addicts, criminals, and perpetrators of abuse, restitution is an especially important component of healing—one that can potentially help bring a sense of closure for all parties involved.

Teshuvah from Fear versus Teshuvah from Love

In classic Jewish thought it is understood that there are different levels of teshuvah, each one leading to a different outcome. The lowest level is repentance out of fear, or *teshuvah mi'yirah*. This level refers to an awakening motivated by the fear of negative consequences or punishment that will result if one does not make needed changes. For instance, when a smoker begins experiencing respiratory distress, he may decide to give up smoking out of fear that his continued use of tobacco will lead to serious health consequences. Similarly, after a client of mine was arrested for drunk driving and had his license suspended for six months, he finally began to take his sobriety seriously. The fear of permanently losing his license did a lot more than all my cautioning and admonitions to help him resolve to finally stop drinking.

Fear, as we all know, can be a powerful motivator of change, yet even more powerful, say the rabbis, is repentance stirred by love. This level of teshuvah, known as *teshuvah mi'ahavah,* is a state of being in which one awakens to the unity of all being and becomes consumed by an all-pervasive love of the divine. How does one awaken? In the words of Maimonides, "When a person contemplates God's great and wondrous works and creatures and from them obtains a glimpse of His wisdom which is incomparable and infinite, he will immediately love Him, praise Him, glorify Him, and yearn with a powerful yearning to know His great Name."[9] This love can be so overpowering, according to Maimonides, that "one becomes possessed like one who is so lovesick that his attention cannot be distracted from the particular woman that he loves, rather he thinks about her at all times, whether sitting, rising, eating or drinking."[10]

When we experience this kind of spiritual awakening, every area of our lives is radically transformed. Just as human lovers show one another their best selves and are mirrors for one another's perfection, when we fall in love with God our best self is brought forth, our highest and holiest essence shines forth in its perfection. In this state, everything comes to feel connected to everything else; all of life is experienced as part of an awesome unity, and the boundaries that separate us from ourselves and one another dissolve. So, too, the limits imposed by linear time are dissolved; past, present, and future converge, opening up the possibility that the effects of the past can be transformed and illuminated by the light of the Infinite One. At the level of teshuvah mi'ahavah, one's mistakes are not just forgiven, say the rabbis; they are actually transformed into a force for good. As the Talmud puts it, "Repentance [inspired by love] is so great that premeditated sins are accounted as though they were merits."[11]

Resh Lakish, the scholar quoted in this passage of the Talmud, was himself a repentant sinner. He had been a gladiator who, under the influence of Rabbi Yochanan ben Zakkai, became a religious Jew and Torah scholar. The intense passion that Resh Lakish had previously directed toward physical power and bodybuilding became channeled into Torah study and spiritual practice. Being himself a ba'al teshuvah, or master of repentance, Resh Lakish understood how the repentant sinner's past could add fuel to fire his passion for holiness so that he comes to stand at a higher spiritual rung than the perfect tzaddik, one who never strayed off the path. Regarding such individuals the Talmud says that "in the place where repentant sinners stand even the completely righteous cannot stand."[12]

One of my teachers once staged the following demonstration in order to show, in concrete terms, how teshuvah mi'ahavah operates. First she gathered a group of students in a large circle. Next, she stretched a knotted-up rope across the circle and asked two students to hold on to its ends. She then cut away the knotted-up mess in the center of the rope and tied the newly cut ends of the rope back together. When she did this, we were all forced to take a few steps toward the center of the circle to accommodate the rope's shortened length. She then asked us what we had noticed. When one of the students noted that the circle had grown tighter and more intimate as a result of her cutting and retying the rope, my teacher responded that that was exactly what teshuvah accomplishes. "Sometimes," she explained, "our lives become so entangled that we become like a useless rope, caught up in knots. When this happens we just have to cut the mess away and repair the rope. But if we think of ourselves as standing at one end of the rope and God at the other, then the repaired rope actually brings us closer to God than we might have been had we never severed the connection. Such is the power of teshuvah!"

When we fall off the path and seemingly lose touch with our connection with God (our true self), a deep longing for reconnection may be activated in us. Often, this longing is stronger than anything we might have known had we never fallen off the path. These longings of the soul, the soul's yearning to return to its original state of connectedness, can put a person on more intimate terms with the divine than he might have been had he never experienced the lapse in connection. Like the loss of a loved one, says Rabbi Joseph Soloveitchik, sin (the loss of a connection with one's true self) leaves us feeling lonely and bereft. Just as we often don't know how much we need and love someone until we lose him or her, in the spiritual domain, we don't sufficiently appreciate our attachment to God until we lose our way and experience the resulting alienation. Through teshuvah, a deep longing to regain our original closeness and connectedness to God is unleashed in us. For the ba'al teshuvah (returnee) this longing can be so strong that it propels her past the spiritual level of the tzaddik, one who has never left the fold. According to Soloveitchik, the ba'al teshuvah possesses a unique capacity—the power to elevate sin. "A man who has sinned and has repented," he writes, "may be able, if he proves worthy, to utilize the dynamism of the forces of evil which had enveloped him before and elevate them, and to make them operate on behalf of the forces of good."[13]

This level of teshuvah, which Rabbi Soloveitchik refers to as "repentance of redemption," has the power to transform sinner into saint, and to transmute alchemically our worst character flaws into virtues.

Teshuvah as Spiritual Alchemy

This same theme weaves itself throughout the writings of the Hasidic masters, but it is most clearly articulated in the teachings of Reb Tzaddok Ha'Cohen of Lublin, one of the most brilliant Jewish thinkers of the nineteenth century. Unique among the Hasidic masters in that he combined brilliant Talmudic scholarship with a psychologically astute understanding of human nature, Reb Tzaddok spoke about teshuvah in relation to character refinement. Taking off on the rabbinic notion that the ba'al teshuvah stands at a higher rung than the tzaddik who never tasted sin, Reb Tzaddok suggests that our wounds and deficits can lead us to our own unique path of redemption.

> By the very quality in which one is lacking or wounded, by that very quality one finds one's unique strength or gift. The Rabbis alluded to this in the Talmud (Sanhedrin 70a) when interpreting the passage "And they (Adam and Eve) sewed garments for themselves out of the leaves of the fig tree." (Genesis 3:7) Through that which was their downfall they redeemed themselves. Similarly, the Rabbis alluded to this same notion in the Talmud Yerushalmi (Berachot Ch. 2) when they said: "The messiah was born on the day that the Temple was destroyed."[14]

Contrary to the Western notion that the apple tree bore the original fruit of temptation, the midrash quoted by Reb Tzaddok teaches us that it was the fig tree. Since Adam and Eve clothed themselves with the leaves of the fig tree, the midrash reasons that the forbidden fruit must have been a fig! The very thing that brought about Adam and Eve's downfall would lead them to their eventual redemption in the form of the fig leaf.

In my clinical work I frequently encounter a variation on this theme. Sometimes people's core wound or symptom contains within it the seed of their own healing and redemption. Jan, for instance, a woman I worked with, suffered from episodes of depression related to her early childhood experience of abandonment. Abandoned as an infant by her teenage mother, she was raised for the first several years of her life in an orphanage. In our work together Jan began to realize that the painful experiences of her early childhood had also left her with a unique capacity for connection and intimacy. From her experience of growing up without a sense of belonging she had developed a special appreciation of the importance of belonging. Friendship and community became extremely important to her. She was, in fact, gifted with a special ability to create a sense of belonging for herself wherever she went. Jan had friends all over the world—people she had met on her travels and through her work in the Peace Corps— with whom she managed to stay in close touch. As a result of her wound, Jan became acutely aware of the preciousness of the people in her life, and she became committed to creating a surrogate family for herself with people all over the world.

Each of us, according to Reb Tzaddok, has some unique wound or personal vulnerability that with loving acceptance may become the means by which we find our greatest gifts and possibly our own unique path to enlightenment. But this kind of spiritual alchemy is possible, he says, only when teshuvah is triggered by love rather than fear, for love alone has the power to reconnect us to our wholeness and to the larger whole of life. This idea is very much in line with contemporary psychology's notion that we must first love and accept who we are right now in order to change or heal anything about ourselves. Love and acceptance alone have the power to bring heal- ing. The mystical practice of devekut, loving attachment to God, opens us up to this possibility of healing. In a state of devekut the "evil" or flaw we seek to eradicate is instead illumined as the follow- ing tale suggests.

A young man once came to Rabbi Yisrael of Rizhin seeking coun- sel as to how he might break or overcome his "evil inclination" (sex- ual impulse or desire). The rabbi's eyes laughed as he looked compassionately at the young man and replied, "You want to break your impulses? You can break your back or your hip, but you will never break an impulse no matter how hard you try. However, if you pray and study and serve God with love and sincerity, the evil *in* your impulses will vanish of itself. In its place will remain a passion that is pure and holy. With this passion you will be able to serve God in truth."

According to Reb Tzaddok, each of us has a particular passion or vulnerability, a personal blind spot that evokes a great deal of attach- ment and desire. This passion can create a blind spot in our lives that will prevent us from seeing life clearly. If we are not mindful of its influence on us, this passion can come to control us. If, however, we find a way to utilize this passion in service of the divine, we restore it to its source in holiness. When we do so, our passion finds its most uplifted expression and becomes a conduit through which we channel divine blessing. In Reb Tzaddok's words: "Every person has a unique passion or desire and that very thing which evokes the greatest amount of attachment or desire is also a vessel for receiving God's blessing, if one returns to God with all of one's heart."[15]

The libidinal drive, for example, is a powerful force in our lives that can have a positive or a negative influence on us. If directed toward divine service, this drive can ultimately fuel our passion for holiness and truth. According to Reb Tzaddok, *chamido d'oraita,* the love and passion for Torah and spiritual illumination, is inextricably tied to our libidinal passion. Interestingly, the Hebrew word *yetzer,* used to denote the libidinal drive, comes from the same root as the word for creativity, *yetzirah* or *yetziratiut.* All our passions and creativity come from the yetzer; by means of teshuvah, the yetzer's life-enhancing, creative potential is activated. Instead of acting as a hindrance in our lives, it then fuels our passion for holiness. The same is true for all our passions and desires. Illuminated by the light of teshuvah, each one potentially brings a unique blessing into our lives.

CHUCK'S STORY

Reclaiming Integrity

In my spiritual guidance work with Chuck, Reb Tzaddok's teachings on teshuvah helped inspire him to transform one of his most distressing character flaws—namely, dishonesty—into a passion for truth-telling. When Chuck first came to see me, he was caught in a web of lies. It wasn't that Chuck was maliciously dishonest; yet he had become somewhat of a compulsive liar because he was simply afraid to tell people the truth. What was most troubling about his dishonesty was that it had become habitual; Chuck confessed that he often found himself telling small lies about things that he really did not have to hide.

As a result of his dishonesty, Chuck's personal life had become entangled in knots. Instead of confronting the difficulties he and his partner of several years were having, he found himself emotionally withdrawing from the relationship and having an affair with another woman. To cover his tracks he repeatedly lied to his partner about his whereabouts. Chuck recognized that this was a pattern he had fallen into many times before, and one he was not proud of. Several other friendships and intimate relationships had fallen apart because of his dishonesty in the past. Chuck knew he had to face his fear of telling the truth or else he would just go on ruining all his intimate relationships.

As we explored the origins of his fear, Chuck revealed that he had grown up in a family where the unspoken rule in the house was not to tell the truth. It's not that anyone told him to lie; it's just that no one really wanted to hear his truth. His mother, who was frequently ill when he was a child, was too weak, both physically and emotionally, to take an interest in Chuck's inner life. His father was a classic workaholic who was mostly absent from the family. The few times during childhood when Chuck had attempted to speak out about his true needs and feelings, he was told he didn't know what he was talking about or that his feelings were simply wrong. Feeling ashamed of his unrecognized, unmet needs, Chuck learned to shut up and hide his true self. Basically, he learned to tell people what *they* wanted to hear rather than the truth. But the strategy that had helped Chuck survive his childhood was now wreaking havoc on his life as an adult.

It was not easy for Chuck to reveal this problem to me because he felt tremendous shame about his lack of courage. In our work together I challenged Chuck to find a way to transform this personal weakness into a strength. I suggested that instead of giving in to his fear of telling the truth, he could make a commitment to being honest at all costs. From his past mistakes Chuck knew firsthand how dishonesty could destroy a valued relationship. More than many others, he could appreciate the value of telling the truth.

Though reluctant at first, Chuck decided to take on my challenge. He decided to try to be honest at all costs. At first it seemed as though

Chuck became honest almost to a fault, saying what he was thinking or feeling without regard for its consequences or appropriateness to the situation. For a while he seemed to have lost touch with all sense of tact and timing. He seemed to need to do this in order to overcome his natural tendency to avoid conflict. Over time, however, Chuck began to discern when, where, and how to speak his truth. He even took some workshops in developing better communication skills and found that he became more and more skillful at fearlessly speaking out. Chuck's newfound gift for truth-telling served him both in the professional and personal arenas, bringing him much satisfaction. He discovered that his worst inadequacy, his fear of communicating the truth, had compelled him to develop a special gift for honest communication.

Teshuvah and Psychotherapy as Time Travel

Time transcendence—the temporary experience of standing outside the flow of linear time—occurs both in mystical states and in the course of psychotherapy. It is an experience that seems to facilitate healing on the physical as well as the emotional and spiritual planes. In the spiritual domain we find that by getting in touch with our eternal selves we touch a realm beyond time in which we are able to heal and transform the workings of time. The experience of teshuvah—the return to a state of connectedness with the infinite and eternal dimension of our being—also involves a kind of reverse time travel, as it were, from the future to the past. As Rabbi Joseph Soloveitchik writes, "Man lives in the shadow of the past, future and present simultaneously." Teshuvah reverses the flow of time so that "the future determines the direction and indicates the way [by transforming] the trends and tendencies of the past."[16] In effect, the higher state of consciousness that we achieve through teshuvah enables us to shine light back to the time of the sin, illuminating the past and allowing us to view it more benignly and creatively.

For when teshuvah is inspired by love, we gain access to the healing power of YHVH, the Infinite One. This name for the divine—which, as I have pointed out, is a composite of the Hebrew words *hayah* (was), *hoveh* (is), and *yihiyeh* (will be)—puts us in touch with a realm beyond time and space, the infinite realm, in which we are freed from the determinism of linear time. Thus, the mistakes we have made in the past can be recontextualized by the good deeds we may achieve in the future, and instead of the past determining the future, the future determines and gives meaning to the past.

Rabbi Shneur Zalman of Liadi adds a more mystical dimension to the experience of teshuvah from love. He describes teshuvah from love as an opportunity to experience the "time before time"—the primordial time before creation, when all things were one and unbroken. He adds that

> when man takes this to heart—that the entire universe is under time, while the entirety of time is but as a single moment before God, Who is above time and before Whom time's divisions do not apply at all—his heart will burn as a flaming fire and his soul will dissolve (in yearning) to cleave to Him.
>
> Thus, "Teshuvah preceded the world." This is not to say that it existed before the world was created; for if there is no world there is no sin, no iniquity, and no teshuvah. Rather, this means that teshuvah with a dissolution of the soul reaches higher than time and space.[17]

Time Travel in Therapy

Psychotherapy also employs a variety of "time travel" techniques that facilitate the healing of childhood pain and past traumas. It is generally accepted that the unconscious mind is not bound by time. In the unconscious, events and emotions from the past, even the distant past, can be experienced with the same immediacy as if they were happening now. In therapy, as in dreams, time may be experienced as expanded or contracted. (A dream snippet that takes only a few seconds of clock time may include a plot so thick it would take hours to experience in reality.) Using such tools as free association, guided visualization, or hypnotic trance, which take advantage of the powers of the unconscious mind, therapists can guide clients back in time to a particular trauma or painful memory of the past. And when the client reaches out compassionately from the healthy adult self to the memories of hurt from the past, healing begins to occur. As with teshuvah, the pain of the past is touched and transformed by the love and compassion we bring to it from the present. In effect, our painful memories of the past are healed as they are recontextualized by the higher state of consciousness we have reached in the present.

At such moments in therapy, clients often experience a transforming shift. Instead of trying to forget the pain of the past, we feel a deep connection to all of who we *are,* who we have *been,* and who we *are becoming.* At those moments we are completely at one with the many parts of ourselves. All the different voices within us unite under one tallit (prayer shawl) and say, "Amen, so may it be!" Such transformational healings occur when we can finally look back and see how everything we have endured, all the pain and suffering as well as the mistakes we have made, has led us to become who we are today. When we can embrace it all with a sense of forgiveness for ourselves and others, and for God as well, our healing is complete.

ANCIENT RITUALS OF REPENTANCE

According to observant Jews, rituals of repentance play an important role in maintaining the emotional and spiritual well-being of the entire community. In particular, the days of repentance associated with the High Holy Days serve an important communal healing function. In many ways, these sacred rites of repentance serve a healing function that parallels that of psychotherapy in our contemporary, secular lives. In fact, people turn to psychotherapy today expecting it to take the place of these religious rites, which once enabled people to achieve healing and forgiveness.

Every year during the days surrounding Rosh Hashannah, the Jewish New Year, and Yom Kippur, the Day of Atonement, observant Jews actively engage in repentance. These days, known as the Ten Days of Repentance (*asseret y'mai teshuvah*), are a time for self-reflection, for letting go of anger and guilt, and for mending interpersonal rifts in the community. They are also a time to focus on how our lives have steered off course so that we can reset our inner moral and spiritual compass. And they are a time when Jews go out of their way to ask one another and God for forgiveness for the ways they have wronged one another in the past year, so that resentments and interpersonal conflicts are not carried into the new year.

In ancient times, observance of the High Holy Days included a series of shamanistic rites performed by the high priest in the Jerusalem Temple. Yom Kippur essentially served as a sacred communal *therapeia*, geared at restoring harmony for the individual person within himself and in relation to God, his loved ones, and the community. We no longer perform these sacred rites, but we can gain insight into the integrative, healing power of teshuvah by understanding their symbolism.

The first rite, known as the scapegoat offering, or *se'ir le'azazel,* involved drawing lots over two identical goats. One was chosen to be sacrificed in the Temple, while the other was sent off alive to *azazel* (the wilderness) after the priest had confessed and transferred all the sins of the people onto it.[18] On the surface it may seem as though the scapegoat offering is a highly dualistic rite, but according to the thirteenth-century Spanish mystic and biblical commentator Nachmanides, the scapegoat was actually a rite of divine unification. By making an offering to azazel, or the "other side," he says, the high priest was presenting a *shochad la'satan,* a gift or bribe to Satan.[19] The intent of this offering was to extract a blessing from Satan and thereby turn the "prosecution" (*kategor*) into a "defense" (*sanegor*). Thus, the scapegoat rite symbolically suggests that on the holiest day of the year one must extract a blessing even from one's nemesis. Even God and Satan must make amends on Yom Kippur, so that nothing that exists remains outside the realm of the divine "One." Everything that is "outside" or "other" must be restored to the "inside," so to speak. The spiritual challenge of Yom Kippur is to heal and transform all the sins and mistakes of the past so that *all* things may be restored back (teshuvah) to their source.

In psychological terms, the unification of God and Satan can be seen as symbolizing the reintegration of that which was previously split off from consciousness or relegated, in the Jungian sense, to the "shadow," those parts of the self that are unacceptable in one's conscious image of oneself. We might also view the rapprochement between God and Satan as a metaphor for the psychological capacity for integration of good and bad. In Nachmanides' mystical interpretation, the scapegoat ritual, far from banishing one's bad self to the netherworld or azazel, does the opposite. Through this rite, Nachmanides suggests, we attempt to make peace with the satanic, "evil" side of our nature. As is often the case, the mystical interpretation of the text stands diametrically opposed to a literal reading. As I have pointed out, nonmystical Judaism's concern with separating out good from evil is turned on its face in the mystical tradition's nondual view of the divine. On Yom Kippur, the holiest day of the year, we are all invited to become high priests and priestesses and to enter the holy of holies together, that place where all things are essentially *one*. On this day of at-one-ment, when we attempt to heal all the fragmented, split-off parts of ourselves, even God must make peace with Satan, God's dark or destructive side.

Nachmanides points out that if the scapegoat rite were performed on any other day of the year, it would have been considered idolatrous, for normally no offerings were allowed outside of the Temple. Yet on Yom Kippur such an "external" offering becomes not only a mitzvah but also a rite of divine unification. Nachmanides concludes that this transformation of what would ordinarily be a sin into a mitzvah hints at the power of teshuvah to transform our sins into merit and to illuminate all the dark places within us.

Another one of the unique rites performed on Yom Kippur in Temple times was the incense offering, or *ketoret*. This rite was performed daily by the priests in the outer sanctuary of the Temple, but it was performed only once a year, on Yom Kippur, in the holy of holies, or *kodesh kodashim,* the innermost sanctuary of the Jerusalem Temple. The performance of this rite, by the high priest alone, was the spiritual climax of the holiest day of the year. When the high priest emerged safely from the kodesh kodashim after offering the ketoret, the entire community gathered to celebrate this joyous holiday of forgiveness and at-one-ment through dance and mating rituals.[20] In these celebrations, the women were said to have danced in the vineyards wearing "borrowed" white clothing. This act of "borrowing" created a sense of economic equality. No one could appear to be "above" anyone else. During this dance rite, the men would pick their future brides—not knowing if they were wealthy or poor. This mating rite was seen as an earthly reflection of the Israelite nation's reconciliation with God on this holy day of at-one-ment. This is a far cry from the somber holiday that Yom Kippur has become over the ages since the Temple was destroyed and the Israelites were exiled from their land![21]

In the mystical tradition, the ketoret was understood to be a symbol of unity and interconnectedness within and among people. According to Jewish law, it had to be made from eleven different spices, including *chelbenah,* or galbanum. Though chelbenah itself is foul smelling, it was an essential ingredient of the sweet-smelling ketoret offering, for according to legend, when the chelbenah was joined with the ten other ingredients, it actually added sweetness to the ketoret's sweet fragrance.

The inclusion of the chelbenah in the ketoret suggests that when we are joined together as a community, we atone for one another. Even the sinners and schleppers among us add to the perfection and fragrance of the whole. In commemoration of the chelbenah, on the eve of Yom Kippur prior to the chanting of the opening Kol Nidre prayer, Jews recite the following invocation, which formally welcomes the sinners among them to join in and be accepted back into the community: "With permission of God and the permission of the community we hereby give ourselves permission to pray alongside the sinners."

Hasidic thought also applies the symbol of the chelbenah to the intrapsychic realm. Just as unity among all Jews, from sinners to saints, is a requisite for achieving atonement, so, too, according to this way of thinking, each of us must welcome and reintegrate our own inner chelbenah on Yom Kippur. In this interpretation the chelbenah is taken to symbolize that quality or part of ourselves that is least developed and least desirable—our shadow, if you will. To the degree that we deny or reject this part, it remains split off and becomes an adversarial force in our lives. The inclusion of the chelbenah among the sweet spices of the ketoret teaches us that we must integrate our weaknesses and vulnerabilities into the totality of our being. When we do, they can actually add potency and sweetness to our lives.

In my own life and in my work as a therapist I have repeatedly found this to be true. Only by deeply accepting our vulnerabilities and integrating them into the totality of our being can we transform them into strengths. Our greatest gifts and deepest wounds are inextricably bound together. When we unify our being, each part of the self finds its place in the context of the whole. Rabbi Kook writes that by sinning a person enters "the world of fragmentation, and then every particular being stands by itself, and evil is evil in and of itself and it is evil and destructive. When he repents out of love there at once shines on him the light from the world of unity, where everything is integrated into one whole, and in the context of the whole there is no evil at all. The evil is joined with the good to invest it with more attractiveness, and to enhance its significance. Thus, the willful wrongs become transformed into real virtues."[22]

The vital message of both of these ancient Yom Kippur rites—the scapegoat and the incense offerings—is that no part of the self, nor any individual community member, may be cut off from the whole. In order for us to come into our wholeness, all parts of the self must be held together as one. And when we join together as a collective, something greater constellates than the simple sum of individuals. Joined together, we atone for one another, for what one of us may lack another makes up for, and one person's weakness may evoke another's strength. In community, then, we find our wholeness and healing. On Yom Kippur, Jews cease to view themselves as isolated individual persons but as members of an interconnected web, a community in which each person takes responsibility for the sins of the collective. This sense of communal responsibility and interconnectedness is reflected in the Yom Kippur confessional prayers, which are always chanted in the plural: We have sinned, we have stolen, we have hated, and so on.

Yom Kippur is a time when we each gather up the broken pieces of our lives—as the ancient Israelites gathered up the broken pieces of the first tablets—and try to reestablish a sense of wholeness and coherence both as individual people and as a community. Despite whatever has been broken or shattered through our own mistakes or fate itself, Yom Kippur, the day of at-one-ment, gives us a chance to heal and be whole once more.

MEDITATION ON SELF-FORGIVENESS

Begin this meditation by taking a few minutes to relax and get centered, using whatever meditative practice works best for you, or simply spend time paying attention to your breath. Throughout this meditation, if you find yourself becoming distracted, simply bring your awareness back to your breath.

Now I want to invite you to open up your heart to the possibility of forgiving yourself—of truly and wholly forgiving yourself. See if you can breathe in a sense of spaciousness in your being, the spaciousness of an open heart, a heart that is willing to love, accept, and forgive.

We all have parts of ourselves and stories from our past that we have tucked away and cut ourselves off from because we have been unable to forgive ourselves. We all have unresolved traumas, humiliations, and losses; and many of us have a hurt inner child whom we have banished from our lives and forced to live in hiding and in isolation, exiled from our hearts.

In this state of openheartedness and spaciousness allow an image or memory from your past to surface in your mind—a memory or image of yourself from a time when you were deeply hurt but were unable to acknowledge and embrace your own pain with an open heart. See if you can embrace that memory or image with a heart filled with love, acceptance, and forgiveness. If an image of your child self arises, take that child into your arms and hold him or her and say, "I forgive you, I forgive you. I'm so sorry for the pain and isolation you have had to endure. It wasn't your fault." Now say, "I forgive you" to your child self using your own name ("_____, I forgive you").

As you welcome the child back into your heart, you may also need to ask her for forgiveness for the times you were not able to be there for her in the past. Ask the child what she needs from you in order to forgive *you*. Let yourself receive forgiveness from your child self.

Take as long as you need to bring some resolution or healing to your troubling memory. When you feel complete, see if any other image or memory arises, and once again see if you can embrace what comes up with compassion and forgiveness, welcoming the memory or image with an open heart. Take as long as you need to bring some resolution to this situation as well.

Now bring all your different images of yourself together, merging the adult and child selves, bringing the past and the present together in your heart, letting yourself feel and acknowledge how much the person you have become has to do with that past. See if you can look back and acknowledge how everything you have been through, even your worst mistakes, has led you to become who you are today. See if you can embrace it all with a sense of forgiveness for yourself and for others, and for God as well.

8

THE MYTH OF MESSIANIC REDEMPTION

The Wound That Heals Us

God creates the healing before the illness.
—*The Talmud, Megillah 13b*

In ancient myth and among many tribal peoples, we find that healing powers are often bestowed as a gift of the gods to a person who is wounded or vulnerable. In shamanistic societies, for instance, would-be shamans commonly undergo an initiatory illness, experiencing extreme states of disintegration and personal suffering. Out of these death-rebirth rites, shamans receive the power to heal others.

The motif of the wounded healer also appears in Greek mythology, in the paradoxical figure of Chiron the centaur, famous for his wisdom and knowledge of medicine. Though he is a source of inexhaustible cures, Chiron himself, according to certain versions of the myth, suffers from an incurable wound, having been accidentally pierced by a poisoned arrow shot by Hercules. In the archetypal figure of the wounded healer, we see again and again that healing powers can be accessed as a result of the experience of being wounded.

In Jewish lore it is the *mashiach,* or Messiah, who most clearly embodies the archetypal image of the wounded healer. Each of the mythic figures associated with the messianic lineage is portrayed as wounded, though each is wounded in a different way. By examining these ancient legends as well as the myth of messianic redemption, we can learn a lot about the process of healing, for ultimately the Messiah symbolizes the power to heal and raise up all that is fallen in the world.

In the following Talmudic legend, the Messiah's woundedness is portrayed quite literally as a physical wound:

One day, Rabbi Yehoshua ben Levi was meditating near the entrance to the tomb of Rabbi Shimon Bar Yohai, in the Galilee, when he had a spontaneous mystical vision in which he encountered the prophet Elijah. He used the opportunity to ask Elijah a number of important questions, including "When will the Messiah come?" Instead of answering Rabbi Yehoshua's question directly, Elijah suggested that he go and ask the Messiah directly. Rabbi Yehoshua expressed wonderment as to where he would find the Messiah and how he would recognize him, and so Elijah instructed him to go to the entrance of the gates of Rome and there he would find the Messiah sitting among the poor, the sick, and the wretched. How would he tell the Messiah apart from the others? While all the others are busy untying *all* their bandages and then retying them all at once, the Messiah will untie and rebandage each wound separately (one at a time), in order to be ready at any moment, should he be called to reveal himself.

Elijah then took Rabbi Yehoshua on a mystic vision to the gates of Rome, where the rabbi encountered the Messiah and asked him when he would be coming. The Messiah replied simply, "Today!" whereupon Elijah explained that "today" refers to a passage from Psalm 155: "Today, if only you will hear his voice." In other words, the Messiah was prepared to reveal himself immediately if only we were ready to receive him.[1]

The image of a Messiah who sits among the wretched and poor, dressing his own wounds, suggests that messianic healing powers derive from an intimate connection with suffering. As with all wounded healers, the Messiah's healing powers derive from the knowledge of a wound in which he forever partakes. His compassion for humanity's suffering derives from his own experience of suffering.

This particular image of the Messiah bears a surprising resemblance to the Christian image of Jesus as the suffering servant of God. No doubt, some of the emotional appeal of the Christ figure is due to the universality of human suffering. People long to have their own pain reflected back to them in a divine mirror. The Talmud's image of the Messiah as wounded and suffering no doubt serves a similar function, mirroring divine compassion and empathy for the human condition.

In another series of striking legends, however, the Messiah is portrayed in a way that is quite different from the traditional portrayal of the Christian savior. In these legends, the Messiah's woundedness is no longer literal but familial, a matter of lineage. What I'm referring to is the much-repeated motif of "tainted origins" that surrounds the birth of King David, the first messianic prototype. A far cry from the myth of Jesus' immaculate conception, King David's lineage is replete with stories of sexual scandal, incest, and sin. According to scriptures and midrashic legend, David's ancestors on both the maternal and paternal sides engaged in illicit or at least questionable sexual unions.[2] Not only were King David's ancestors sinners, but he himself committed several grave sins as king, including adultery and murder.[3]

What is particularly striking about the King David legends is that they stand in striking contrast to the story of his predecessor, King Saul, who, apart from his failure to obey God's command in the war against Amalek, made no mistakes. Yet for the single mistake of not executing the King of Amalek and taking spoils of war, he lost his kingship.[4] Biblical commentators all ask why Saul was punished so severely for a single mistake, while King David, who committed the two cardinal sins of adultery and murder, was forgiven. Not only was David forgiven, but he was also chosen to become the messianic prototype on whom eternal kingship was bestowed. The answer given by several commentators is that instead of acknowledging his mistake, Saul made excuses for it, whereas King David immediately confessed his sins when confronted by the prophet Nathan's reprimand. He then spent the rest of his days engaged in sincere repentance, as reflected in these verses from Psalm 51, which he wrote: "Be gracious to me, O God, according to Your steadfast love; through

Your great mercy, blot out my transgressions. Wash me thoroughly from my iniquity, and cleanse me from my sin. For I acknowledge my transgressions; and my sin is ever before me. Against You alone have I sinned and done that which is evil in Your eyes."

As the one chosen to be the messianic prototype, King David provides a model in which the redeemer need not be perfect, but he must be able to face his failings with honesty and humility. It is the integration of power with vulnerability and saintliness with sinfulness that characterized the Jewish Messiah. The Messiah's impure and tainted origins suggest that in order to raise up all that is fallen in this world, the Messiah must himself be intimately connected to the pain and evil that need redemption. Since redemption involves the transformation of darkness into light and impurity into holiness, the Messiah himself must be connected to impurity. Thus, only a wounded healer/repentant sinner can become the messianic redeemer.[5]

The rabbis extended this notion to leaders in general. In the words of the Talmud, "One should not appoint anyone as leader of a community, unless he carriers a basket of [impure] reptiles on his back, so that if he becomes arrogant, one could tell him: 'Turn around and look behind you.'"[6]

In contrast to our contemporary secular leaders, with their hypocritical self-righteousness, the rabbis considered the existence of skeletons in the family closet or a tainted past as an advantage for leaders because of its humbling effect. In choosing the repentant sinner as the prototype for its redeemer, Jewish theology embraced imperfection rather than perfection as its ideal. This stands in striking contrast to contemporary American culture, where our leaders are rarely given a second chance. In fact, politicians leap on any opportunity to expose their opponents' flaws, creating an atmosphere in which it is practically impossible for leaders to openly admit their mistakes and express their remorse. Yet it is precisely this ability to admit one's errors and to suffer the private as well as the public humiliation that repentance entails that qualifies one to be a true Jewish leader.

Another extraordinary Jewish teaching, which appears in numerous different midrashic sources, suggests that "the Messiah was born on the very day that the [Jerusalem] Temple was destroyed."[7] This saying, which was said in reference to the destruction of the second Temple by the Romans in 70 c.e., is based on the mystical notion that the brightest light emerges out of the moment of greatest darkness. The symbol of a redeemer who is born at the moment of greatest pain and loss teaches us that life is cyclic, that death and birth are linked, and that every ending is followed by a new beginning. According to a tale told by Martin Buber:

> They asked Rabbi Pinhas [of Koretz] "Why should the Messiah be born on the anniversary of the destruction of the Temple—as the tradition has it?" "The kernel," he replied, "which is sown in earth, must fall to pieces so that the ear of grain may sprout from it. Strength cannot be resurrected until it has dwelt in deep secrecy. To doff a shape, to don a shape—this is done in the state of pure nothingness. In the husk of forgetting, the power of memory grows. That is the power of redemption. On the day of destruction, power lies at the bottom of the depths, and grows. That is why, on this day, we sit on the ground. That is why, on this day, we visit graves. That is why, on this day, the messiah is born.[8]

In order to understand the meaning and deep healing message implied in this teaching, one must remember the spiritual and national significance of the Jerusalem Temple in ancient Jewish life. As I mentioned earlier (chapter 3), the Jerusalem Temple was a unifying force for the Jewish people both in the practical and mystical sense. It served as a symbol of Jewish national sovereignty and as a gathering place where all the different tribes came together on the pilgrimage holidays. Its existence symbolized the deep bond of love between God and Israel and stood for the union of all opposites—of heaven and earth, masculine and feminine, spirit and matter. The Temple's destruction marked an unparalleled cataclysmic event in the history of the Jewish people. To this very day, Jews mourn its destruction and pray daily for the Temple's rebuilding, which is seen as a symbol of the future redemption.

The belief that the redeemer and the possibility of redemption are born out of the very ashes of destruction serves a powerful therapeutic function. Similar to a hypnotic technique used in the treatment of trauma, this myth creates an emotional link between the experience of devastating trauma and ultimate optimism—the hope of redemption and rebirth. The Messiah's birth on the day that the Temple was destroyed constitutes what the cultural anthropologist Victor Turner calls a polar-archetype, linking the opposite poles of destruction and redemption into a single narrative. Like the Lurianic myth of the shattered vessels, it redefined an event that had been experienced as a national catastrophe as an event that would ultimately lead to transformation and renewal. By doing this, it provided a renewed sense of hope and faith for a people disillusioned by defeat and exile.

The myth of the birth of the Messiah on the day of the Temple's destruction draws on the symbolism of the moon cycle, central to all Goddess-based religions. As the new moon follows the darkest night of each month, moon-watching teaches us that endings are always followed by new beginnings. Despite its repudiation of the Goddess cult, Judaism incorporated many of the spiritual values and symbols of this ancient feminine wisdom. We see this clearly in the figure of the Messiah who is said to embody the regenerative power of the moon—the ability to bring renewal and new hope to all humanity. Jews pride themselves in being moon-watchers, for the Jewish calendar is essentially a lunar one. In fact, in the monthly ritual of sanctifying the new moon (*kiddush ha'chodesh*), Jews dance under the moonlit sky, and while jumping up and down, they point to the waxing crescent moon and evoke the eternal memory of the first messianic king: "David, the King of Israel, lives forever!"

Messianic Motifs in Healing

In Hasidic teachings, the Messiah came to be seen not just as an actual savior of humanity but also as a power within each soul that can bring about healing and transformation. The messianic spark, or *nekudat mashiach,* as it is known in Hebrew, is what enables each of us to transform the difficult circumstances of our lives into something meaningful and holy. It is awakened whenever we discover the divine force of healing moving through our lives at the darkest of moments.

Whenever I work with a client going through a devastating loss or major life crisis, these teachings are present in my heart. At certain points in treatment I may use the myth of the Messiah as a means of encouraging clients to find the redemptive possibilities hidden within their difficult circumstances. Timing, however, is everything in bringing these kinds of teaching stories into treatment. In the midst of a personal tragedy, people typically need just to sit with their feelings of hopelessness and despair and feel our empathy for their pain and our support for them. Our presence enables them to bear the unbearable. There comes a point, however, when seeds of "redemption" can be delicately planted, as I did with Sarah, a woman whom I counseled after her husband of twenty years left her.

For the first year after her separation, Sarah was filled with deep rage and grief. She could not get over feeling terribly betrayed and wronged. Her faith in herself and in God had been shattered as a result of her husband's abandonment of her, for her marriage had been a religious one. After many months of being empathic to her anger, I began to sense that Sarah was becoming a prisoner of her own anger and feelings of injustice. She seemed unable to view her situation in any other way than as a victim.

Something shifted for Sarah, however, when I brought up the symbolism of the Messiah's birth on the day the Temple was destroyed. Somehow, this particular metaphor seemed to touch her deeply, and she was particularly moved by the personal application of this myth to her own situation. It offered her hope in place of her despair and hinted at how this ending in her life might lead to some new beginning. After months of feeling totally devastated, Sarah finally started acknowledging that a part of her had been dying in the marriage and that the ending of the relationship, no matter how painful and devastating it had been, was also giving her back herself. Though she was still in a lot of pain about the breakup of her family, she began to sense that in her aloneness she was reconnecting in a profound way with her true self—a self she had unfortunately sacrificed in order to be loved.

During the next few months of treatment Sarah began exploring how she had surrendered too much of her autonomy for the sake of the marriage and had all too often put her own goals on hold in order to keep the peace. Slowly she began to realize that her divorce was a necessary step in her own healing—not one she would ever have chosen consciously but something that was needed in order for her to emerge into the fullness of her own being.

Sarah's realization meant that it was time to let go of her anger and begin to work on forgiveness. During this process, I continued using the metaphor of the destruction of the Temple to acknowledge how tragic the breakup had been but also to show how a redemptive force had been released in her as a result of it. Though Sarah would never again have the wholeness of her nuclear family, as a consequence of the breakup she was finally becoming the person she deeply longed to be.

Like Sarah, we can each learn to face and come to terms with the "endings" in our lives with far less fear and resistance when we develop faith in the redemptive seed that is planted every time we shed an old skin. And by identifying such archetypal themes as the destruction of the Temple and the birth of the redeemer in our personal lives, we learn to see our own personal dramas through a much wider lens. And when our personal dramas are mirrored by the larger mythos, we feel less alone in our personal pain, which now becomes part of *the* pain of a universe that is perpetually dying and renewing itself. When we become aware that this process is occurring in all of existence at all times, from the macrocosmic down to the microcosmic, cellular level, we begin to take our lives a little less personally, in the sense that we see we are not unique or alone in our suffering. In saying this, I do not mean to discount the experience of painful feelings. Rather, I am suggesting that when we view our lives through the larger mythic lens, we begin to experience our lives as part of a much greater matrix of meaning in which every transition we undergo, whether it be a death, divorce, or illness, may initiate us into the larger mysteries of life.

HEALING FROM ADVERSITY AND ILLNESS

When adversity and illness are viewed as an essential and vital force in human growth and transformation, not just as things to be endured or overcome, they are granted a sacred role in our lives. Jungian analyst C. Jesse Groesbeck points out in his essay "The Archetypal Image of the Wounded Healer" that "when sickness is vested with such dignity, it has the inestimable advantage that it can be vested with a healing power. The *divina afflictio* [divine affliction] then contains its own diagnosis, therapy and prognosis, provided of course that the right attitude toward it is adopted. The art of healing was left to the divine physician in ancient times. He was the sickness and the remedy."[9] When seen as a rite of initiation rather than as a disfiguring or disabling force, every illness becomes a path to a particular healing or personal gift. If we listen deeply to its message rather than try to eliminate it, illness may heal *us* instead of the other way around. Perhaps this is what the ancient Talmudic sages were suggesting when they said, "God creates the healing before the illness."[10]

The atemporal notion that God creates the healing before the illness suggests that when we need to heal in a particular way, the divine healer may bring about symptoms or situations that will force us to manifest that healing power. The intended outcome is healing; the means to healing, at certain times, may be an illness or other unanticipated crisis.

The notion that what wounds us can also heal us is hinted at in a number of biblical stories. During their journey in the desert, for instance, the Israelites are attacked and poisoned by snakes, and Moses is instructed to heal the wounded by making a bronze snake for them to gaze at. Using a replica of that which smote them in order to bring healing, Moses learns the secret of homeopathy, healing *like* through *like*. Even the material Moses uses to construct the replica of the snake is connected with the snake itself, for the Hebrew word for bronze is *nechoshet,* a play on the word *nachash,* or snake.

And the wounding and healing are one and the same in yet another way. As Numbers 21:6–8 makes clear, it was God who both sent the snakes and advised Moses on how to heal the victims:

> Then the Lord sent fiery serpents among the people, and
> they bit the people, so that many Israelites died. And the
> people came to Moses and said, "We have sinned against
> you; pray to the Lord to take the serpents away from us."
> So Moses prayed for the people. And the Lord said to
> Moses, "Make a bronze serpent and set it on a pole, and
> every one who is bitten, when he sees it shall live."

The notion that both the wounding agent and the healing process are the same suggests that illness and healing derive from a unified divine source. "He who wounds also heals," said the ancient Delphic oracle. And because illness and healing are so deeply connected, our symptoms often become the path to our healing.

More evidence for this notion of illness as healing can be found in the way the child's immune system is formed. It is only through repeated exposure to germs and the repeated experience of illness that the exquisitely complex immune system develops the ability to fight off illness. In this sense, illness supports the development of health—the two are inseparable. In fact, health is not possible without illness. So, too, in the realm of the soul. Certain powers of the soul can emerge only when we struggle with adversity. Though none of us would ever consciously choose to be ill, when we are lifted out of the secure confines of our ordinary lives by an illness or trauma, we discover new qualities and strengths in ourselves that we may never have imagined ourselves to possess.

Whenever I have worked with people who have undergone a significant period of illness, they all express a sense of not being the same person they were prior to the illness. And almost invariably, they are filled with a strange sense of gratitude for the changes that the illness brought about, though they never would have consciously chosen to go through it.

Similarly, survivors of trauma who undergo treatment often find that they feel healthier and stronger than they ever did prior to the trauma. It seems that in situations of extreme stress, the assault on our characteristic coping mechanisms compels us to shift to a more complex level of functioning. In effect, traumatic events force us to manifest new coping mechanisms and new strengths that we might never have come by otherwise.[11]

WRESTLING WITH ANGELS

The biblical story of Jacob wrestling with the angel is a classic example of healing and blessing coming on the heels of a wounding experience. The story, told in Genesis 32, takes place on the night of Jacob's return from exile after twenty-two years away from his family and homeland. As Jacob spends the night all alone, preparing to confront his estranged brother, Esau, with whom he has painful unfinished business from childhood, he is attacked by a man (or, in Hebrew, *ish*) with whom he wrestles until dawn.

The fight begins with Jacob wrestling what appears to be an earthly adversary, but it progressively becomes more surreal and symbolic until Jacob's outer struggle comes to mirror his inner struggle—the struggle to make peace with his shadow side, the part of him that he had always projected onto Esau. Though Jacob is injured in his ordeal, he ultimately prevails and is blessed by his adversary with a new name, a spirit name—Israel, or Godwrestler. As Genesis tells it, the angel said, "Your name will no longer be Jacob but Israel because you have wrestled with God and with man and prevailed."

When we examine the biblical narrative, it seems that the transformation from trauma to blessing and injury to healing occurs when Jacob realizes the divine nature of his adversary—that indeed he is not just a man, an ish, but an angel, or messenger of God. Out of this realization Jacob names the site of his struggle *Peniel*—the face of God—and declares, "I saw God face to face and my soul was saved."

We are all a lot like Jacob in that sense. For it is when we encounter the face of the divine in our struggles and adversities that our wounds become a source of blessing. In discovering the divine hand moving through and shaping our lives, we uncover a deeper meaning to our existence. This restoration of meaning is itself a profound source of healing.

MEANING WITHOUT BLAME

In any discussion about the spiritual meaning of illness or adversity, it is extremely important not to get stuck in old paradigms that are based on a system of moral accounting for God's ways. The old paradigm, based on the Talmudic notion that there is no suffering without sin, attempted to justify all human suffering by establishing moral cause and effect—essentially by blaming the victim. This approach appeals to the primitive psyche in us that wants to know that things are not entirely random and out of control in the universe. However, in seeking to view God as always fair and in control, we often end up blaming ourselves and others unfairly for their fate.

Clearly, it is important for anyone dealing with illness to explore the possible causal connections between their illness and any destructive habits and behaviors that are in their power to change. People need to feel empowered to do what is in their control to positively affect their health. Self-reflection can be a very helpful tool, enabling us to take responsibility for our actions and change behaviors that are clearly self-destructive. However, to the degree that life is rarely a purely cause-and-effect affair, and people who are ill are already burdened by excessive guilt, overly simplistic theories of moral accountability are not entirely helpful. We need to balance the view that our minds and health habits play an important role in our health and wellness with a humble respect for the mysterious element of life. Sometimes there is no *why*.

Even the Talmud acknowledges that there are times when suffering cannot easily be accounted for. It suggests that there is an acausal form of suffering, which it sets apart from all other forms of suffering. It advises the afflicted, "If you find that suffering is upon you, search your ways. If you have searched and not found any wrongdoing, consider the possibility that you are remiss in spiritual work or study of Torah. If after extensive soul-searching you can find no hint of guilt or spiritual lacking, know that your suffering is suffering from love."[12]

It's not entirely clear what the Talmud means by "suffering from love." On the surface it seems to be one of those classic rabbinic "reframings" of reality, based on the idea that what seems bad on the surface may mask some hidden goodness. It may feel as though God doesn't love us when we suffer without obvious reason, yet the Talmud tells us such suffering may on the contrary be an expression of love, as it often has the effect of bringing us close to God. There is no causality operating in this case, but simply the mysterious phenomenon that suffering has the potential to bring us to intimate terms with the spirit. It can awaken love.

In my therapy work I find that when people get hung up on the question of "why is this happening to *me,*" they invariably are led either to self-pity (*"oy veh iz mir!"*—"woe is me!") or to excessive self-blame ("it's all my fault"). The question of "why me?" tends to induce feelings of anger and frustration, for no matter how much we search for reasons for our suffering, it rarely makes sense from the perspective of "fairness." We so much want the universe (God) to be "fair," but sometimes it just isn't. And when we can't come up with a good answer to the question of why, it's easy to lose whatever faith in God we may have.

The Talmud, in fact, tells a story about a famous scholar and mystic named Elisha ben Abuyah, who lost his faith when he saw a man die while performing a mitzvah deemed to prolong one's life. According to the Torah (Deuteronomy 17:6–7), "If you happen upon a bird's nest on the path, in a tree or on the ground, whether there be baby birds or eggs and the mother bird is sitting on the babies or eggs, do not take the mother with the offspring. Send the mother free and take the babies for yourself so that things will be good for you and your days will be lengthened." When Elisha ben Abuya saw a man fall to his death while performing this mitzvah, he concluded that "there is no justice and there is no judge."[13] In telling us this tale, the Talmud seems to be directing us to let go of the need to always find direct, causal connections between human deeds and reward or punishment. Life is not always going to be fair, and we don't deserve everything that happens to us, good or bad!

Beyond Causality

The Teleological Perspective

I find that questions of teleology, addressing the ultimate end or purpose of things, lead to a much more helpful discourse on meaning than questions of causality. When we look at things from the teleological perspective, we begin to ask questions such as

- Where is this experience potentially taking me, and who might I become as a result?
- How can I grow by being fully present to my experience?
- What is God revealing to me through this particular revelation of divinity known as illness?

This acausal, forward-looking approach to the quest for meaning eliminates the cycle of self-blame with which most ill people are already overburdened. I particularly like the last question because it frames illness as just another face of God. But meditating on any of these questions or others like them instead of the "why me?" sort transforms the experience of illness into a revelatory one rather than just another excuse to beat up on oneself. And when we view illness as emanating from the same divine source to which we turn for healing, illness and healing become a single meditation leading us to an appreciation of the nondual nature of God.

In my work with cancer patients and people dealing with medical and disability issues, I have found this approach to be quite helpful. When my client Carol was undergoing radiation and chemotherapy for breast cancer, she was stuck in a classic self-blame cycle. She repeatedly said she was feeling as though she were being punished by God with her illness. She felt as though she were dirty in some way and must have deserved what she was going through.

I realized that Carol's irrational self-blame was masking some unresolved childhood pain that was resurfacing at this difficult time in her life. As we explored this together, Carol revealed that she had been sexually abused as a child by one of her uncles. This abuse had gone on over the course of the many years that she spent lots of time at her uncle's house. Carol's parents had been so preoccupied with their own difficulties throughout her childhood that she never felt she could bring her needs to their attention, and so she had never brought the abuse up with them. All in all, Carol grew up seeing herself as a burden to others and did not feel entitled to having her own needs met.

Seeing her illness as a punishment from God, a sign of her unworthiness, Carol seemed to be merging her childhood experience of neglect and abuse with her experience of being a cancer patient. In Carol's mind God had become an extension of her neglectful caretakers; her cancer was proof she was not lovable. This kind of unconscious merging of one's experience of God with one's internal image of parents and early caretakers is a way that faith commonly becomes distorted.

I suggested to Carol that instead of seeing her cancer as a punishment from God, she might open herself up to the possibility that God was right there with her in her illness, compassionately holding her. This notion had a radical effect on Carol. Instead of feeling punished by God with her condition, she began to see how her illness was connecting her with God. It was also leading her to connect with parts of her core self that she had never touched. With a lot of encouragement, Carol joined a spiritual support group and slowly began letting others in on her loneliness and shame. She also started attending meditation and art classes, and found herself expressing parts of herself that had been untouched since childhood. As Carol let go of the shame associated with being a cancer patient, she began to allow others to support her through the difficult times she was facing. For the first time in her life Carol felt a deep sense of connection with God, her core self, and her community, all as a result of her illness.

The side effects of the radiation treatments Carol was receiving continued to be trying. The fatigue she experienced in the days and weeks following treatments was difficult to bear. Carol also experienced the radiation treatments themselves as humiliating, and she asked me to help her devise a spiritually uplifting meditation she could use during and after the treatments. Together we came up with the practice of imagining the radiation to be a conduit of divine heal-ing light. During the treatments she closed her eyes and simply imag-ined herself to be in the unconditionally loving presence of the Shechinah—the divine feminine. Instead of focusing on the destruc-tive power of the radiation, she imagined it to be a manifestation of the Shechinah's radiant healing light and love. At the same time, she envisioned herself being encircled by all her friends and community, seeing them as supporting her and sending her loving energy for healing.

In the days following each radiation treatment Carol found com-fort wrapping herself in a tallit (prayer shawl) and focusing once more on the same meditation. Carol is currently in complete remis-sion from her cancer, and she has dedicated herself to helping other women who are dealing with cancer and chronic illness.

MEDITATION ON INTEGRATING STRENGTHS AND WEAKNESSES

Take a few minutes to relax and become centered. Now try to get in touch with your greatest strengths as a person by considering questions such as these:

- What are your most powerful spiritual/emotional resources?
- How are you unusually gifted?
- What do other people see as special about you?

Take a moment to feel appreciation for the personal gifts and blessings you possess.

Now try to open your heart also to your own sense of wounded-ness and vulnerability—to the ways in which you have felt hurt, abandoned, unloved, or insufficient. Try to open your heart fully to your wounded self.

As you experience both your strengths and vulnerabilities at once, you can hold your whole self in loving embrace.

See if you can begin to recognize how your strengths and weak-nesses are connected, deriving from a common source. Discovering this connection can lead to a profound sense of self-acceptance and self-forgiveness. See if you can offer thanksgiving for it all—the bitter as well as the sweet.

It is only by breaking open entirely,
by allowing our heart and whole being
to break open again and again,
wider than we ever thought possible,
that the unbreakable jewel is revealed:
the belovedness of being itself,
the radiant diamond that we have always been.
By loving, truly loving every aspect
of who we are,
an inexplicable laughter is born
from the deepest sorrow,
an exquisite song emerges
from the most terrifying scream,
the most tender child is awakened
through the hateful murderer,
our purest holiness is revealed
by our willingness to embrace
the very thing that most frightens us
and we find unexpectedly the treasure
where we least expect it to be.
Often in the most disavowed part
of who we are.

—RASHANI, "AGAIN AND AGAIN"

9

Moving from Judgment to Compassion

Great are the righteous for they transform
judgment into mercy.
—*Midrash Bereishit Raba 33:3*

At first God thought to create the world through the
quality of judgment (*din*), but realizing that the world
could not endure at this level, God added on the
quality of compassion (*rachamim*).
—*Midrash Bereishit Raba 12:15*

One Friday morning a group of Hasidim set out for the town of Lublin to spend the Sabbath with their teacher, the legendary clairvoyant Reb Ya'acov Yitzhak, also known as the Seer of Lublin. Reb David of Lelov, whose deep love for animals earned him a reputation as a gifted horse whisperer, was among this group of disciples. After encountering several obstacles and delays on their way, the group arrived just as the sun was about to set Friday afternoon. Fearing they would be late for Sabbath prayers and miss the seer's holy teachings, the group hastily abandoned their horse and carriage and ran off to the synagogue—everyone that is, except Reb David. When the seer realized that Reb David was missing, he sent the others to look for him. Where did they find him? In the livery, feeding the horses. When they asked him what he was doing there, he responded that all the others had run off without thinking to feed and water the horses, who were weary from the arduous journey, and so he had stayed behind to do just that.

Reb David was a Hasid in the truest sense of the word, a lover of the divine, and his love for God was expressed through his deep compassion for all creatures and all living things. It was absolutely clear to Reb David that by observing the mitzvah of *tzaar ba'alei chaim,* the commandment to prevent the suffering of animals, he would obtain more closeness to God than by seeking spiritual uplift-ment in the synagogue. Reb David understood that it is in the expression of compassion—the love and care we extend to all living things—that we find the divine presence; for ultimately compassion, or *rachamim,* as it is called in Hebrew, is God's very essence.

Jewish mysticism teaches that we come close to God only when we "walk in God's ways"—that is, when we embody the divine quality of compassion. In the following midrash, the thirteen attributes of divine mercy revealed to Moses at Mount Sinai form the template for the practice of compassion:

> "Walking in all His ways": (Deut 11:22). What are the ways of the Holy One? "A God compassionate and gra-cious, slow to anger, abounding in kindness and faithful-ness, extending kindness to the thousandth generation, forgiving iniquity, transgression and sin" (Ex. 34:6). This means that just as God is gracious and compassionate, you too must be gracious and compassionate. . . . Just as God gives freely to all, you too must give freely to all. Just as God is loving, you too must be loving.[1]

Spiritual development, according to the rabbis, is measured by how much compassion we embody. We see this in the legends surrounding Moses' spiritual development. According to legend, Moses' first en-counter with God occurs when his compassion for one of the animals from his flock leads him to the site of the burning bush. Chasing after one of his flock, Moses finds the vulnerable creature drinking from a stream at the foot of Mount Sinai. As his heart goes out to this creature, he receives his prophetic initiation. The midrash explains that "the Holy One of Blessing saw that Moses was gentle and compassionate; [and] that he was the kind of shepherd who would sacrifice his own life to save one of God's flock. For even were one of his sheep to stray into Midian, Moses would go to rescue it."[2]

In his ethical-mystical treatise *The Palm Tree of Deborah,* the sixteenth-century rabbi Moshe Cordovero defines compassion as the desire to seek the well-being of all fellow creatures. Compassion, he teaches, is the ultimate fulfillment of the command to love one's neighbor as oneself, the mystical imperative to experience the interconnectedness of all being. Cordovero urges us to

> do good to whomever needs your goodness. . . . You should desire the well-being of your fellow creature, eying his good fortune benevolently. Let his honor be as precious to you as your own, for you and your fellow are one and the same. That is why we are commanded: "Love your neighbor as yourself. . . ."
>
> Let your compassion extend to all creatures, neither despising nor destroying any of them. For Wisdom spreads over all created things: mineral, vegetable, animal, and human. Each was created in Wisdom. Do not uproot anything that grows, unless it is necessary.[3]

Through compassion, Cordovero writes, we not only come to resemble God, but we actually have the power to open up the flow of divine compassion in the universe. Changing the usual "as above, so below" to "as below, so above," Cordovero suggests that our actions here on earth influence the heavens because God needs our mercy in order to fully manifest divine mercy. "Just as you conduct yourself below," writes Cordovero, "so are you worthy of opening the corresponding sublime quality above. Exactly as you behave, so it emanates from above. You cause that quality to shine in the world."[4]

Interestingly, the Hebrew word *rachamim* comes from the same three-letter root as the word *rechem,* womb, suggesting that compassion makes us womblike, nurturing of life. With compassion we enable all things to grow into their most beautiful and complete form. To be truly nurturing of life and growth, however, our compassion must become flexible, like the womb itself, allowing us to expand or contract as needed; for at times compassion requires that we extend our boundaries and give of ourselves, and at times it requires that we hold back and restrain from giving.

In order to become a conduit for the flow of divine compassion, many of the Hasidic masters made compassionate awareness the central focus of their spiritual healing practice. They taught that each day of our lives, we have many opportunities to view things either from the perspective of judgment—*din*—or compassion—rachamim. When we view reality from the perspective of din, our vision may be objectively correct from an absolute perspective, but we are often missing the point of it all, which is that all of life needs healing and fixing, and we are part of the process. When we see life through the lens of rachamim, with eyes filled with love and compassion, we become healers, and we have the ability to shape reality in a positive way. Ultimately our compassion and love have the power to bring healing.

FINDING THE GOOD

Among the Hasidic masters, Rabbi Levi Yitzhak of Berditchev, also known as Levi-Yitzhak Derbaremdiger the merciful, stands out as one who truly perfected the practice of compassionate awareness. Levi Yitzhak was a legendary master of the "good eye," one who could bestow blessing by seeing the good in others.

A classic tale of Levi Yitzhak describes a conversation he had with a certain Jew whom he encounters eating in public on *Tisha B'av,* the ritual fast day commemorating the destruction of the holy Temple in Jerusalem. Levi Yitzhak said to the man, "Surely you have forgotten that it is Tisha B'av?" "No," replied the man brazenly, "I know it is." "Then surely you do not realize that we are commanded to fast on Tisha B'av?" "No, I know we are supposed to fast," said the man. Once again giving the man the benefit of the doubt, Levi Yitzhak said to him, "Perhaps you are sick, and the fast would endanger your health." "No, rabbi," answered the man. "I am quite healthy, thank you. May there be many in Israel as well as I am." At that moment Levi Yitzhak looked up to heaven and said, "Master of the Universe, look down from heaven and see who is like your people Israel, a holy nation. A Jew would rather declare himself a sinner than permit a false word to escape his lips!"[5]

On another occasion, Levi Yitzhak was heading to synagogue for the traditional *selichot* services on the eve of the Jewish New Year when a sudden downpour forced him and his personal assistant to seek shelter under the awning of a tavern. The assistant peered through the window and saw a group of Jews feasting, drinking, and reveling. Growing impatient, he urged Levi Yitzhak to see for himself how these Jews were misbehaving when they should have been in synagogue praying to God for forgiveness. Instead of looking, Levi Yitzhak rebuked his assistant, saying, "It is forbidden to find fault with the children of Israel. They are surely reciting the blessings for food and drink. May God bless these holy Jews." The assistant, still feeling judgmental, peered into the tavern once more and heard two Jews telling each other about thefts they committed. He told this to the rebbe, hoping finally to convince him of their wickedness. Refusing to see them as other than righteous people, Levi Yitzhak exclaimed, "If that is so, they are truly holy Jews, for they are confessing their sins before Rosh Hashannah. As you know, no one is more righteous than he who repents."[6]

In choosing to focus selectively on the good in others, Levi Yitzhak was embodying *midat ha'rachamim,* the divine attribute of compassion. This practice of focusing on the good in each person was further developed by Rabbi Nachman of Breslov. From his work as a soul-healer he learned that when we selectively focus on the little bits of good that exist in each person, we enable those bits of good to expand and slowly overcome the bad. By choosing to focus on what is right in people instead of what is wrong, we have the power to lift them up. This, according to Rabbi Nachman, is what the rabbis meant when they said that we must always "tip the scales of judgment toward the side of mercy" and judge every person as *pure* (literally, *meritorious*),[7] as described in Rabbi Nachman's collected teachings, *Likutey Moharan:*

> You should know that one must judge every person in such a way as to tip the scale of judgment to merit; even someone who is evil. One must search and find some small aspect of goodness in him and judge him favorably [*lekaf zechut*]. Through this you tip his scale toward the good and enable him to do teshuvah. This is what is meant in the passage [Psalm 37] "In just a bit there will be no evil one and when you glance at the place where the evil one [*rasha*] stood, he will no longer be there." This passage teaches one to tip the scale of judgment in the direction of merit. . . . Even if you see he is evil, you must search to find some goodness—some area where he is not evil. . . . And one must also find this in oneself.[8]

The Hebrew expression—*zechut*—that Rabbi Nachman uses to signify the tipping of the scales toward the side of merit also suggests pureness—*zach*. To tip the scales toward zechut is to intentionally focus on that essence which is most pure in each person—to see the person's highest and holiest potential, his or her essential divine being, that place deep inside that is untouched by problematic symptoms or defenses. The same challenge goes for ourselves, says Rabbi Nachman. We have to be compassionate with ourselves and connect with our own inner goodness and purity in order to lift ourselves up from whatever fallen state we may be in.

Rabbi Nachman's teaching is actually a powerful therapy technique, one we can use in our daily life as well as in our work as healers. The way we see each other has a profound influence on each other's unfolding. By seeing the goodness and wholeness of others, even when they are unable to see it in themselves, we open up the space for them to become who they are truly meant to be.

If we were to apply Rabbi Nachman's teaching to therapy, we might begin to think differently about how to help people heal. Instead of focusing on what is wrong with people, we might begin to focus on what is right about them. Far too often, therapy is ineffective because it becomes too focused on people's problems and symptoms while ignoring their unique strengths and capacities.

Rabbi Nachman himself applied his practice of selectively focusing on the good as a treatment for depression and melancholy. He intuitively understood that depression can distort people's perception of themselves and their lives in such a way that they become overly focused on the negative. In fact, when we are depressed, we tend to magnify the bad and forget all the good parts of ourselves, to the point that the bad overwhelms the good. By forcing ourselves to acknowledge the little bits of good that exist, we effectively challenge our own distorted perceptions. Acknowledging the good—however small it might be—helps us regain a sense of balance and perspective. Rabbi Nachman suggests:

> One must try at all times to be joyous and to distance oneself from depression. Even if you look within and find no good . . . this is the work of the *"ba'al davar"* (the evil one) who wishes to cast you down in depression and dark bitterness, God forbid. It is forbidden to fall into this. One must search and find some good in oneself. How is it possible that one did not do some mitzvah or good deed all of one's life. . . . One must find some good point in oneself in order to restore a sense of life and in order to find joy. . . . One must continue to search more for other good things, even if the good parts are mixed with much bad. Even so, one should extract the good point and gather all the good points.[9]

Unfortunately, many of us spend a great deal more time sitting in harsh judgment (din) than practicing compassion (rachamim) or forgiveness. We are more concerned with what's wrong with ourselves and others than with what's right. We obsess about our own imperfections and are all too ready to criticize our friends, family, and associates whenever they fall short of our expectations. When we get stuck in our "judging minds," life begins to seem like an endless series of disappointments! And when we relentlessly judge and find fault with ourselves and others, we unfortunately often end up worsening the problems we think we are trying to remedy.

Friendships and relationships, for instance, frequently break up because we spend too much time and energy focused on what's wrong with them and what's missing from them rather than on building from what is right about them. If we constantly tell our partners what they are doing wrong, we cause them to lose confidence in themselves, and they begin to feel inadequate. The same with education. Teachers who spend too much time punishing bad behavior, rather than reinforcing good behavior, find that their students become increasingly difficult to control. The sense of failure tends to reinforce itself with continued failure. If instead teachers give their students positive feedback—reminding them of what they have done right instead of what they have done wrong—they will build the students' self-confidence. Feeling more confident that they can succeed, children become motivated to try to do their best.

Retraining ourselves to be loving and compassionate with ourselves and others rather than judgmental and critical is not always so easy when we have grown up in critical home environments. Many of us, unfortunately, have been taught from a very young age to be absolutely merciless with ourselves, and by extension, we are harsh with others. We never know when to give ourselves a break and say *"dayeinu"*—it's enough! *genuk*! Yet with practice and mindfulness we can learn to catch ourselves when we get stuck in our judging/critical minds and lovingly redirect ourselves to focus on the good.

Compassion during Times of Illness or Disability

There is no other time when self-compassion is more crucial than when we are struggling with an illness or disability. Rebecca, a middle-aged woman I worked with for several years, taught me some deep lessons about the importance of compassion for those struggling with illness. Rebecca started therapy after becoming stricken with an autoimmune disease that greatly restricted her energy and ability to function. There were many days when Rebecca could barely get herself out of bed, let alone work or do errands. Having worked full-time her entire adult life as a teacher and administrator, Rebecca was facing, for the first time, the terrifying possibility that she might not be able to support herself anymore. Rebecca already suffered from lifelong bouts of depression and anxiety, and she had very poor self-esteem. Her current condition only worsened matters.

Like so many depressed individuals, Rebecca was caught in a painful cycle of self-blame and self-punishment. Instead of finding a way to comfort herself when she was in debilitating pain, she would beat herself up emotionally for being unable to function. Rebecca's feelings of self-hatred and worthlessness inevitably resulted in the worsening of her physical symptoms, which in turn made her feel even worse about herself.

Having been the victim of severe and chronic emotional abuse throughout her childhood, Rebecca had internalized a chorus of vicious inner voices that were ready to defeat her at every turn. No matter what she did or how hard she tried, the voices were ready to attack her, much as her own immune system seemed to be doing. Though I tried in every way I knew to help Rebecca become more gentle and compassionate with herself, nothing in my bag of therapist tricks seemed to help. When repeated attempts to treat her depression with medications failed, I realized I was going to have to approach treatment in an unconventional way.

Since Rebecca had sought me out as a therapist because of my Jewish spiritual orientation, I decided to begin drawing more freely on the wisdom of the Jewish mystical tradition in our work. As I began talking to Rebecca about her relationship to God, I discovered that she had a deep and rich inner spiritual life, but her notions of God were confused by the painful overlay of childhood trauma. Her image of God had, in effect, become confused and merged with her internalized images of her parents. As a result, she was experiencing her illness as a punishment from God and as evidence of her basic unworthiness. This attitude echoed what her parents had told her when they abused her—that she deserved to be punished because she was bad.

In therapy I worked together with Rebecca on developing a meditative practice whereby she would envision herself through God's eyes—eyes of loving-kindness—instead of through her parents' cruel and critical eyes. My intention was to help Rebecca gain a new perspective on her situation, one based on self-love and self-acceptance rather than self-blame. This simple practice was tremendously healing for Rebecca, bringing about a radical shift in her experience of herself. Instead of constantly viewing herself as her critical, judgmental parents had viewed her, she opened up to experiencing the enduring and eternal dimensions of her being—that part of herself that was not defined by what she did or how her body looked or functioned on any given day. Instead of seeing herself as damaged goods, she began to experience herself as a beloved spark of the divine.

Over the course of several sessions I introduced Rebecca to some of the mystical folklore on the Shechinah—the mythic figure of the Kabbalah associated with God's feminine and unconditionally loving side. My hope in introducing these legends into Rebecca's therapy was that this powerful, loving image of the divine might offer an antidote to her parents' negative, critical voices, which she had internalized.

The Shechinah is portrayed in Talmudic legend as a deeply compassionate, motherly spirit who goes into exile with her children (the Jewish people) and wanders in their wanderings, empathically suffering along with them in all their trials and ordeals. The Shechinah is often portrayed as a loving presence that comes to help all those in need. She is said to visit and comfort the sick and she hovers above the heads of those who are ill and bedridden.

In Kabbalistic myth, the Shechinah evolved into a veritable Goddess figure whose psychological function seemed to be to balance out the overly punitive, judgmental characteristics of the lone patriarchal God of the Bible. She appears in numerous legends as fiercely defending Israel against God's wrath. As a religious symbol, the Shechinah reintegrated the loving and repressed feminine aspects of God that somehow had been lost by earlier generations.[10]

The notion that the Shechinah is especially present and available to us during times of illness and personal distress was particularly helpful to Rebecca. Wrapped in a tallit (prayer shawl), symbolizing the Shechinah's loving and protecting embrace, Rebecca learned to meditate on divine compassion. This practice enabled her to feel more compassion toward herself, particularly when she was feeling discouraged by her painful and often debilitating symptoms.

Experiencing God as the loving and compassionate Shechinah has helped Rebecca differentiate between the echoes of her parents' critical voices and God's truly loving voice within her heart. Instead of being angry at herself when she is in pain, Rebecca has learned to lovingly embrace and support herself, modeling herself after the Shechinah, who lovingly embraces all those who suffer.

Over time Rebecca has begun to honor her illness as revelatory—a face of the divine—and as a meeting place between her and God. She has also acknowledged that her illness not only was the catalyst for her spiritual awakening but was also, in a strange and paradoxical way, healing her; for so long as Rebecca was well, she was forever hooked into the game of trying to satisfy the unreasonable demands of her inner critical voices. Yet no matter how hard she tried to please them, she never felt she was good enough. It was only when her illness forced her to quit playing the game of conditional self-love that she began to heal into unconditional self-love.

Though Rebecca has not completely silenced her critical inner voices, she has developed the ability to change the channel, by becoming a channel for the divine. Through prayer and spiritual practice she has been able to break away from many intractable, self-defeating patterns that, I'm convinced, conventional therapy alone could not have changed. Most important, Rebecca's negative self-image has healed as she has begun to see and experience herself in relationship to the infinite. Rebecca's physical condition has not changed, but she has found a way to live compassionately and gracefully with the conditions she suffers from. Instead of being something she is constantly angry at herself and the universe about, her illness has come to be the path she walks to God, albeit not an easy one.

SPIRITUAL ATTITUDE ADJUSTMENTS

In Jewish spiritual lore, we find that, like Rebecca, many of the great sages and prophets had to overcome their harsh judgmental and critical tendencies before they could fully come into their healing powers. Reb Zusia of Hanipol, for instance, who became famous for his ability to spiritually heal even the most wicked people, didn't start out with healing powers. As the following tale describes, he gained his healing powers only after realizing how destructive his judgmental tendencies could be.

One day, Reb Zusia went to the house of study of his teacher, the Maggid of Mezerich. When he walked in, he saw a man trying to convince the Maggid to join in a business venture with him. Being clairvoyant, Zusia saw that this man had a long history of getting involved in dishonest dealings and business scams. Without hesitating, Reb Zusia blurted out this information to the Maggid, causing the man to leave in total embarrassment. Reb Zusia immediately regretted what he had done. He realized that by criticizing the man and pointing out his faults, he had shamed him, and in doing so, he had failed to open doors of healing and repentance for him.

Having witnessed the incident, the Maggid, wise teacher and healer that he was, understood that Zusia's psychic powers were getting in the way of his work as a healer. And so the Maggid blessed him, asking that from that day on Zusia only be able to see the *good* in others, even if they did something bad right in front of his eyes. And indeed, from that day on, Reb Zusia became blind to the evil in others. Even if someone sinned right in front of his eyes, he saw only the good in that person, and any bad action Zusia saw performed by another he experienced as though it were his own wrongdoing.[11]

Zusia's practice of taking upon himself the misdeeds of others may seem a bit extreme, but for the tzaddik, everything that is brought to awareness is there for the purpose of healing and fixing. In order to heal others, the tzaddik must first join with them by identifying with their flaws. Then, by fixing the subtle evidences of those very flaws within himself, the tzaddik opens up the gates of repentance and healing for both himself and the person in need of healing. In a sense, the tzaddik becomes a lightning rod for *midat ha'din* (the divine attribute of judgment) by taking the judgments upon himself while extending rachamim to others.

Some version of this identification process goes on with all healers. In order to heal someone else, healers must be able to empathize and connect with the pain or problem they seek to heal in another. Being truly empathic demands that one continually tap into one's own reservoir of pain in order to sense the pain of others. In this sense, empathy forces us continually to work on healing and fixing ourselves as we identify and join with others in pain. Ultimately, our ability to connect and feel empathy and compassion for others is our most powerful healing tool.

There is a saying in the ethical treatise *Pirkay Avot* (Ethics of the Fathers) that one should not judge another person unless you have stood in the exact same place as that person.[12] The Ba'al Shem Tov understood this saying as a suggestion that if we find ourselves judging others, it is probably because we *are* standing in the exact same place as they are. Indeed, the faults we find most disturbing in others often exist within us! Otherwise, we would not have noticed or recognized them.

Because they experience all of reality as interconnected, the tzaddikim (plural for *tzaddik*) know that if they witness or experience something, they are, in some subtle way, connected to it. So if a sin or character flaw has been brought to their awareness through the actions of another, this is in order to awaken them to the need to fix that characteristic within themselves—and not to judge the characteristic in the other person. The tzaddik's identification with the sins or flaws of another person was often very subtle, like the resonance that one musical instrument can evoke when its own vibration causes a similar note to vibrate in another instrument standing nearby.

Shifts in the Divine Countenance

In the rabbinic imagination, it is not just we who must struggle to overcome our own judgmental tendencies; even God is portrayed as struggling to allow divine compassion to overcome divine judgment. According to the Talmud, God prays, "May it be My will that My mercy should suppress My anger, and that My attribute of mercy should dominate all My other attributes, so that I may conduct Myself with My children with mercy, and that I should deal with them, not according to the strict letter of the law [but do for them more than they have rightfully earned]."[13] Perhaps it's a bit of a projection on our part to imagine that God struggles with his own attributes, much as we do. But according to Jewish legend, God's struggle to overcome the attribute of judgment (midat ha'din) goes all the way back to Genesis, where the unfolding of creation is described as a dynamic dance between the divine qualities of judgment and compassion—din and rachamim. The opening passage of Genesis suggests that creation is initiated by Elohim—the name associated with *gevurah,* divine judgment: "In the beginning *Elohim* created the heavens and the earth" (Genesis 1:1). Indeed, as the Kabbalah teaches, creation began with an act of divine gevurah as the Ein Sof (Infinite One) withdrew its light in order to make room for a finite, boundaried world to exist.

Though creation is initiated by Elohim, when we look further into the text of Genesis, we find that another name—YHVH—is added: "This is the story of the creation of heaven and earth. On the day that *yhvh*-Elohim created earth and heaven" (Genesis 2:4). Commenting on this name discrepancy, the midrash suggests, "At first God thought to create the world through the quality of din (truth/judgment), but realizing that the world could not endure at this level, God added on the quality of rachamim (compassion)."[15]

This midrash can be a bit confusing if taken too literally. It's not that God had a change of mind or heart but rather that the process of creation involved a blend of the energies of YHVH and Elohim—of love and limits, of rachamim and din. The multitudinous finite forms created by Elohim exist only to reveal the love and unity of the timeless Infinite One. These two names actually coexist and balance one another as complementary, yin-yang aspects of reality that are interdependent and inseparable. If we look at the dynamic relationship between Elohim and YHVH from the perspective of modern-day physics, we might say that while Elohim continually creates structure and form, YHVH is characterized by the absolute freedom and chaos of subatomic particles, which seemingly obey no steadfast rules. While Elohim operates according to the linear and deterministic laws of nature, YHVH exists at a level of reality where causality no longer operates.

The rabbis taught that at any given moment we have the power to shift the figure-ground relationship between these two aspects of the divine. In kabbalistic parlance, we have the ability to "sweeten the judgments." When we open ourselves to a consciousness of YHVH's love and compassion, Elohim steps aside, as it were, making room for the unpredictable and even the miraculous to occur, for the limits and karmic laws of justice embedded in creation by Elohim exist only as a gateway through which the boundless love of the Infinite One can be revealed. The responsibility for opening the curtain on finite reality and revealing this love rests with us. This is essentially what Jewish spiritual healing is all about—namely, enabling the forces of din to be overpowered by the forces of rachamim.

Each of us can participate in this healing work of *hamtaka* (sweetening) by simply keeping our hearts open when we encounter harsh or painful situations. Our compassion, then, has the power to mitigate the forces of din that we encounter. For instance, when we support and lovingly care for those who are ill or suffering, we sweeten an experience that would otherwise be harsh and unbearable (din).

Similarly, when we find a way to transform situations of anger and discord between people into harmonious, loving connections, we sweeten the judgments. There's a story about the Rebbe of Talno, who was once passing through a town of a rival rebbe when a Hasid of that rebbe threw a stone at him to let him know he was unwelcome in their town. Instead of becoming angry at his assailant, the Rebbe of Talno reached out and caught the stone, keeping it as a cherished reminder of the love and devotion of a Hasid for his rebbe. Instead of focusing on the hostile aspects of the stone thrower's behavior, the Rebbe of Talno sweetened the judgments by finding the sparks of light, the hidden goodness in what would otherwise be considered an aggressive act. By doing this, he also diffused any harsh judgments that may have come down from heaven as a result of the Hasid's unrighteous actions.

In a similar fashion, Levi Yitzhak of Berditchev refused to get angry when the wife of one of the *mitnagdim*—a group of religious Jews who vehemently opposed the Hasidic movement—threw the full contents of a garbage can on his head as he walked through a marketplace. Instead, he went to the synagogue and said to God: "Don't be angry with her, Lord, it's not her fault. Poor woman, she wishes only to please her husband. Can you blame her for that?"[16]

Doing this kind of spiritual healing work may not be suitable for everyone, for it demands an unusual degree of self-transcendence as well as a knack for not taking life too personally. And, clearly, there are times when it may not be appropriate or advisable to try this kind of work. If, for instance, someone is hurting us or taking advantage of us, it may be necessary to assert ourselves and set firm limits with that person before we work on transcending our feelings.

There are, however, many situations in our daily lives when we do have the power to "sweeten" things, particularly in relation to our own harsh judgments about ourselves and others. We also have many opportunities to transform angry and aggressive verbal exchanges into respectful, loving exchanges. We have the power to set the tone of conflicts so that our discourse with others is characterized by mutual compassion and empathy. And ultimately, when we succeed at transforming potentially contentious relations into mutually empathic exchanges, we open up the flow of divine rachamim in our own lives. For as the rabbis said, "According to the quality one uses to deal with others, by that very quality is one dealt with."[17]

THE HIGH HOLY DAYS AS HEALING PARADIGM

Every year during the High Holy Days, Jews engage in communal healing rites of forgiveness and atonement that are aimed at moving the cosmic energies from "judgment" to "compassion." The cycle begins on Rosh Hashannah, the Jewish New Year, and culminates ten days later on Yom Kippur, the Day of Atonement. These ten days, known as asseret y'mai teshuvah (Ten Days of Repentence) are a time for self-reflection and spiritual realignment. On Rosh Hashannah, the drama of creation is ritually reenacted. To the rather eerie, mystical sounds of the shofar, or ram's horn, the Jewish New Year is ushered in, and time itself is renewed as the liturgy proclaims, "Today the world is conceived!" The sounding of the shofar, which resembles the sound of a person weeping and wailing, is intended to awaken us from our spiritual slumber. Crying out like a woman in labor, the shofar beckons us to give birth to ourselves, so that we may begin anew, like a newborn, free from the karmic residue of the past.

According to the Kabbalah, the shofar—which is actually shaped like a birth canal, narrow at one end and broad at the other—symbolizes the movement we attempt to effect within ourselves (and in the cosmos at large) from the constricted space of din, or judgment, to the expansive state of rachamim, compassion and forgiveness. Before the shofar is sounded, a passage from Psalm 118 is chanted that is suggestive of this movement: "From the narrows I call out to you; answer me in the divine expanse."

The shofar's power to effect a shift from din to rachamim in the divine and human realms rests on its ability to break open even the most well-barricaded of hearts. And so the rabbis of old often went to great lengths to find a shofar blower who was truly righteous and spiritually adept at this healing art. Once a year, the Ba'al Shem Tov devoted himself to preparing his disciple Rabbi Wolf Kitzis to blow the shofar by instructing him in all the holy intentions and meditations on the various divine names brought down by the Kabbalah. Rabbi Wolf carefully wrote these meditations down on a piece of paper, which he slipped into his pocket in order to use prior to blowing the shofar. When the awesome moment came, Rabbi Wolf searched his pockets, but he could not find the note, for it had slipped out of his pocket on his way to synagogue. Grieved that he would have to blow the shofar without the holy meditations he had been taught, Reb Wolf broke down and wept with a humbled heart.

After the prayers, the Ba'al Shem Tov said to him, "In a king's palace there are many chambers and each door has its own particular key. But there is one tool which can open *all* the doors and that is the ax. The kabbalistic meditations are the keys to the gates of the upper worlds, where each gate requires its own particular meditation. But a broken and humbled heart can burst open all the gates and all the heavenly palaces. Your tears today did just that."[18]

During the High Holy Days we attempt to storm the gates of heaven by breaking down the walls that keep us separate from our innermost being, our very own heart. Moved by the shofar's evocative cry, we open up to that place inside us that is gentle, compassionate, and forgiving. And as we make that shift within ourselves from din to rachamim, say the rabbis, we enable God to move "from the throne of judgment to a throne of mercy."

The High Holy Days provide an important model for all Jewish healing, which ultimately is about moving life toward the expansive energy of love. Jews, of course, have to do this by indirection. The High Holy Days are structured so that we move toward rachamim by first leaning into the quality of din. Rosh Hashannah, which celebrates the creation of the world, is also considered to be a day of judgment, *Yom ha'Din,* a time for deep soul-searching and repentance, for realigning ourselves morally and spiritually with our highest potential. Rosh Hashannah is ultimately a time for personal reckoning with midat ha'din (the divine attribute of judgment and perfection). However, by leaning into the quality of din on Rosh Hashannah, it is believed that we effect an opposite movement in the divine, causing God to move from a throne of judgment to a throne of mercy. When we consciously impose midat ha'din upon ourselves, God (Elohim) is in effect freed up to manifest mercy (YHVH). A useful analogy to this process comes in the parent-child relationship. When a child makes a mistake and feels regret, all on its own, for having made the mistake, it is often unnecessary for the parent to discipline the child. The parent may instead feel inclined to say to the child something on the order of "It's OK. I forgive you. Don't feel so bad, for you have already learned so much from your mistake." Like the child in this example, we use the quality of din on Rosh Hashannah to judge ourselves and make needed changes in our selves. This constructive use of din, judgment, enables us to become worthy of being forgiven and pardoned by God (and by ourselves) on Yom Kippur.

Yom Kippur comes at the climax of the Ten Days of Repentance, as we open ourselves to the divine face of love. As we chant the thirteen attributes of divine compassion that form the refrain of the Yom Kippur liturgy, we envision God as sitting on a throne of compassion. These thirteen attributes, known as the *shlosh esray midot rachamim,* were revealed to Moses on Mount Sinai following the sin of the golden calf. After losing his temper with the people and shattering the first tablets, Moses beseeches God to teach him how to be a more patient and compassionate leader. When Moses says to God, "Show me your ways" (Exodus 33:13), he is asking for spiritual guidance as to how he can overcome his own impatience and anger with the people. One also senses that at the same time that Moses is trying to understand his role as leader, he is also trying to help God remember God's own compassionate, forgiving nature. And, in fact, as God reveals the divine attributes of compassion to Moses, God simultaneously pardons the Israelites for the sin of the golden calf. Thus, through his longing to understand and embody divine compassion, Moses succeeds in influencing the heavenly realm, bringing about the needed shift in the divine countenance from judgment to compassion.

To what degree our own thoughts, prayers, and deeds actually influence the heavenly realm is not so easy to measure or document. Yet, it is clear that the energy we put out into the world tends to evoke a similar, sympathetic vibration. While our judgment of others tends to elicit judgment toward us, our compassion often invites a loving response in return. Our outer lives frequently come to mirror our inner lives. This is perhaps what the author of the Zohar was suggesting when he wrote that our repentance and realignment with the divine will helps to evoke mercy in the supernal realm: "Once when Rabbi Abba was studying with Rabbi Shimon, he said to him: 'I have often enquired about the [spiritual] significance of the shofar but I have never yet received a satisfactory answer.' Rabbi Shimon replied: 'When the supernal shofar—that which contains the illumination of all—removes itself and does not shine on the people, then [divine] judgment is aroused. But when the people [repent] and realign themselves with the divine will as they hear the sound of the

shofar below, the sounds ascend on high to awaken the supernal shofar of mercy. As a result, judgment is removed.'"[19]

The Book of Jonah
A Lesson in Divine Mercy

The theme of divine compassion is revisited once more on the Day
of Atonement when the Book of Jonah is read during the afternoon
prayers. The Book of Jonah tells the tale of a reluctant prophet.
While Moses was adept at performing the shuttle diplomacy demanded of prophets (bringing the people to repent while at the same
time convincing God to forgive), Jonah is unwilling to perform this
task. In fact, Jonah is so averse to carrying out his prophetic calling
that he foolishly attempts to flee from the face of God, as the opening
lines of the Book of Jonah reveal:

> The word of YHVH came to Jonah, the son of Amitai
> (Truth) saying: "Rise up and go to Nineveh, the great city
> and proclaim judgment upon it, for their wickedness has
> come before Me." And Jonah arose to flee to Tarshish from
> the face of YHVH and he went down to Jaffe and found a
> ship.

Jonah's adamant initial refusal to perform his prophetic mission to
the people of Nineveh is rather enigmatic. While scriptures offer no
direct explanation for his behavior, commentators offer a variety of
possible interpretations. On the most literal level, it seems that Jonah
does not want to become a catalyst that will help the people of Nineveh to repent. Why? Some commentators suggest that Jonah flees
because Nineveh is the capital of Assyria and Jonah knows prophetically that the Assyrians will later invade the land of Israel and exile
the northern Kingdom of Israel. Whatever his reason for fleeing,
Jonah feels so strongly about his position that he prefers to die rather
than have the people of Nineveh be given the chance to repent and be
forgiven. And by fleeing from his prophetic calling, Jonah is refusing

to be used as an instrument of God's plans. But as Jonah eventually learns, it is impossible to flee one's destiny and divine calling.

According to another interpretation of Jonah's intransigence, he simply does not believe in divine pardon and compassion. He is more concerned with "God's honor" than the plight of humanity, and he would rather see the Judge of all the earth bring judgment upon the wicked rather than give them a second chance. This position is reflected in his later rantings at God when he finally does go to Nineveh and the people immediately heed his cry. Instead of rejoicing in the effectiveness of his prophetic voice, Jonah angrily criticizes God for being merciful and long-suffering. As Jonah 4:2 says,

> Jonah was great displeased and grieved and he prayed to
> YHVH saying: "Oh God, isn't this exactly what I said when
> I was still on my own soil. This is why I fled to Tarshish,
> for I knew that You are a gracious and compassionate God,
> slow to anger, abounding in kindness and relenting of
> punishment."

The very attributes of compassion and mercy that God revealed to Moses at Mount Sinai become angry complaints in the mouth of this prophet. He can't bear the fact that God is "gracious and compassionate," "slow to anger," "abounding in kindness and relenting of punishment." Rather than invoking these attributes as a prayer on behalf of humanity, Jonah spits them out as sour grapes.

As if in protest, Jonah then proceeds to camp out on the outskirts of the city of Nineveh and waits to see what will happen. It is as though he is holding out hope that perhaps the people will return to their evil ways and God will yet punish them, or at least Jonah will have the chance to say to God, "I told you so," when the people of Nineveh revert to their wicked ways. This, however, is not what happens. Instead, God teaches Jonah a very personal lesson in the flesh about the universal need for divine compassion.

According to the text, YHVH-Elohim causes a *kikayon,* a gourd plant, to sprout up overnight to protect Jonah from the scorching desert sun and wind.[20] As it is related in Jonah 4:6, Jonah rejoices over the kikayon, though he expresses no gratitude for this unearned act of grace. Elohim then invites a worm to destroy the kikayon and brings on a hot desert wind. As the kikayon withers, Jonah is left vulnerable to the elements and is smitten with heatstroke. Jonah turns suddenly angry and asks once more to die, this time not out of ideological zeal but because of his own loss of creature comfort. Jonah both takes God's mercy and grace for granted and is deeply distressed when it is withdrawn. As if to poke fun at the overly zealous prophet, scriptures describe Jonah's outrage over the ruined kikayon using a similar expression to the one used for his outrage over God's pardoning of Nineveh. In doing so the text highlights the deep gap between Jonah's self-righteous indignation and his own human vulnerability.

The book of Jonah then ends enigmatically, with God asking the prophet a rhetorical question that points out the vast distance between God's compassion and human understanding: YHVH said "You felt compassion for a gourd for which you did not labor and did not cause to grow, that materialized overnight and perished overnight. And I, should I not feel compassion for Nineveh, the great city, in which there are more than a hundred and twenty thousand persons who do not know their right hand from their left, and many beasts as well?"

Since it is unclear from the text whether Jonah has learned God's intended lesson or not, the midrash attempts to answer that question. According to the midrash, Jonah is indeed humbled by his experience and upon reflecting on his experience with the kikayon, he acknowledges the universal need for rachamim: "At that moment he [Jonah] fell upon his face and said [to God], 'Conduct Your world according to Your attribute of compassion as it is written: Compassion and forgiveness belong to YHVH, our God' (Daniel 9:9)."[21]

As we read the book of Jonah on the Day of Atonement, we realize that we are all a bit like Jonah—self-righteous, ungrateful, and extremely vulnerable. While we expect God to be compassionate with us, we are not always ready to extend our compassion to others. And, unfortunately, much like Jonah, we rarely learn the importance of compassion without enduring hardship and pain in our own lives.

Suffering and Compassion

The following tale about Rabbi Yehudah Hanasi, the famous second-century scholar and redactor of the Mishneh (oral tradition), describes how he was transformed by years of personal suffering from somewhat of a heartless character to a deeply compassionate being. According to the tale, Rabbi Yehudah suffered from a terrible pain syndrome for thirteen years. The onset of his painful symptoms coincided with a certain incident, as did the remission of his symptoms.

One day, Rabbi Yehudah happened to be at a slaughterhouse when a calf that was being taken to the slaughter broke away and hid his head under Rabbi Yehudah's skirt, as if in terror. Rabbi Yehudah's response to the calf was "Go, because this is what you were created for." In response to his heartless reaction to the frightened calf, it was decided in heaven that Rabbi Yehudah would have to learn compassion the hard way—through his own suffering.

From that very day on, the Talmud recounts, Rabbi Yehudah was plagued by a horrible, chronic case of kidney stones. His pain upon going to the bathroom was so severe that his neighbors timed the feeding of their noisiest animals to those times when Rabbi Yehudah went to the bathroom, hoping their cries would drown out his heart-wrenching screams.

One day thirteen years later, Rabbi Yehudah witnessed his household helper mercilessly sweeping a cat, or some say a weasel, out of the house. He beseeched her, "Be gentle with him, 'for God's mercy is upon all his works'" (Psalms 145:9). At that very instant, the Talmud tells us, Rabbi Yehudah's painful symptoms abated, his own compassion having aroused the compassion of the heavenly court.

The serendipitous disappearance of Rabbi Yehudah's painful physical symptoms coincided with his spiritual healing into compassion. This great scholar, who knew all the secret passageways of the Torah and the law, was a foreigner to the pathways of the heart until his own suffering awakened his compassion. After thirteen years of unrelenting pain, Rabbi Yehudah no longer judged whether the creature in front of him deserved mercy or not. His heart was simply open.[22] If we go beyond the literal tale, perhaps the Talmud is suggesting that at the deepest level we are healed only when our hearts open wide and we become channels for God's mercy.

MEDITATION

Finding the Seat of Compassion

The symbol of the two divine thrones and God's shift from the seat of judgment to the seat of compassion are powerful healing images—ones that can be called upon at any time, not just on the High Holy Days. Whenever you notice that you are stuck in a place of judgment, whether of yourself or of someone else, try to imagine what it would be like if you stepped away from the judging position and viewed the same person or situation from the perspective of rachamim. You can try practicing this as a meditation in which you visualize these two qualities—judgment and compasion—literally as two seats. Imagine yourself getting up and moving away from that seat of judgment and sitting on a seat of compassion. As you see yourself sitting on the seat of compassion, let the judgments go and allow your heart to open wide. Feel the warmth that fills you as you embrace yourself and all of life from a place of mercy and compassion.

After practicing this meditation daily for a while, see if you can sustain it for a whole day. You will be surprised by how many opportunities there are in the course of an ordinary day to come from a place of compassion rather than judgment.

SHECHINAH MEDITATION

Opening Ourselves to Unconditional Love

Take whatever time you need to relax and get centered, paying close attention to your breath, or *neshima,* letting it connect you with your neshama, or soul. With each breath you take, feel how you are ensouling the body through the breath. With each breath, feel how you are weaving conduits of connection between the different levels of your being.

Now imagine that you are sitting in the presence of a luminous being, a being of pure light and love, a being in whose presence you feel completely, unconditionally loved and accepted for all of who you are. (If that's difficult to imagine, try to conjure up the image of someone you know who has taught you the meaning of unconditional love. If there wasn't such a person in your life, try to imagine one.)

As you continue to meditate, allow yourself to experience what it feels like to be seen and lovingly embraced by the Shechinah—the divine feminine. Really try to let go of how you ordinarily see yourself and allow the judging, critical voices be silent. As you open up to being in the presence of the Shechinah, let yourself feel deeply loved and accepted for all of who you are.

As you slowly and gently come back to your ordinary awareness, notice how you may feel differently about yourself or the problems you are dealing with in your current life. Try writing in a journal about your experiences during and after this meditation.

PART THREE

Sheleimut
WHOLENESS AND INTEGRATION

It is no coincidence that the root word of whole, health, heal, holy, is *hale* (as in hale and hearty). If we are healed, we become whole; we are hale and hearty; we are holy.

—MADELINE L'ENGLE

10

WHOLENESS AND THE PARADOX OF HEALING

There are two types of truth. In the shallow type,
the opposite of a true statement is false. In the
deeper kind, the opposite of a true statement is
equally true.
—*Neils Bohr*

I grew up thinking that only Jews knew of
the healing powers of chicken soup. So I was surprised one day to
hear a radio broadcaster report the results of a multicultural contest
for the best chicken soup wisdom. In this particular contest, the Jewish chicken soup took first prize for the cook's astute perception that
chicken soup is "good for you but bad for the chicken." That line
stuck in my mind for years as epitomizing the Jewish mind. For
better or for worse, Jews always look at things from multiple vantage
points. Nothing is ever simple to Jews.

Jewish mysticism teaches us how to walk a middle path that finds
the balance point of each of life's many contradictions. In order to
avoid either/or solutions to life's complicated problems, Jewish
thought finds that contradictory notions can coexist within a larger
truth. When centuries of rabbinic discourse were recorded in the
Talmud, for example, *all* of the opinions and arguments of the sages
were included—not just those whose words accord with Jewish law.
Though Jewish law sided with the opinions of the academy of Rabbi
Hillel, the opposing perspectives of the academy of Rabbi Shamai

were still honored as sacred teaching. In fact, a heavenly voice was said to have brought resolution to the decades of debate between these two rabbinic academies by proclaiming that opinions from both academies "are words of the living God."[1]

Jewish tolerance for contradiction and ambiguity is quite apparent in Jewish humor. I'm reminded of the story of two Jews who go to their rabbi for mediation of a conflict. The first man presents his case, and the rabbi says, "You are right." Then the second man presents his case, and again the rabbi says, "You are right." At this point the rabbi's wife cries out, "But Rabbi, how can they both be right?" To which he replies, "You are also right!"

The Jewish penchant for contradiction and paradox is also reflected in the Hebrew language itself. A fascinating thing about many Hebrew words is that they can imply both a thing and its opposite. For instance, the word for stranger, *nochri,* comes from the same root (*nun-kaf-resh*) as the word for recognition, *hakara.* Paradoxically, the stranger is someone who lacks recognition. And once he receives recognition he will cease to be a stranger.[2]

Similarly, the Hebrew root *chet-tet-aleph,* which usually implies sin (*chet*), can also be used to refer to the purification from sin, as we find in the ninth verse of Psalm 51, which says, "Purify [*te'chateini*] me with hyssop and I shall be purified." The fact that so many Hebrew words combine opposite meanings suggests that the Hebrew language itself is based on a worldview that sees all opposites and polarities as deeply connected to a unified source. In Torah study, when a Hebrew word has ambiguous meanings, all meanings of the word must be taken into account, even if they contradict one another, for truth is essentially multilayered, and frequently it is contradictory. Hebrew words seem to follow the principle of physics where, as Neils Bohr suggested, a great truth is one whose opposite is also true.

Dialectical reasoning lies at the core of Jewish thought; and paradox is one of the fundamental features of kabbalistic doctrine. Everything in this world, according to the Kabbalah, is essentially revealed through its opposite manifestation: God's very unfolding through creation is understood by the Kabbalah to be a paradoxical process, for divinity is *revealed* through a process of *concealment,* or tzimtzum;

unity is revealed through multiplicity; and the divine nothingness (ayin) is realized through the existence of "somethingness" (yesh). Similarly, the existence of evil makes possible the revelation of goodness, while darkness lends light its luminosity.

In therapy we find that the ability to recognize and appreciate the complexity and paradoxical nature of life and of people is, in fact, one of the crucial components of psychological wholeness. This ability, along with the capacity to integrate good and bad feelings about ourselves and others, is at the heart of emotional maturation. Without these capacities, life can be a wild roller coaster ride, alternating between all-good and all-bad feeling states.

Yet so many people suffer from an inability to live with paradox and contradiction. They are stuck in an either/or universe where different feeling states are experienced as mutually exclusive. To experience any one feeling, they have to cut off or deny all other feelings that seem to stand in contradiction. This black-and-white, simple-minded thinking leaves little room for the many shades of gray that characterize our daily existence. As a result, such people often feel threatened by intimate relationships and other situations that generate mixed emotions or demand emotional flexibility. As anyone who has ever been intimate knows, the people we most love and admire can, at times, disappoint and hurt us. To be able to forgive and go on loving and trusting our intimates demands that we have the capacity to hold on to our love even when we are angry, to remember the good even when things feel bad, and most important, to see people (ourselves included) as *whole* beings, in all their strengths and weaknesses.

Western education, with its basis in the formal laws of logic and linearity, has an unfortunate tendency to reinforce either/or thinking. We are taught that things are either true or false, good or bad. We are trained to win arguments in a debate rather than come up with a compromise solution or consensus. The startling idea that truth can be multilayered, unpredictable, and contradictory is generally not a part of Western thinking. It is our nonacceptance of paradox that leads to so much confusion in both our personal and interpersonal lives.

Our inability to see life in all its shades of gray also contributes to political impasse. When politicians portray the world as consisting of "good guys" and "bad guys" rather than considering the many complicated factors that make our "enemies" hate us, we reinforce an us-them mentality that leads to war. The truth is, sometimes the bad guys and the good guys are the same guys! And if we could begin to look at our own contribution to world problems, we might find a way to resolve our international conflicts without resorting to violence.

An important part of many Jewish spiritual practices involves creating harmony between contradictory notions or balance between opposing energies. For to heal the soul, one must be able to integrate and contain the opposing forces that exist inside us within a larger, unified field of being. It is within this God-field that we find the spaciousness within which all opposites can be united. God is ultimately the union of all opposites, writes the nineteenth-century rabbi Aaron ha'Levi Horowitz of Staroselye: "The entire purpose of creation and the interlinking of all the worlds . . . is in order to reveal His wholeness exactly from its opposite. . . . For the main principle of wholeness is that within the One even opposing contraries may be integrated."[3]

We live in a world of such great fragmentation and particularization that we all deeply long for something that can make our broken-into-pieces lives feel more whole and unified. Jewish mysticism and spiritual practice offer just that—a way to experience life from the perspective of unity, or yichud. This is probably one of the reasons that the Kabbalah is so popular today. The ability to be comfortable with contradiction and celebrate life's many paradoxes is key to the Kabbalah's understanding of healing, since we always live in two worlds at the same time—this world of finite reality and the world of the spirit, where none of the laws of the material plane seem to exist. We exist both as body and as soul. We are finite beings bound by time and place, yet simultaneously we are connected to the infinite. We are separate and unique individuals, yet we are also deeply interconnected—existing within an ineffable unity in which all our particularity dissolves.

Jewish spiritual practices enable us to live as citizens of both the upper and lower worlds. In this lower world, where multiplicity and polarity are the rule, we heal into wholeness, or sheleimut, by making ourselves into vessels that can contain opposites. Healing, from the perspective of the upper world, is about opening ourselves to the experience of yichud, or unification, by tapping into the realm in which duality ceases to exist. These two qualities, sheleimut and yichud, operate synergistically in all kabbalistic healing. Having experienced yichud, or unity, we are better able to tolerate paradox because we will have found the whole that connects the many disparate parts. And by attaining sheleimut—psychological wholeness and integration—we are more able to hold on to and apply the insights we gain from the experience of unity to our actual lives.

Unfortunately, a lot of spiritual seekers attempt to ascend the spiritual ladder without ever looking deep enough inside to prepare themselves to be whole vessels. Many people, in fact, use spirituality as a defense against experiencing life's painful complexity. The Kotzker Rebbe, known for his pithy sayings and absolute commitment to truth, cautioned his followers not to use spirituality in order to avoid dealing with psychological issues, saying, "If a person looks at the heavens before he gazes within himself, he is liable to fall into a hunter's trap."[4] I would add to the Kotzker Rebbe's warning that when we lack psychological wholeness, our spiritual experiences, though perhaps momentarily satisfying, tend to remain unintegrated and disconnected parts of our experience. So an important first step on the journey of healing involves developing sheleimut.

SHELEIMUT

In Jewish mysticism, wholeness is understood to be essentially paradoxical. The Hebrew word for wholeness, *sheleimut,* which comes from the same Hebrew root (*shin-lamed-mem*) as *shalom* (peace), is not seen as a static condition but as the dynamic interplay of opposites balancing one another. The very letters in the common root *shin-lamed-mem* suggest that wholeness involves the balancing of polar forces, for the first letter, *shin,* signifies fire; while the last letter, *mem,* signifies water. It is when water and fire, symbols of creation and destruction, coexist in balance that we find wholeness and peace. In this sense peace and wholeness exist paradoxically when opposites are contained within a unifying vessel.

A similar notion appears in the *Sefer Bahir* (the Book of Illumination), one of the earliest known kabbalistic works, first published in the twelfth century in Provence. According to the *Sefer Bahir,* the first and last letters of the word *shalom—shin* and *mem*—symbolize the angelic pair Michael and Gavriel, whose essences stand in opposition to one another. Michael, the angel of loving-kindness, is associated with the letter *mem*, which stands for water (*mayim*), while Gavriel the angel of strict judgment and limits, is associated with the letter *shin,* which signifies fire (*esh*). The liturgical passage "may he who creates peace [shalom] in the heavens make peace among us" (Job 25:2) alludes to God's efforts to make peace between these two angels with opposing energies.[5] We can extrapolate from this teaching that wholeness—sheleimut—involves the dynamic balance of opposing tendencies that exist within each of us.

In the Bible, Jacob is the only character who is described as having become *shaleim,* whole.[6] But this title is not conferred upon him until he undergoes a deep process of inner transformation. In this process Jacob must go beyond his familiar, limited sense of himself and find a way to incorporate his shadow—the disavowed and disowned parts of himself that he has projected onto his brother, Esau. He must also shift from being the plain and honest man he was in his youth to becoming a much more complex and paradoxical figure.

In his youth Jacob is described as a simple and sincere man, an *ish tam* (Genesis 25:27). Unlike his brother, Esau, who has acquired the cunning and duplicity of the hunter, Jacob's "heart and mouth are congruent," according to Rashi.[7] There is no contradiction or tension between his inner experience and his outer expression. And having led a protected life, Jacob is also somewhat naive. Unlike his brother, who is prototypically male in both his appearance (he is hairy) and in his actions (he is a hunter and an outdoorsman), Jacob "dwells in the tents," close to his mother and the womenfolk. While Esau is his father's favorite, "Rebecca loves Jacob," (Genesis 25:28) and sees him as the more worthy spiritual heir to his father's legacy. And so, when Rebecca hears that Isaac plans to give Esau the special blessing of the *be'chor,* or firstborn male, she begins to plot a way for Jacob to "steal" his brother's blessing.

This is the point in the biblical tale where Jacob begins to shift from his old identity as a simple and sincere man to take on some of the more complex aspects of his brother's character. Under his mother's instruction, Jacob disguises himself by dressing up in his brother's animal-skin clothes. He does this to appear "hairy" and to "smell" like his brother, so as to trick his father into thinking that he is Esau. Rebecca cooks a feast of savory meats that taste like Esau's venison and with this charade Jacob pretends to be his brother so that he might receive the blessing of the firstborn. However, as soon as Jacob begins impersonating his brother, his identity begins to expand to take on some of Esau's characteristic cunning. In so doing he begins the process of incorporating his shadow.

After stealing his brother's blessing, Jacob's life, as he has known it until then, falls apart. He can no longer go back to living peacefully "in the tents" as before. Instead, he is compelled to flee for his life and go into exile, for Esau plots to kill him in revenge. Forced to leave the comfort and security of his family and homeland, Jacob must learn to survive in exile as an outsider, as other. The "paradise" of his youth is replaced by a journey into "paradox" in which he will learn how to be whole by enduring heartbreak, and he will achieve a sense of integrity by grappling with disintegration and fragmentation.

It all begins when Jacob falls in love with Rachel and he is invited into her father's home. Rachel's father, Laban, who also happens to be Jacob's maternal uncle, is a bit of a scoundrel. In dealing with Laban, Jacob meets his match in cunning and must learn how to survive by his wits. He must become truly shrewd, for he will be repeatedly swindled and taken advantage of by his uncle. After working for seven long years in order to obtain Rachel's hand in marriage, Jacob is deceived on his wedding night, when he discovers that Laban had put Leah under the marriage canopy instead of Rachel. As extraordinary as it may seem, Jacob does not realize this until the next morning when he awakens and finds Leah in his bed.

(Evidently the women of that time were modestly veiled at their weddings!) When Jacob confronts his father-in-law about this treachery, he is told that it would not have been proper to marry off the youngest before the eldest. Why Laban did not tell this to Jacob in advance is unclear. But according to mystical readings of the story, Jacob's unconscious marriage to Leah was foreordained. The one who deceived his own brother was fated to become the victim of deceit himself. In fact, Jacob's deceit in stealing his brother's blessing is revisited upon him "measure for measure" when he unwittingly marries Leah. Just as Isaac blesses Jacob without realizing whom he is blessing, Jacob marries Leah without being conscious of whom he is marrying.

Though Jacob is eventually allowed to marry Rachel in exchange for yet another seven years of labor, things will never be quite the same as he had dreamed. Jacob's life will inevitably be fragmented and fractured by the rivalries and tensions that developed between his two wives and their offspring.

But Jacob's unintentional union with Leah has additional meaning as well. According to Rabbi Mordecai Yosef of Izbitz, author of the *Beis Ya'acov,* Jacob's union with Leah came from the "hidden world" (*alma d'itkasia*)—a realm beyond conscious awareness.[8] In contrast, Jacob's marriage to Rachel was from the "revealed world" (*alma d'itgalia*)—the realm of the conscious mind. Though these Aramaic phrases come from the Zohar, the thirteenth-century magnum opus of the Kabbalah, they seem to correspond with Freud's notion of the conscious and unconscious mind—the alma d'itgalia being the conscious mind and the alma d'itkasia being the unconscious mind. In the same way that Rachel's beauty was apparent, Jacob's love for her was apparent to him. Jacob's connection with Leah, on the other hand, is much more hidden and mysterious, just as her beauty was more subtle and hidden than her sister's. In Genesis 29:17, the Torah makes a point of contrasting their beauty, "And Leah's eyes were tender; and Rachel was beautiful in her appearance and beautiful to behold." Yet, Jacob's journey toward wholeness involves navigating these two kinds of love—the love for a partner he has consciously chosen as well as the love of a partner who enters his life in opposition to his conscious desires.

In the midrash, Jacob's marriage to Leah is seen as part of the "package deal" of having usurped his brother's birthright and blessing. Leah, suggests the midrash, was connected to Esau and had been destined to marry him. When Jacob stole his blessings, he also became heir to this aspect of his brother's destiny.[9] In its uniquely metaphoric style, this midrash is teaching us about the inner work of integrating the shadow. When Jacob incorporated the more complex aspects of Esau's character into his own being, he became privy to a deeper kind of self-knowledge. His union with Leah symbolizes this deeper knowledge.

Jacob's marriage to Leah also has additional spiritual significance. According to Rabbi Mordecai Yosef, this story teaches us that sometimes the highest and holiest things in our lives come about from a place that is above and beyond our conscious choosing. The meaning and blessing inherent in them is often initially hidden from our awareness. So, too, with the shadow—that part of ourselves that we consciously reject. In order to be whole we must learn to accept and incorporate this aspect of our being into our conscious image of ourselves. Jacob initially scorns and resents Leah, as he initially is unable to appreciate his brother's, Esau's, worth. However, over time, he comes to love Leah and appreciate her beauty—as he realizes that her beauty is more subtle and hidden than that of her sister. The (pro)creativity of Jacob's union with Leah is revealed through their many offspring, and it is Leah's son Judah who becomes the chosen leader of the tribes and is the progenitor of the messianic lineage. Sometimes, those very things that come into our lives not according to our *conscious* choice or conscious desire turn out to bring us the greatest blessings.

In his transformation from *temimut* to sheleimut, from sincerity to wholeness and authenticity, Jacob must expand beyond the realm of the known and certain (alma d'itgalia) and venture into the unknown and complex realm of the unconscious (alma d'itkasia). He must discover the good that is hidden in those aspects of his destiny and character that he initially rejects. He must also learn to balance his desire for truth and simplicity with the reality of living in a world of duality and duplicity. Instead of living in harmony with the *one* woman he consciously chooses, he must learn to navigate the complexities of a bifurcated family. With two wives who are sisters and rivals, plus twelve sons (and one daughter) who are often in conflict with each another, Jacob must make peace with imperfection and fragmentation. Yet, somehow, in mastering all these difficulties, and in finding a way to integrate all the opposing forces within his own being, Jacob comes to sheleimut, wholeness.[10]

In the Kabbalah, Jacob also came to be associated with the divine attribute of truth, *emet*. It may seem ironic that the biblical character that wrestled most with deceit and dishonesty became, for the mystics, a symbol of truth. Yet, the phrase from Micah 7:20 "give truth to Jacob" made its way into the weekly Sabbath afternoon liturgy.[11] At the climax of the Sabbath, when the spirit of Jacob is said to be present, a blessing of wholeness descends upon all those who observe the Sabbath. Having learned the painful consequences of dishonesty, Jacob became an *ish emet,* a man of truth.

Ultimately, Jacob's healing journey provides a paradigm for all of us, who, according to the *Sefat Emet,* must learn to live with integrity in this world of illusion, *alma d'shikra.* Like Jacob, we all must reckon with the illusion of multiplicity and separateness to come to the truth of God's unity.[12]

THE SEPHIROT

An Integrated Model for Wholeness

The importance of learning to balance polarities in the pursuit of wholeness is reflected in the Kabbalah's doctrine of the ten sephirot, the divine attributes with which divinity continually creates and interacts with creation. The sephirot describe the process of divine unfolding or emanation—how the Infinite One, through a dialectical process, became clothed in the multiplicity of finite forms, or vessels. They can also be understood as a ladder of ascent by which humankind can come to identify with the creator. By learning to emulate the sephirot, we come to embody the divine attributes of wholeness.

The sephirot are arranged as paired energies—one primarily generative (masculine), the other primarily receptive (feminine)—that stand in balanced relationship with one another, with a middle point in between to integrate them.[13]

For example, in the system of the sephirot, *chessed*, lovingkindness, is balanced by gevurah, the divine ability to set limits. Both chessed and gevurah are essential for wholeness. Love without the limits and discernment provided by gevurah can be misinformed and even destructive. The kind of problems that result from loving and giving to a child without ever setting limits are clear evidence of the need for such a balance. But in much more subtle ways, all loving energies need boundaries within which they can be expressed; for when chessed has no limits, it can lead to its opposite. Similarly, if gevurah is not tempered by chessed, it can lead to cruelty and judgmentalism.

According to the Kabbalah, the middle point that stands between the sephirot of chessed and gevurah is associated with the quality of rachamim, or compassion. *Rachamim,* which, as we have seen, comes from the same Hebrew root as *rechem,* or womb, represents the perfect balance of love and limits. Like the womb, whose wisdom lies in its ability to expand and contract appropriately in order to sustain life, rachamim is the place where the expansive energy of love finds its perfect expression based on the true needs of a worthy recipient—not just the needs of the giver. It is a love that neither smothers nor spoils. It is a love that is flexible, expressing itself at times by saying yes and at other times by saying no. Rachamim is not a static middle ground but the flexibility to expand and to contract. It is not lukewarm but hot or cold, depending on what the situation calls for.

In the Kabbalah, Jacob is not only identified with truth; he is also associated with the *sephirah* (plural of *sephirot*) of rachamim. As a result of his journey of self-integration and healing, Jacob becomes someone who can move freely between the poles of chessed and gevurah, responding to each life situation as it demands. Unlike his father, Isaac, who was very much associated with the introverted, restrained quality of gevurah, and unlike his grandfather Abraham, who tended toward extreme chessed and extroversion, Jacob found

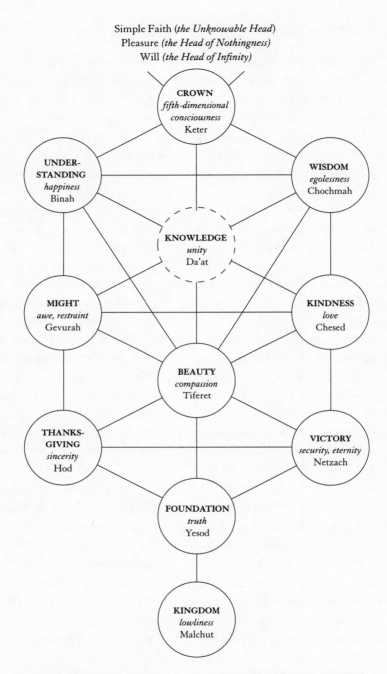

Simple Faith (*the Unknowable Head*)
Pleasure (*the Head of Nothingness*)
Will (*the Head of Infinity*)

CROWN
*fifth-dimensional
consciousness*
Keter

**UNDER-
STANDING**
happiness
Binah

WISDOM
egolessness
Chochmah

KNOWLEDGE
unity
Da'at

MIGHT
awe, restraint
Gevurah

KINDNESS
love
Chesed

BEAUTY
compassion
Tiferet

**THANKS-
GIVING**
sincerity
Hod

VICTORY
security, eternity
Netzach

FOUNDATION
truth
Yesod

KINGDOM
lowliness
Malchut

The Ten Sephirot and Their Inner Life Force of Experience

From *Kabbalah and Consciousness* by Allen Afterman (New York: The Sheep Meadow Press, 1992). Reprinted with permission.

the balance point of rachamim. This sephirah is also known as *tifferet,* or beauty, in the Kabbalah, for where there is true balance between opposites, beauty exists.

CHESSED AND GEVURAH IN THERAPY

On countless occasions the paradoxical wisdom of the sephirot has guided me in both my personal life and my work as a therapist. For those of us who often get caught between conflicting needs and inner tendencies, the sephirotic system offers an integrated model for wholeness.

Some years ago, I counseled a woman named Susan who was experiencing problems in all of her relationships. Susan had a classic chessed-gevurah imbalance: she was unable to balance her loving and angry feelings. As a result, her self-esteem levels fluctuated wildly, and her interactions with friends and family oscillated between extremes of selfless giving and angry outbursts or withdrawal. She would run herself ragged trying to satisfy the many needs and demands of her family, friends, and community, never stopping to take time out for herself. Then, periodically, Susan would become exhausted to the point of falling apart, and she would either start screaming at everybody and everything or lock herself in her room for hours. During these episodes she felt stuck in all-bad feelings, about both herself and others. And as Susan turned from willing servant to name-calling, ranting lunatic, her children began to feel terrible about themselves, while her husband was shocked and frightened by Susan's outbursts. He didn't have a clue that his wife had been building up so much resentment until it was too late.

Susan's problems stemmed from her inability to put limits on her basically loving and expansive nature and from her difficulty integrating mixed emotions. The contradictory aspects of her nature were basically at war with one another. Her image of herself as a giving and loving person kept her from saying no to others, even when she needed to. And when Susan could not live up to her own unrealistic self-expectations, her feelings about herself would plummet into the garbage pail, taking along those she most loved.

In counseling Susan, I used the symbolism of the sephirot to give her a new way of understanding her problem. Having been raised in a very large Orthodox Jewish family where selfless giving was the ideal (and somewhat of a survival mechanism), Susan had never developed a healthy sense of personal boundaries. She experienced her boundaries only after she had been pushed way past her limits. Yet setting limits was not something she could do without feeling selfish and unrighteous. After learning about the necessity of balancing chessed with gevurah, however, Susan began to appreciate how these energies are interdependent and that they need and support one another. Slowly she began to realize that the limit-setting quality of gevurah need not negate her essentially loving nature, and she began to find ways to comfortably set limits with her loved ones. By seeing gevurah as an essential counterpart to chessed, Susan learned to be more balanced. She realized that by withdrawing from time to time she could avoid getting angry at her intimate others. Learning to recognize the moment when she needed to manifest gevurah by taking time for herself, and doing so without feeling guilty, helped Susan become more balanced. She also needed to adjust her ego ideal—the standard to which she was holding herself—to match her real self, who she discovered was a person with needs of her own as well as someone who cared for the needs of others.

In a variety of ways, Susan's dilemma is one we are all caught in. Our inner polarities may be different from hers, yet when we learn to see them as parts of a whole, we can live our lives with greater harmony and balance, giving each tendency its needed expression.

MEDITATION ON SHELEIMUT

The following meditation is aimed at helping you develop sheleimut—the ability to hold and contain opposing forces within our selves.

Take a few moments to relax and become centered, anchoring your awareness in your breath. Breathe slowly and deeply, breathing in relaxation and healing energy, breathing out whatever you need to let go of right now in order to be fully present.

As you continue to pay attention to your breath, imagine that with each in-breath you are breathing in a divine out-breath. And as you breathe out, send your exhalation back to its source in the divine.

Now imagine that in your right hand you hold the energy of chessed—loving-kindness. Feel your life-affirming, expansive flow of love, the joy of saying YES to life. Anchor this energy in your right hand, so it is there when you need it.

Imagine that in your left hand you hold the power of gevurah, the ability to limit the outward flow of energy. Feel your power to say no and set limits when needed, and your ability to channel your love selectively. Feel the power of deep introversion, of keeping your energy and attention inward. Anchor this energy in your left hand, so it is there when you need it.

Now you are holding the energies of chessed and gevurah together, at once, in your being. Feel the inward- and outward-flowing energies dance together inside you. Become shaleim, a vessel of wholeness, a vessel that can contain opposites.

As you continue this meditation, see if you can bring other polarities that you wrestle with into your awareness at this time: introversion/extroversion, male/female, thinking/feeling, oneness/separateness, particularism/universalism, and so on. See if you can hold on to these different polarities at once.

Now see if you can simultaneously hold on to your good and bad feelings about someone or something by placing your good feelings in one hand and your bad feelings in the other. Allow yourself to experience the mix and complexity of your emotions, and as you do this, feel your capacity to be whole.

11

FINDING GOD IN ALL THINGS

Nondualism and the Psychological Capacity for Integration

There is nothing outside of me. I am YHVH and there
is nothing else. Forming light and creating darkness;
making shalom [peace] and creating the evil. I am
YHVH (the infinite one) who does all these.
—*Isaiah 45:6–7*

When you train yourself to hear the voice of God in
everything, you attain the quintessence of the human
spirit.
—*Rabbi Abraham Isaac Kook*

In Jewish lore there are many stories about
the troubles that can be caused by naive piety. The following story,
about a pious fool, or *hasid shoteh,* is adapted from a joke I once
heard. It both makes fun of those who take their faith in God too
literally and points out the dangers of naive faith.

A huge storm was once approaching the town where Yosela lived.
As the storm clouds darkened the sky, the weatherman urged everyone to get out of town, but Yosela said, "I won't worry. God will
save me." The morning of the storm, the police went through the

neighborhood with a sound truck telling everyone once again to evac-
uate. Yosela once again said, "I won't worry; God will save me." By
the time the storm drain backed up and there was an inch of water
standing in the street, a fire truck came by to rescue Yosela, but he
told them, "Don't worry, God will save me." The water rose another
foot. A National Guard truck came by to rescue Yosela, but he told
them once more, "Don't worry, God will save me." The water rose
some more, and Yosela was forced up to his roof. When a boat came
by to rescue him he told the people in the boat, "Don't worry, God
will save me." The water rose even higher, and Yosela was forced up
to the very peak of his roof. Finally, a helicopter came to rescue him,
but he shouted up at the people in the helicopter, "Don't worry, God
will save me." When the water rose above Yosela's house, he eventually drowned. When he got up to heaven, he said to God, "I've been
your faithful servant ever since I was born. Why didn't you save me?"
God replied, "First I sent you a fire truck, then the national guard,
then a boat, and then a helicopter. What more do you want from me!"

I like this story because it captures a central teaching of Jewish
mysticism, namely that God can be found in *all* things—from the
storms that threaten us to the many agents of rescue and healing that
are sent our way when we are in trouble. Unfortunately, we are all a
little like Yosela, the naive Hasid in this story, in that we stubbornly
wait for God to appear as some version of the all-powerful, God-in-
the-sky, scorekeeping, all-good parent we may have wished for in our
childhood fantasies. Unfortunately, such outmoded, dualistic notions
of God interfere with our ability to perceive the actual presence of the
divine in our lives. When our faith is based on the naive expectation
that God appear in transcendent, wondrous form, we are likely to lose
our faith when we experience life's difficult and darker dimensions.

Yet it is precisely during the dark times of personal crisis that we
most need faith. Whatever brings us to spiritual searching as adults,
in order to develop a mature relationship with the divine, we must
deepen in our understanding of God and faith. What we may have
learned in Sunday school or even in yeshiva often doesn't speak to
our deepest questions about life, for much of traditional Jewish

discourse is stuck in a dualistic understanding of God—the belief that God is somehow apart from us or separate from anything.

The bottom line is that how we understand God affects how we understand ourselves and life itself. In a sense we become *like* the God we design. In embracing a nondual understanding of the divine, the Kabbalah teaches us to embody a unified perspective in which the different and often contradictory aspects of reality might be seen as parts of a whole. As we shall see, this view supports the development of healthy psychological coping mechanisms such as the capacity for mutuality, tolerance, integration, and empathy. In contrast, when we conceive of God as all-good, transcendent, or separate from us, we unwittingly reinforce the illusion of duality, and dualisms of all kinds reinforce the use of primitive psychological coping mechanisms such as splitting and projection, which can be extremely destructive.

Splitting is a coping or defense mechanism that originates in our earliest infancy, when we experience each moment of reality as being something unto itself. Without the mediating experience of thought and memory, infants under the age of two tend to experience reality in a fragmented, all-or-nothing fashion—either powerfully wonderful or powerfully terrible. If you have ever spent extended time with a young child, you have probably noticed how their moods tend to shift rapidly. One moment they may be completely peaceful, while the next they may burst into tears, only to be followed a moment later by laughter and glee!

While rapidly shifting mood states are perfectly normal in the young child, when, as adults, we make use of splitting as a defense mechanism (a means of avoiding pain!) we are regressing to this more primitive stage of development. Essentially, when we use splitting we are distorting reality by separating out a *part* of reality from the *whole*. Its use during adulthood can lead to many destructive outcomes, as we shall see in a moment.

In normal, healthy development, children overcome the tendency to use splitting by acquiring two crucial psychological capacities—object constancy and the capacity for integration. Margaret Mahler, a psychoanalytic thinker from the contemporary school of thought known as object relations theory, was the first to describe this process, which she referred to as separation-individuation. At around the age of two, Mahler suggests, as children begin to understand that they are *separate* from their caretakers, they face the developmental challenge of achieving "object constancy"—the ability to remember that their caretakers still exist and love them even when they are absent or are temporarily frustrating the children's desires. Without object constancy, the experience of separation or frustration triggers intense, unbearable anxiety. Object constancy, then, enables children to tolerate the anxiety attendant upon separation and individuation. With it they can learn to balance their need for a dependable adult with their growing sense of autonomy and independence.

The child's growing awareness of her autonomy and separateness from others also coincides with another developmental challenge: learning to reconcile the contradictory emotions of love and hate. The capacity for integration, as it is called in object relations theory, enables us to embrace a larger, more multidimensional sense of the world, in which we can simultaneously hold on to good and bad images and feelings about ourselves and others. Integration is essential for sustaining intimate relations, for it allows us to remember our love even when we feel hurt or angry, and it enables us to see others as whole persons with both strengths and weaknesses. Integration also makes life's ups and downs more bearable, for it helps us remember the big picture.

When, as adults, we use splitting as a defense mechanism, we tend to see things in black and white, with few shades of gray. In mistaking the part for the whole, we experience emotional states that are either all good or all bad, with no emotional middle ground. We may become extremely depressed or enraged because we have singled out something bad in ourselves or others and focused on it as though it were the whole story. And if we make important life decisions while we are in a split state, we are likely to make poor choices because our decisions will be based on only a fragment of the whole truth.

For instance, in a split state we may say or do extremely destructive things that can undermine a perfectly good friendship or relationship. Our inability to remember our "good" feelings when we are frustrated or angry can cause us to exaggerate our "bad" feelings.

Splitting also leads to the use of other primitive defense mechanisms such as projection, for when owning a feeling makes us feel all bad about ourselves, we are more likely to want to rid ourselves of it by projecting it onto others. In extreme cases, this process of disownership can lead us to devalue or even demonize others. We see this process at work in many fundamentalist religious traditions, which use projection and splitting in order to expunge God of all darkness and evil. In attempting to construct a God who is "all good" and "all light," they must project evil and darkness onto some identifiable "other" (Satan or some other scapegoat), who can then be hated and destroyed. Much human suffering owes its existence to the prevalence of splitting and projection, which are, unfortunately, sanctioned and reinforced by many fundamentalist religious traditions.

While the capacity for integration enables us to see ourselves and others as whole beings, nondual awareness allows us to experience God's unity and wholeness. From a nondual perspective, nothing exists outside of God, and so all things—even evil, death, and suffering—can be experienced as part of a greater unity. Nondual spiritual experiences support the use of higher-level psychological coping mechanisms, such as integration as well as empathy, tolerance, and acceptance. The realization that God and life are tremendously mysterious and full of paradox enables us to appreciate that opposites coexist and are parts of a whole that contains both good and bad. The existence of evil or suffering need not be viewed as negating the existence of God. In fact, in Jewish legend, even Satan is characterized as just another one of God's angels or messengers, one who ultimately serves a helpful role in the larger divine scheme of things, for Satan's role as tempter and trickster offers us the opportunity to exercise our free will to choose the good over the bad.

Even evil, according to the Kabbalah, is an aspect of God, for nothing exists outside of God. As Luria's cosmology myth suggests, good and evil have been intertwined in an intricate knot since the beginning, when God's infinite light had to be veiled in order for an embodied, finite universe to come into being. The very creation of this finite realm necessitated the tzimtzum, or hiding of God's infinite unity and its cloaking in the dynamic dualism of a creation *seemingly* separate and apart from the Creator. Were it not for this tzimtzum, the light of the infinite would otherwise obliterate us with its brilliance. Paradoxically, we live in a world in which God's love and goodness could be revealed only through a certain degree of its concealment. And because of this concealment, evil arises. However, as the mystics teach us, evil has no independent existence; rather, its existence is part of the revelation of God's infinite being.

Despite the psychological advantages of nondual awareness, there is a danger in embracing the belief that everything is a part of divinity—namely, that we may become passive in the face of suffering or human evil. At the same time that mystical awareness teaches us to see evil as an aspect of divinity, we are also commanded to fight evil and right the world's wrongs. Paradoxically, everything may be in God's hands, but ultimately God uses *our* hands to set things right and bring about justice in this world. In other words, nondualism is no excuse for passivity. In fact, Judaism teaches that in relation to the suffering of others, we must act as though there were no God.

For instance, when we encounter a poor person, instead of saying to ourselves that it must be God's will that he is poor or that God will provide for the poor man or woman, we are instead commanded to act as though there were no God and we alone are responsible for helping that person.

In counterpoint to the mystical position that sees everything as a part of divinity, normative Judaism's focus is on making moral distinctions and ethical judgments. The ability to separate out good from evil (or kosher from nonkosher) is an essential part of being a Jew, and we are commanded to take responsibility to heal the suffering and evil that surround us. Yet at the same time, the mystical perspective challenges us to experience the perfection of all that is—because it is all a manifestation of the Divine One. Most important, for the purpose of our discussion, the nondual perspective challenges us to experience our *own* suffering as a face of the divine, since there is nothing outside of God.

UNDERSTANDING EVIL

The problem of the existence of evil, according to biblical legend, goes back to Adam and Eve, who were expelled from the Garden of Eden for eating from the tree of knowledge of good and evil, or *etz ha'daat*. When Adam and Eve ate the fruit of the tree of knowledge, the awareness of and capacity for evil are said to have been born. Though a literal reading of the Eden myth seems to suggest a rather dualistic understanding of "good" and "evil," in the Kabbalah this myth is understood from a nondual perspective.

The Hebrew word used in the Bible to denote "knowledge" is *da'at*. This same word, which is used to describe the "tree of knowledge," is also used by scriptures to connote union and conjugal relations.[1] In fact, *da'at* is the word used throughout the Book of Genesis to imply sexual union. So *etz ha'daat' tov ve'ra*—the tree of knowledge of good and evil—can also be understood to mean the tree of the *union* of good and evil. As the nineteenth-century kabbalist Rabbi Chaim of Velozin wrote, Adam and Eve's eating of the forbidden fruit symbolizes the inevitable mixing of good and evil that was the outcome of creation. As Rabbi Chaim wrote,

> The forces of evil were mixed inside [Adam], and so, too, in all the worlds. And this is the meaning of the tree of knowledge [da'at] of good and evil—that they were joined and mixed together inside him [Adam] and in all the worlds—the good and evil together—one, actually, inside the other—because the meaning of "da'at" is union, as it is known in the esoteric knowledge.[2]

Thus it seems that eating from the tree of knowledge does not lead simply to an awareness, or knowledge, of good and evil but to a blurring of the boundaries between the two. Ever since Adam and Eve partook of *etz ha'daat,* good and evil have been mixed together so that there is nothing of a holy nature that is not also accompanied by a certain measure of its opposite.

According to this understanding, Adam and Eve's eating the forbidden fruit was not so much a sin but an unavoidable stage of human and cosmic development. It parallels the experience we all go through as we grow up and take our own steps toward separation and individuation. Banishment from the garden of oneness is inevitable for all incarnate beings, as each of us must struggle with separateness and aloneness as soon as we leave our mother's womb and become separate and unique beings. With each step we take toward individuation, we, too, partake of the forbidden fruit.

It is unfortunate that a literal reading of the Bible portrays Adam and Eve's act of self-assertion as sinful and punishable with banishment from the garden and alienation from God. Such a literal interpretation paints a dualistic picture of right and wrong. In fact, parents who act as punitively as God does when their children assert their independence often sow the seeds of emotional disturbances that take many years to sort out! Instead, children need to feel their parents' support and acceptance of their steps toward self-assertion and self-definition.

It was this overly dualistic reading of the Eden myth that the Kabbalah attempted to reframe in its alternate creation myth, for in the myth of the shattered vessels God comes to share responsibility for having created a flawed universe in which imperfection and the potential for evil are woven into the very fabric of the creation. It seems that whenever Jewish myth or practice appears overly dualistic, the Kabbalah offers another, more integrated perspective.

So why should all this have to be so problematic? Clearly, it was God's intention to create a universe in which particularization and individuation would come into play. This is where the tree of life comes in.

The Tree of Life
The Unity That Integrates All Polarities

While the Eden myth seems to focus almost exclusively on the tree of knowledge of good and evil, there was another tree in paradise— the tree of life. While Adam and Eve were prohibited from eating the fruit of the tree of knowledge, nothing is said about the fruit of the tree of life. There is a midrash, however, that suggests that if Adam and Eve had only waited a few more hours—until the beginning of the Sabbath—they could have safely eaten from the fruit of the tree of knowledge by eating it together with the fruit of the tree of life.

In contrast to the tree of knowledge that is the source of all dualities, the tree of life symbolizes the unity of all being. It is often depicted as an inverted tree whose roots grow in heaven and whose branches contain all existence. On the Sabbath, the Jewish day of rest, humankind is given an opportunity to eat from the tree of life—to experience life from the perspective of oneness. On the Sabbath, say the Hasidic masters, creation is restored to its root in divine oneness, for by refraining from "doing" on the Sabbath, we return to the ground of all "being." The Hebrew word for Sabbath, or Shabbat, comes from the root *shav,* which means to return or be restored. On the Sabbath, we are each given a chance to return to the garden of paradise, as it were, so that we might be nourished by the tree of life.

By suggesting that Adam and Eve could have eaten from the fruit of the two trees if only they had waited till the Sabbath, the midrash is teaching us about the very goal of creation. Indeed, it is a message to all of us that by linking our need for self-assertion and separation (the tree of knowledge) with an awareness of our inseparability from all being (the tree of life), we reach what may be described as messianic consciousness, in which unity and duality dance harmoniously together, each one mirroring the other as another manifestation of the One.

Because they ate the fruit of the tree of knowledge by itself, Adam and Eve mistook a part of reality for the whole, sundering the paradoxical unity of all things, which are both one and separate. When we split apart these two interdependent energies (oneness and separateness), we are exiled from the garden and from our true nature. Healing is about finding our way back to the tree of life—to the unity that integrates all polarities. It is about finding a way to enjoy the fruits of our differentiation along with the fruits of our connection with all being.

Many Jewish spiritual practices serve a healing function precisely because they are aimed at rejoining and rebalancing life's essential polarities. For instance, the wording of the daily liturgy reminds us that life is a mix of light and darkness, good and bad. According to the Talmud, we must "mention the characteristic of the day at night-time and the characteristic of the night in the daytime."[3] In the morn-ing prayers we say to God, "You form light and create darkness, you make peace and create all," and in the evening prayers, we say, "You create day and night, you roll away the light in face of the darkness and darkness in face of light. . . . You cross over from day and bring on the night and divide between day and night, God of hosts is his name." The consistent linking of light with darkness within Jewish liturgy serves an integrative, healing function that teaches us to re-member the whole out of which the different parts of reality emanate.

Jewish mysticism teaches us that things are not always just what they appear to be on the surface. Reality and truth are always multi-layered, and the boundaries between what is good and what is bad are not always so clear-cut. What may seem bad on the surface may paradoxically turn out to be good, and vice versa. This appreciation that reality is multilayered is expressed in a famous midrash that at-tempts to explain the difference between "good" (*tov*) and "very good" (*tov me'od*) in God's musings over the different aspects of creation:

> Rabbi Huna said . . . "Behold it was good" [Genesis 1:4]. This refers to good fortune. "Behold it was very good" [Genesis 1:31]. This refers to suffering. It may seem strange that suffering should be seen as *very* good! How-ever, it is through the experience of suffering that people come to experience life in the world to come. . . . "Behold it was good;" this refers to the good inclination [human altruism]. "Behold it was very good;" this refers to the evil inclination [the libidinal drive that is seen as the origins of human selfishness].[4]

Rabbi Huna's intentional blurring of the boundaries between what we ordinarily think of as good and what we ordinarily think of as

bad is an attempt to show us that good and bad are so deeply intertwined that they cannot be separated. Necessary evils like death, suffering, illness, and human desire are part of a larger whole that is
essentially very good. These things whose goodness is not quite so
apparent are not just *good* but *very good* because they contain a much
more mysterious, hidden, and paradoxical goodness than the things
whose goodness is more obvious.

The blurring of distinct boundaries between what is good and
what is bad is apparent not only in the Kabbalah but also in the
natural world, where no natural substance is ever entirely good or
bad. In fact, what is good for us may at times also be bad for us. For
instance, cholesterol comes in two forms—one that is primarily good
(HDL), and one that is primarily bad (LDL). Yet, even the so-called
bad cholesterol is necessary and critical for cell growth. In fact, without this "bad stuff" you would die. Similarly, eicosanoids, which
serve as the glue that holds the human body together, operate in pairs
that function in opposition to each other. Though made by every
living cell in the body, eicosanoids are difficult to isolate; however,
they are the ultimate regulators of cellular function. A balance of
their opposing actions is the key to good health, whereas imbalance
leads to disease. For example, so-called good eicosanoids prevent
platelet clumping in blood cells, while so-called bad eicosanoids promote clumping. Too much clumping can lead to blood clots that can
cause heart attacks or stroke; too few of the clot-promoting eicosanoids and you could bleed to death when you got cut. Optimal
health involves the dynamic balance of good and bad eicosanoids.

In human physiology and in the natural world, cutting-edge
thought defines optimal health as the dynamic balance of good and
bad elements, not the eradication of something that is wholly "bad."
No natural substance is ever entirely good or entirely bad and too
little of a "bad" thing can be as dangerous as too much of a good
thing. Nature, essentially, seeks balance. This intermixing of good
and bad forces in nature is, perhaps, the manifestation of *etz
ha'daat*—the tree of the mixing of good and evil—in the physical
realm.

As in nature as a whole, there is also a balance of light and dark and good and evil inside each of us. In fact, the rabbis of old believed that great souls often have to struggle with great forces of evil. As one of the Talmudic masters once said, "A person who is greater than another will also have a greater 'evil inclination.' "⁵ In this popular rabbinic dictum, the "evil inclination," or *yetzer ha'ra,* refers to the libidinal impulse or sexual drive. Although referred to as evil, the yetzer ha'ra was never seen as truly evil in Jewish thought, for without it the rabbis recognized there would be no passion or impulse to create or procreate. The yetzer, however, needs to be kept in check and properly channeled. Otherwise, it can control us and cause us to act selfishly and destructively.

A number of different spiritual communities have had to deal with great teachers, rabbis, and gurus who fell prey to their yetzer ha'ra. Stories abound of leaders who have abused their spiritual authority and acted as sexual predators. A number of years ago, it came out that one of the beloved Jewish teachers of my generation, someone who had a tremendous influence on a huge number of people, had been a womanizer. There had always been rumors about his sexual misconduct with women, but after his death such a large number of these stories emerged that it simply became too big a problem to ignore. Since he had been one of the most important and influential figures in my own spiritual development, I became fascinated with the process that evolved. Basically, his followers became divided into two camps. A large number of his most devout followers simply refused to believe the allegations. Their extreme idealization of this teacher made it impossible for them to incorporate his misdeeds and "shadow" self into their overall image of him. At the same time, others became completely disillusioned by the stories that emerged, and they embarked on a campaign to smear his reputation and discredit all his teachings and work.

In my own community I found myself in the center of a stormy conflict that threatened to break the community apart between those who came out against this teacher and those who advocated a more measured and forgiving response. For me, the challenge seemed clear. We needed to hold on to an integrated image of this teacher as both a saint and a sinner all wrapped together as one. It seemed important to honestly face this teacher's unconscionable behavior with women. We needed to talk openly about these very painful matters and express our sense of disillusionment. Those who had been victims needed us to listen to their pain, and we needed to take measures to make sure this kind of abuse of spiritual authority would not happen again in our community. Yet knowing firsthand the deep love, wisdom, and generosity of spirit that this teacher possessed, it also felt important that the enormous legacy of spiritual teachings and good deeds that this rabbi had left behind not be subjected to a wholesale rejection.

As I worked with people in the community who were struggling with these issues, I came to appreciate deeply how the capacity for integration is crucial in dealing with life's most complex and confusing situations—those in which the greatest good and evil seem to be mixed up all in one. I saw this unfortunate situation as an opportunity for us to learn that great souls have the potential for great wrongdoing if they don't deal with their own inner darkness—and that we can be spacious enough within our own being to hold on to the mix of good and bad both in ourselves and in others.

Cultivating Equanimity and Faith in Times of Pain

Rabbi Ya'acov Yosef of Polonoye, the master scribe of the Ba'al Shem Tov, taught that "in every pain there is a holy spark from God, but it is concealed with many garments. When a person focuses on the fact that God is present even in the pain, the garment is removed and the pain vanishes."[6] Likening God's essence to that of a snail, Ya'acov Yosef also wrote that just as the snail's garment, or shell, both contains it and is part of it, so too the garments of the divine are part of its essence. Suffering, according to Ya'acov Yosef, is one of the divine garments. The work of tikkun, or healing, in the mystical tradition, has to do with finding and revealing the divine sparks of light that lie scattered throughout creation and are hidden in the most unlikely of places, including pain itself.

The Hebrew word for garment, *beged,* also connotes betrayal, *bagad*. As all garments hide what is underneath them, they potentially betray the truth, while removing a garment reveals the truth. We often feel betrayed by God when we are in pain because our suffering has a tendency to eclipse or hide God's love. When we find a way to connect with God despite our pain, we remove both the garment and our sense of betrayal. And when the garment of our suffering becomes a vehicle of our spiritual awakening or healing, we actually redeem the sparks of divinity that are contained in it. Yet we all know that when we are in pain, it is difficult to access nondual awareness. We may welcome God as our healer, but we usually struggle with finding God in our pain or illness. In fact, pain and suffering often cause our universe to contract, imprisoning us in a painful sense of isolation and separation from others. To the degree that we do think about God when we are in pain, it is often because we feel unfairly singled out and punished by God. Our suffering during life's difficult times may also be intensified by the belief that we shouldn't be suffering, that somehow we are failing at life when we are sad or ill or things simply go wrong for us.

Western medicine's general attitude toward illness doesn't help matters. In its war against death and disease, Western medicine reinforces a dualistic and adversarial attitude toward illness and suffering. Focusing exclusively on the elimination of symptoms, it fails to honor the sacred role of illness in our lives. Fortunately, this is beginning to change as holistic thinking has begun to influence the practice of medicine.

Jewish mysticism teaches that when we accept that pain is an inevitable part of living, a face of God, our suffering actually diminishes. As we overcome our habit of judging and categorizing our experiences as either "good" or "bad," acceptable or shameful, succeeding or failing, we can experience life's vicissitudes as parts of a divine whole that includes each thing as well as its opposite. When we can find God in all that we experience, in the raw and painful as well as the happy and good aspects of our lives, our faith matures.

Reb Zusia of Hanopil, one of the most beloved of the Hasidic masters, is said to have lived through many trials and tribulations, yet he always sustained a deep faith in God's love. A story is told about a Hasid who went to the Maggid of Mezerich asking for help in dealing with his many personal problems. He wanted to know how he could possibly live up to the teaching that one must praise and thank God for suffering just as much as for well-being, receiving it with the same joy and equanimity. The Maggid replied by telling the Hasid to go to the Beit Midrash, the yeshiva where Reb Zusia studied, and ask him. The Hasid went and found Reb Zusia sitting in tattered, dirty clothing, looking as though he hadn't eaten in days. When he asked Reb Zusia his question about suffering, Reb Zusia replied, "You certainly have come to the wrong person. You should go ask someone other than me, for I have never experienced suffering." Amazed to hear Reb Zusia's response when he saw clearly how poor and uncared for Reb Zusia was, the Hasid left knowing what it was to accept suffering with love.[7]

Reb Zusia was so connected to God's love and unity that he did not pay much heed to his own suffering and deprivation. For him there were no "garments" of betrayal. But for those of us who lack the deep faith and humility Zusia possessed, it's not so easy. We can, however, begin to lessen our suffering by approaching life with fewer judgments and dualisms.

Depression

Embracing the Dark Times

The phrase from Isaiah quoted at the opening of this chapter, "forming light and creating darkness; making peace and creating the evil," points to a vision of the divine as embodying all the forces of light and darkness, the creative as well as the destructive. Isaiah's powerful proclamation of God's absolute nonduality was, unfortunately, sanitized by the rabbis, who, when editing this verse for the liturgy, replaced the phrase "creating the evil" with the euphemism "creating all things."[8] I suppose the rabbis were afraid that Isaiah's words would be misconstrued in some way. Perhaps Isaiah's image of God sounded too much like one of the Near Eastern goddesses of love and war or the Hindu god Shiva, who is seen both as creator and destroyer. Yet by attempting to exclude evil from God's domain, rabbinic Judaism unwittingly reinforced the splitting of good and evil into distinctly separate domains. This subtle act of editing also robbed Judaism of the potent and integrative image of divinity that fortunately is resurfacing in today's religious discourse.

Why fortunately? From a psychological standpoint, it is much easier to deal with life's vicissitudes when our notion of the divine expands to include the darkness as well as the light. When we stop splitting life into two distinct categories that we label either good or bad, it is also easier to accept our own pain and woundedness.

A good deal of what goes on in therapy involves helping people accept and bear their painful feelings. Ironically, for many, the painful symptoms that have brought them into treatment arose in response to their avoidance of pain. At the beginning of treatment, people often have the fantasy that therapy will somehow eliminate their pain and exorcise their wounded selves. They are typically disappointed when I suggest that in order to heal, they will need to learn how to embrace and express their pain more fully, instead of trying to get rid of it. It is only by integrating *all* of who we are, including the hurt and wounded parts, that we become whole. As we overcome our aversion to pain and develop a healthy acceptance and even curiosity about whatever we are experiencing, our symptoms not only reveal important information to us, they actually begin to heal us at a deeper level.

Depression, for example, involves a painful set of symptoms that arise when we have pushed away parts of the self. Depression may result from suppressed grief over a loss that we never mourned, or it may arise when we have lost touch with an essential part of our core self. Depression can also be the result of anger that we have suppressed and turned against ourselves. The symptoms of depression often serve to slow us down and redirect our attention from the outer world to our inner selves, so that we can focus on self-healing and integration. When attended to with care and compassion, depression can lead us to recover what we need in order to be whole.

Judith, a woman who was suffering from severe depression following the end of a relationship, discovered the healing role of depression in our work together. When I first started working with Judith, she was so depressed she could hardly get out of bed in the morning. I sensed Judith was very angry toward her ex-partner for giving up so easily on the relationship when things became difficult between them. Judith, however, was not consciously in touch with this anger; instead, she seemed to be directing her anger toward herself by constantly blaming and berating herself for the demise of the relationship. Judith's self-flagellation also extended itself toward the symptoms of her depression. She had always been such a high-functioning, active woman that she could not forgive himself for being so depressed and unproductive. Not being able to function made her feel worthless.

Judith's self-loathing attitude seemed to add fuel to the fire of her depression. The more anger she directed at herself, the worse her symptoms became. I knew that Judith would not be able to overcome her depression until she adopted a more compassionate and accepting attitude toward it. I repeatedly encouraged her to be gentle with herself, to stop beating herself up for being depressed. But it wasn't until I suggested to Judith that she start honoring and attending to her depression as though it were a sacred revelation that she took in what I was saying.

As she began to think of her depression as a sacred revelation, Judith stopped being so angry at herself and instead became curious about what the depression might be here to teach her. She began to notice that certain childhood memories and feeling states were becoming available to her as the depression enabled her to drop down to another level of her being, one that she typically tuned out when she was able to function optimally in the outer world. In particular, Judith began getting in touch with how another traumatic loss, one from her childhood, was piggybacking on her current experience of loss. Judith's mother had become ill and died rather suddenly when she was thirteen. At the time, she lacked the emotional means for dealing with this trauma because no one helped her grieve the loss. And in the absence of appropriate comfort and emotional support, Judith mistakenly concluded that she ought not feel the sadness she was feeling. Instead, Judith felt ashamed of her grief and attempted to bury her pain by throwing herself into a frenzy of activity and overachievement. Though it may not seem entirely logical, children often internalize a sense of shame for their unrecognized feelings.

In therapy Judith began to recall and relive the trauma of her mother's untimely death. This belated grief work enabled her to separate out her childhood grief from her current sadness and anger over the ending of her relationship. Judith and I worked together on both the present and the past, focusing on how she might hold her sadness with greater compassion. She began to learn how not to push away her own experience, no matter how painful it was.

To facilitate the expression of Judith's childhood grief, we devised a "belated mourning ritual" together in which she set aside a full month to focus intensively on her mother's death. During this month Judith spent time each day writing in a journal about her memories of her mother and her feelings around the time of her mother's death. She also spent time each day meditating next to an altar she had erected, on which she placed some old pictures of her mother and herself as a child next to a lit candle.

At the end of the month Judith invited a group of close friends for a closing ceremony to mark the end of her mourning period. In this ceremony Judith read the poetry and prose she had written and shared memories about her mother. She also recited the *Kaddish,* an ancient Aramaic prayer recited by mourners. By having her friends present as witnesses to her process, Judith felt publicly validated for a pain that she had felt compelled to hide in childhood. The shame she had internalized as a result of hiding this pain would still need to be worked through in therapy, but the ritual provided Judith with a long-overdue "coming out."

Judith's recovery from depression coincided with her deepening awareness and acceptance of how wounded she really was. Paradoxically she felt more whole following the depression than she had ever felt before, for she was finally able to put old ghosts from the past to rest and reclaim an essential part of her identity.

Facing the Darkness

Embracing the dark times, such as depression or illness, as a face of the divine is the quintessential Jewish expression of faith. Perhaps for this reason, the Jewish oral tradition begins with instruction in spiritually navigating the night. The Mishneh, which is the authoritative compendium of Jewish law, opens with a discussion of the appropriate time for reciting the Shema at night. "From what time," it asks, "may one recite the Shema in the evening? From the time that the priests enter (their houses) in order to eat their ritual offering, until the end of the first watch. These are the words of Rabbi Eliezer. The Sages say: 'Until midnight.' Rabbi Gamliel says: 'Until the dawn comes up.'"[9]

Embedded within this legalistic discussion about the evening prayer time is a hidden spiritual teaching: We begin the spiritual journey by facing the night or the darkness, affirming our faith in God's oneness. The Shema is a prayer that teaches us to see all of life—the darkness as well as the light—as part of a whole. The Shema's proclamation: "Listen Israel, YHVH [the Infinite One] is Eloheinu [our God], YHVH is one," teaches that the differing manifestations of the divine—YHVH and Elohim—are actually one and the same. YHVH, traditionally associated with God's loving, compassionate nature, and Elohim, God's limit-setting, judicial quality, are ultimately part of one seamless unity. Jewish spiritual practice begins with the recitation of the Shema at night—in other words, with knowing that everything we experience emanates from the same divine source. Ultimately, there is only God.

What if we stopped breaking down reality into opposing halves: good and bad, black and white, liberal and conservative, us and them? What if instead we viewed everything—ourselves, our relationships with friends and family, life on earth—as if it were a shattered vessel, splintered into many pieces, and our job were to join the pieces of the whole back together, liberating the sparks of light and truth from each part? This is, in large part, the Kabbalah's healing message.

ILLNESS AS REVELATORY: THE BURNING BUSH

One of the most potent healing symbols in the Torah appears in the story about Moses' first encounter with YHVH at the site of the burning bush. The story takes place while Moses is tending Jethro's sheep in the Sinai desert. According to the biblical narrative in Exodus 3:2–4, Moses is led to the mountain of God known as Horev. There, "an angel of YHVH appeared to him as a flame in the heart of the bush. And he looked and behold, the bush was burning, however, it was not consumed [by the flame]." Instead of backing away from this awesome and mysterious vision, Moses decides to move closer, to see what is being revealed to him. When God sees that Moses has gone out of his way to look, the Torah reveals that "Elohim called to him from the midst of the bush and said: 'Moses, Moses.' And he answered, 'Here I am.'"

Many beautiful and creative interpretations have been offered to explain the unusual symbolism of this vision. One explanation suggests that everything, even the most ordinary of bushes, is aflame with the spirit of the divine. We don't ordinarily see this underlying level of reality (unless we are on mind-altering drugs) because we walk around content and secure in our separateness. Yet as we step out of our habitual ways of looking at life and bear witness to the extraordinary within the ordinary, the divine force-field that animates all of life reveals itself to us. Only when we stop to take a deeper look at the true nature of reality—namely, that we are all part of a greater unity that underlies the amazing multiplicity of creation—are we initiated into the mystical realm. It is out of this realization that we begin to heal from our own fragmented, solitary sense of self and our hearts, like Moses', open to the suffering of all beings.

What enabled Moses to receive this vision? The midrash tells us that Moses happened upon the site of the burning bush while searching for a baby lamb that had wandered away from the flock in search of water. When Moses found the lamb drinking from a stream near Mount Horev, he rejoiced and embraced the vulnerable creature. It was at that very moment, when Moses showed his own deep care and compassion for a creature under his care, that he heard his divine calling as a prophet and leader. By being a faithful shepherd to Jethro's flock, Moses is groomed to become the shepherd of God's people, the one who would lead them from slavery to freedom.

At the burning bush, God commands Moses to take off his *na'a-laim,* or shoes. This Hebrew word comes from the same root as the word for lock—*na'al.* In his prophetic initiation, then, Moses learns that he must remove that which locks him up and imprisons him. He must take off the garment of his materiality, that which separates him from others and from the ground of all being. When, by removing his shoes, he makes contact with the "holy ground" on which he stands, he is given the gift of vision—to be able to see life through God's eyes, the eyes of divine compassion.

In his vision at the burning bush, Moses learns of God's intimate participation in human suffering. God speaks to Moses out of a lowly thorn bush to convey symbolically that as Israel was suffering under the burdens of slavery and exile, the Shechinah, or divine presence, was suffering with them. The midrash asks, "Why [does God speak] from the thornbush and not from a big oak tree or date palm? The Holy One of Blessing said: I wrote in the scriptures (Psalms 91:15), 'I will be with him in suffering'—as they [Israel] are enslaved, so, too, I am in a narrow place in a bush full of thorns."[10]

The divine name "Ehyeh"—or "I will be"—which is revealed to Moses at the burning bush, implies, according to one midrash, a promise that the Shechinah, or divine presence, will be with Israel throughout their ordeals of the current exile and all future exiles. A similar notion appears in another midrash, which portrays God as being like a twin to Israel who empathically experiences everything that the other twin experiences. This midrash offers a "punny" interpretation of Song of Songs 6:9 ("My constant dove, my perfect one [*tamati*]").

"Do not," this midrash advises us, "read *tamati* 'my perfect one' but *teumati,* 'my twin'—just as in the case of twins, if one of the pair has a headache, its twin also experiences pain, so too, as it were, the Holy One of Blessing says, 'I am with him [Israel] in distress.'"[11]

That the Shechinah is especially present and available to us when we are suffering is a classic teaching from the Talmud. The Talmud also teaches that the Shechinah hovers over the head of one who is ill.[12] In fact, those who perform the mitzvah of *bikkur cholim,* or visiting and tending to the sick, are obliged to sit low to the ground out of reverence for the divine presence. When we perform the mitzvah of bikkur cholim, we encounter the Shechinah's presence, for the divine presence is there both for the person who is ill and for those who are attending to his needs.

Illness, in this sense, may be viewed as a sacred axis or meeting place where God's presence is revealed. Perhaps the visitation by the Shechinah occurs when we are ill because we are more open to experiencing intimacy with the divine when we are ill. As illness thwarts our wills, we potentially become more receptive to God's will. So long as things are going well for us, we mistakenly think that *we* are in control, and this interferes with our ability to be receptive to divine grace. When we are ill, suddenly we know that we are not in control. For many people, this humbling realization can be one of the most positive outcomes of illness.

Paradoxically, then, we may find ourselves spiritually healing at those very times when, according to Western medicine, we are most ill. For as our egos are weakened by the loss of control that we experience during illness, we are freer to experience life from the soul's more humble and unified perspective. Not everyone who suffers from an illness, however, merits this kind of grace. Accepting our pain and helplessness as revelatory requires that we develop a certain measure of humility and equanimity. In order to learn what illness offers, we have to learn not to push pain away. The following meditation can be used to deepen our equanimity in the face of adversity.

MEDITATION AND EQUANIMITY

Jewish mystics of old devised numerous meditations for developing an awareness of God's presence in all things. One of the traditional practices involves meditating on the phrase from the eighth verse of Psalm 16 *"Shiviti yhvh le'negdi tamid,"* which means, "I place yhvh equally before me at all times." Some of the ancient mystics recited this phrase as a continuous mantra in order to become ever mindful of God's loving presence in their lives. When we become mindful of YHVH's presence in all things, we stop judging and categorizing things as good or bad. We can be fully present with whatever the universe is presenting to us at any given moment, for God can be found in all places and in all situations. When we practice equanimity, we learn to accept the universe on its terms, instead of dictating to God how things should be. With equanimity we begin the spiritual work of surrender.

In order to practice this meditation, you might find it helpful to gaze into the letters of the YHVH name, using a traditional Shiviti like the one printed on the next page. Or you can also just meditate on the essence of YHVH, seeing yourself and all of life as part of a seamless unity.

Begin the meditation by paying attention to your breath. Spend the next five to ten minutes relaxing into a steady pattern of breathing in and breathing out, so that all breaths are equal, the in-breath matching the out-breath. You might visualize that with each in-breath you are breathing in God's out-breath and with each out-breath you are breathing into God. Continue this back-and-forth breathing until subject and object merge into one and there is only the one breath of life breathing through you.

Now, whatever is most difficult in your life at this time, bring it to mind and breathe into it, saying to yourself, "Shiviti YHVH le'negdi tamid" (pronounce YHVH as "A-do-nai), and allowing yourself to become aware that YHVH, the Infinite One, is being revealed to you at this time through this very difficult situation. Now do the same with something joyous in your life. Go back and forth between the difficult and the joyous, breathing equally into both, not judging either as good or bad but simply experiencing all life as existing within God.

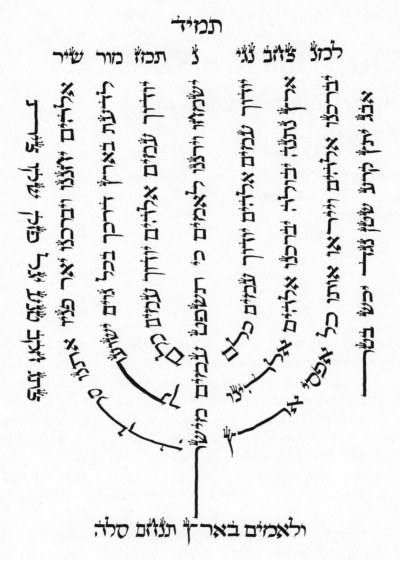

Traditional Handwritten Shiviti

Religious Jews have traditionally used the Shiviti to focus on God's presence during meditation and spiritual contemplation. This Shiviti was handwritten by the Israeli scribe, Ehud Avraham in 2000. This piece is part of the author's personal collection.

I 2

THE FOUR WORLDS
Integrating and Unifying the Self

Remembering is the source of redemption. Exile
persists as long as one forgets.
—*Ba'al Shem Tov*

Once, Rabbi Dov Baer, the son of Rabbi
Shneur Zalman of Liadi, was studying Kabbalah late at night. So
absorbed was he in the great mysteries that he failed to hear the cries
of the baby downstairs. When his father, Shneur Zalman, who was
studying Torah on the floor above him, heard the baby cry, he immediately came downstairs to see what was wrong. When he noticed the
light on in Dov Baer's room, he was surprised to find him awake.
How could he not have heard the baby's cry? After comforting the
crying baby, Shneur Zalman went upstairs and admonished his son
never to be so deep in study that he would fail to hear the cry of a
baby.

On another occasion Shneur Zalman was meditating together with
Avraham, the holy son of the Maggid of Mezerich. Nicknamed the
Angel because of his angelic, awe-inspiring countenance, Avraham
spent most of his life as a spiritual recluse, absorbed in the great
mysteries. In many ways Avraham the Angel was more comfortable
in the upper worlds than in this material world. And so when Avraham and Shneur Zalman ascended the different worlds in their meditation all the way up to the highest level—the world of *atzilut*—

Avraham was at risk of not returning to his body. When Shneur Zalman realized this, he quickly ran and found a bagel, which he proceeded to put in Avraham's mouth to help him become grounded. When the Maggid later thanked Shneur Zalman for acting so quickly on his son's behalf, he added with a touch of humor, "So where did you find the bagel of atzilut?"[1]

Hearing the cry of a baby and finding the "bagel of atzilut" are metaphors for the ability to keep one's feet firmly planted on the earth while traversing the higher realms. Both stories underscore the need to live simultaneously in multiple worlds in order to maintain a sense of balance and wholeness. The Kabbalah understood that we always live in multiple worlds. Just as the Torah is said to have four basic levels of meaning, known as pardes, so too all reality comprises four realms (some say five realms) of being.[2] These four realms—or worlds as they are called in the Kabbalah—exist simultaneously within all things and within each of us. Known as *atzilut* (nearness or emanation), *beriah* (creation), *yetzirah* (formation), and *assiyah* (action or actualization), the four worlds can be seen as corresponding roughly to the spiritual, intellectual, emotional, and physical dimensions of our being. While most contemporary schools of psychology and medicine focus in varying degrees on one or another of these different levels of being, the Kabbalah asserts that we must be able to balance and embody all *four* levels in order to be whole. In this chapter we will examine the symbolism and mythology associated with the four worlds and explore how to apply this multidimensional view of reality to the process of healing into our wholeness.

The four worlds, like the sephirot, describe the progression or process of divine unfolding from infinite being to finite reality.[3] They depict creation as a downward chain of spiritual worlds, or *hishtalshelut,* stretching from the most exalted, hidden realm, known as atzilut, down to the realm of assiyah, the physical plane in which we live.[4] However, since all creation is continually being brought into existence anew, the four worlds are not so much successive phases of creation as simultaneously existing aspects of reality.

INTEGRATING THE FOUR WORLDS

As indicated on the accompanying diagram, the four worlds parallel the process of creation through the sephirot, structuring the ten
divine emanations into a series of stages. Like the sephirot, they
bridge the expanse between heaven and earth, the one and the many,
spirit and matter. Though we speak of the four worlds as though
they were separate realms, they are actually deeply interconnected,
operating holographically, as each contains within it all the other levels of reality.[5] An action in any one of the worlds resonates in all
other worlds. And each of the four worlds, like the four basic
elements—earth, air, fire, water—exists within each aspect of creation in different degrees.

According to one understanding of Luria's myth of the shattered
vessels, the original vessels of creation, or sephirot, shattered because
they were disconnected from each other. While each of them received
the effulgence of divine light, they had no means of communicating
and sharing that light with each other. Because of their isolation they
were unable to form a whole that would be strong enough to withstand the powerful revelation of light from the Ein Sof, the infinite.
It was this state of intersephirotic disconnection that rendered them
vulnerable to shattering. So, too, the disunity of the different worlds
or levels of being is seen by the Kabbalah as the source of individual
and cosmic disharmony. Healing, or tikkun, from a kabbalistic perspective involves the reintegration and reunification of these different
worlds or aspects of being. In the Kabbalah this process is known as
hitkalelut, which is achieved through connection and interinclusion;
recognizing how everything is included in everything, or how the *all*
is in every part.

The process of sephirotic integration mirrors the work of self-
integration that each of us must achieve in order to become whole.
This involves fully embodying and integrating the different dimensions of our being so that they exist in harmonious balance with one
another.[6] If we become overly dependent on any one dimension of
our being to the exclusion of the others, or if the different aspects of
our being become disconnected from one another, we fall into a state

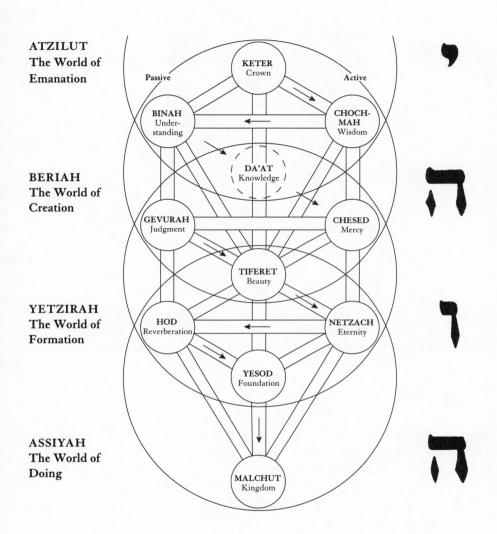

ATZILUT
The World of
Emanation

BERIAH
The World of
Creation

YETZIRAH
The World of
Formation

ASSIYAH
The World of
Doing

KETER
Crown

Passive

Active

BINAH
Under-
standing

CHOCH-
MAH
Wisdom

DA'AT
Knowledge

GEVURAH
Judgment

CHESED
Mercy

TIFERET
Beauty

HOD
Reverberation

NETZACH
Eternity

YESOD
Foundation

MALCHUT
Kingdom

The Sephirot and the Four Worlds

This diagram shows the relationship between the ten sephirot and the
four worlds. It also indicates the correspondence between the four-letter
name of God—YHVH—and the four worlds.

Adapted from *Kabbalah and Exodus* by Z'ev ben Shimon Halevi (York Beach, Maine: Samuel Weiser, 1988).
Diagram p. 22 used with permission of Red Wheel/Weiser.

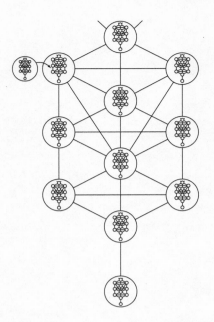

The Holographic Structure of the Sephirot

This diagram shows how each sephirot contains all ten sephirah within it.

From *Kabbalah and Consciousness* by Allen Afterman (New York: The Sheep Meadow Press, 1992). Reprinted with permission.

of imbalance, from which stress and dis-ease can arise. Ultimately, these symptoms of distress serve to call our attention to the lack of balance so that we may do what is necessary in order to restore a sense of inner harmony. In other words, our bodies (assiyah) and souls (atzilut) must become interconnected with our thoughts (beriah) and emotions (yetzirah), so that our physical, emotional, intellectual, and spiritual selves support and balance each other. When these four aspects of our being are in harmonious balance, we become whole vessels, capable of containing the immense light of our full being. If we are not sufficiently integrated, mystical states can pose a danger to our psychic integrity, as the following tale from the Talmud illustrates:

The Tale of the Four Sages

Our rabbis taught: There were four people who entered pardes (the mystical Garden of meaning), namely: Ben

Azzai, Ben Zoma, Acher, and Rabbi Akiva. . . . Ben Azzai gazed at the Shechinah and died. About his (fate) scriptures say, "Difficult in the eyes of God is the death of His loved ones" (Psalms 116:15). Ben Zoma gazed at the Shechinah and went mad. About him scriptures say, "When you find honey, eat what is sufficient for you, lest you be satiated and vomit it up" (Proverbs 25:16). Acher "destroyed the plants" (became an apostate). Rabbi Akiva entered whole (b'shalom) and came out whole (b'shalom).[7]

This tale, which traditionally is understood to be a warning to those who might engage in mystical contemplation without sufficient preparation, is also a tale about the consequences of being unbalanced and unintegrated. Aside from Rabbi Akiva, whom the tale describes as having entered and exited the pardes, or mystical, realm whole (b'shalom), each of the other three sages was damaged by his experience due to a lack of grounding in certain levels of his being.

In this tale, the mystical realm is referred to by the Hebrew acronym pardes (paradise!), a coded reference to the four levels of meaning by which the Torah is classically interpreted. These four levels of meaning, which span the range of meanings from the most literal to the most sublime and hidden, are also a mirror reflection of the four worlds, as indicated on the accompanying chart. (It's interesting to note that the term *pardes* also means orchard. Its use in this legend also hints at the orchard of paradise, where the two original fruit trees-the tree of knowledge and the tree of life—grew side by side.)

Peh-Pshat (literal meaning)—World of Assiyah —Action/Actualization—Physical Realm

Resh-Remez (hint)—World of Yetzirah—Formation—Emotional Realm

Dalet-Drash (deeper word analysis)—World of Beriah—Creation—Thinking Realm

Samech-Sod (secret, mystical meaning)—World of Atzilut—Emanation—Spirit Realm

As indicated in the above list, the *peh* (*p*) of pardes stands for the *pshat* or literal meaning of a text. It corresponds to the world of assiyah, the physical dimension of being. The *resh* (*r*), stands for *remez,* or the symbolic meaning that is hinted at. This level corresponds to the world of yetzirah, or the emotional-expressive dimension. The *dalet* (*d*) stands for the *drash,* or those meanings that can be extracted through deeper analysis of language and word associations or through the imaginative process of the unconscious. It corresponds to the world of beriah, the cognitive-contemplative dimension. And the *samech* (*s*) stands for *sod,* the secret, mystical understanding of the text. It corresponds to the world of atzilut, which is the highest spiritual dimension.

While each of the four sages in the pardes tale was a seasoned scholar and mystic, Rabbi Akiva alone was grounded in all four levels of his being. As mystic-scholar Rabbi Gershon Winkler suggests, he had *both* feet in all four worlds and was able to move freely among the different dimensions of his being. A master of the dance of *ratzo va'shov,* or running and returning, Akiva was able to dance gracefully between paradise and paradox. He knew how to ascend and descend the ladder of worlds without getting stuck in any one level, for he experienced all of life as an integrated whole. Interestingly, Akiva was the only one among the four sages who was happily married and grounded in his mortal existence. He knew that his ascent to the higher realms was in order to return and bring more light and inspiration back into his earthly life.

The pardes tale contains another warning to those engaged in mystical contemplation. It warns of the danger of becoming stuck in any *one* of the four levels of reality. According to the Zohar, this is what happened to each of the other three sages. Each of them had some imbalance in his character that caused him to fixate on a particular level to the neglect of the other levels. Though the Zohar doesn't specify who got stuck where, there are some interesting speculations on the subject.

Ben Azzai, it seems, became so completely absorbed in the spiritual realm, or sod dimension, that he neglected all the other aspects of his being. Like a moth flying into a flame, he was consumed as he gazed directly at the Shechinah; his soul simply left his body to return to its source. Ben Azzai was so ungrounded in the physical realm that on his wedding night, the Talmud tells us, he abandoned his bride to go study the mysteries of the Torah. Unlike Rabbi Akiva, who was able to remain attached to his earthly existence while ascending to heaven, Ben Azzai's yearning for union with the divine overwhelmed his attachment to life and mortal existence. He didn't understand how he might deepen his connection with the Spirit by wrestling with the everyday, mundane challenges of intimate relationships.

Ben Zoma's error was that he aspired to reach a level of self-transcendence for which he was not emotionally prepared; his ego was simply too fragile. Without a solid sense of self to which he might return, the mystical encounter drove him mad,[8] or as Rabbi Winkler suggests, he got stuck in the drash and remez levels of reality, where everything is simply a sign or metaphor for something else. In this tangled web of meanings he lost touch with the literal plane of reality—the simple pshat. According to the Talmud he over-indulged his spiritual yearning, like a person who eats too much honey and becomes sick.

Elisha ben Abuyah, referred to as Acher (Other) in this tale, became an apostate. His loss of faith, we learn from another Talmudic tale, came about as a result of his overreliance on thinking. Indeed, he had been one of the greatest minds of his generation, but in over-emphasizing the rational, he got stuck on the pshat level of reality, and he failed to see beyond the literal meaning of things. As we saw in the tale about his apostasy, Acher lost his faith after seeing a person die while performing the two mitzvot that the Torah specifically says will lengthen a man's days. Perceiving the apparent lack of divine justice in the world, Acher came to the conclusion that "there is no justice and no judge."

Interestingly, Acher's apostasy is described as a destroying, or more literally, a cutting, of the plants, implying that he separated plants from their roots. To take life too literally is to separate things from their source in the deeper mystery. In taking the literal and obvious meaning (pshat) apart from the hidden root source (sod), Acher severed the connection between creation and creator; in effect, he split God in two. His very nickname, Acher, or Other, suggests that by attributing any kind of dualism or "otherness" to God, he too became "other."

In contrast to the story of the apostate Acher, several stories about Rabbi Akiva demonstrate his unflinching faith during times of enormous personal and collective suffering. For instance, when he encountered a fox leaving the site of the holy of holies (innermost sanctum) after the Romans had destroyed the Temple, he is said to have laughed while his companions wept. When asked how he could laugh at such a tragic moment, he replied that in witnessing the fulfillment of Jeremiah's dire prophecy that Zion would be destroyed, he felt reassured that the words, both hopeful and gloomy, of *all* the prophets would be fulfilled. Thus, just as the Temple was destroyed, so, too, was the prophesied future redemption assured. Rabbi Akiva's reply reveals his deep faith in the nondual nature of the divine—his faith that all things, both the good and the bad, exist within God. Being masterful at traversing the different realms, he was able to remember the deeper hidden mysteries, or sod dimension of reality, while experiencing life's tragic dimensions. Rabbi Akiva's faith ran so deep that even while the Romans tortured him to death by scraping his skin off with steel combs, he had the wherewithal to recite the Shema, affirming God's essential oneness.

The tale of the four sages teaches us that in order to be shaleim, or whole, we must be able to traverse comfortably the different levels of reality, from the most concrete and literal to the most hidden and sublime, without getting stuck in any one level. We must also be able to perceive the multiple levels of meaning that coexist within all things and to balance the spiritual, intellectual, emotional, relational, and physical aspects of our being. The true danger, according to the Zohar, is not the act of entering the mystical pardes per se but getting stuck in any one level of reality to the exclusion of all others. Interestingly, the Hebrew word *pardes,* without its last letter, *samech,* which signifies the secret, or sod, level, spells the word *pered (peh-resh-dalet),* which implies separation. Torah without the sod, or mysteries, can lead one to a sense of separation and dualism, rather than the fertile ground of all being, the pardes, where, attached to its roots, all life grows.

In interpersonal dynamics it can be helpful to keep the pardes model in mind, for at times the pshat, or literal, level of what our partners and friends communicate is not truly the deepest level of what they are trying to say. For example, if my husband says something to me with an irritable or critical tone and I respond to the pshat level of what he is saying, I typically respond defensively. If, however, I have the wherewithal to consider that his words also conceal within them remez, drash, and sod levels of meaning, I might consider responding differently. Perhaps he feels neglected by me and would like some attention (remez). Perhaps my own behavior has pushed some unconscious buttons within him (drash). Or perhaps at the deepest (sod) level he is asking for love, albeit in an unskillful way. From experience I have learned that if I respond at one of these deeper levels rather than at the pshat level, I am more likely to facilitate a loving, empathic connection between us.

It is also helpful to keep in mind that every person's soul is rooted most deeply in one or another of the four worlds. Knowing people's soul level can help us better understand their personality type as well as their unique style of communication. This is particularly useful when their soul level or personality type is different from our own. Just as we need to reformat a document that was written in a different computer program than the one in which we typically work before we can interact with it, so also do we need to translate words/actions of those whose operating systems are different from our own.

Jung versus Luzzato: The Four Personality/ Soul Types

The notion that there are four distinct personality types is an important concept in Jungian psychology, where the number four, in general, is seen as a symbol of wholeness. Jung delineated four basic functions that we all use to process reality—namely, intuition, thoughts, feelings, and sensory perception. Though we all have access to all four of these capacities in varying measures, Jung believed that each of us has a primary, or "superior," function (as well as a secondary auxiliary function) upon which we rely most heavily to process information and navigate our way through life. Our personality type, according to Jung, is determined by our most developed function. We also each possess what Jung called an "inferior" function, a capacity that remains more unconscious and undeveloped in us. Part of the work of self-realization, according to Jung, involves developing greater awareness and skill at using all four functions, including our least developed one.

The Kabbalah also delineated four distinct soul types, based on the four worlds. This notion appears in the writings of the famous eighteenth-century Italian kabbalist Rabbi Moshe Chaim Luzzato, who identified souls according to the world in which they are most rooted. Those souls whose roots are from the world of assiyah, he called *nafshot*; from yetzirah, *ruchot;* from beriah, *neshamot;* and from atzilut, *neshamot la'neshamot*—souls of souls. Luzzato's four soul types correspond closely with Jung's four personality types. Nafshot, those souls rooted in the world of assiyah (physical realm) may be seen as sensate types; ruchot, those souls from the world of yetzirah (feeling realm) may be seen as feeling types; neshamot, those souls from the world of beriah (cognitive-contemplative realm) may be seen as thinking types; while neshamot la'neshamot, those souls from the world of atzilut (spiritual realm) are most likely intuitive types.

THE SYMBOLISM OF THE NUMBER FOUR

In addition to enumerating four basic personality types, Jung was also fascinated by the spiritual symbolism of the number four. He noted that the figure of a square, which has four sides, is a symbol of wholeness. When a square appears in a dream, Jung says, it signifies that the dreamer is actively engaged in the process of self-realization, or as he called it, individuation. The square often appears alongside a circle or mandala in dreams as it does in religious symbolism. Jung suggested that when the circle, a symbol of the infinite self, is joined with the square (the symbol of embodied wholeness) it indicates that the natural wholeness of the self is being realized in finite human consciousness. For this reason, mandalas combining the circle and the square are often used in healing rituals and in meditation to restore a sense of wholeness, inner harmony, and balance.

The number four is also a symbol of wholeness and completeness in psychological astrology, where the four elements are seen as the basic building blocks of all material structures and organic wholes, each element being a basic form of energy or consciousness. Though all four elements are said to exist in each of us, every person is consciously more attuned to some types of energy than others. In psychological astrology, personality types are described in terms of a person's most dominant element (earth, air, fire, water) and healing is approached by rectifying excesses and deficiencies in the different elements.

The number four is also prominent in Native American thought, corresponding to the four directions and four winds, the four elements, the four realms (invisible, animal, plant, mineral), and the four seasons (spring, summer, fall, winter). And in Pythagorean numerology, the number four was seen as an embodiment of natural order and balance, while the quadrata, or pre-Christian Greek cross, symbolized the union of opposites.

The number four is also an important symbol of wholeness in Jewish thought, particularly in the Passover Seder, in which the ancestral healing journey from enslavement to freedom is reenacted through storytelling and ritual. In recounting the tale of the Exodus, the Haggadah is punctuated by the ritual blessing and drinking of *four* cups of wine, the asking of *four* questions, and the account of the *four* sons. The four-dimensionality of the Seder night, say the rabbis, hints at the four worlds and God's four-letter name (YHVH) that was revealed through the Exodus. It also hints at the four stages of the redemption, which are reflected in the scriptures' use of four distinct expressions for the kind of help God will give the Israelites. In Exodus 6:6–7, God instructs Moses to "tell the children of Israel, I am YHVH, and I will *bring you out* [*ve'hotzeiti*] from under the burdens of the Egyptians, and I *will deliver* [*ve'hitzalti*] you out of their bondage and I *will redeem* [*ve'gaalti*] you with an out-stretched arm and with great judgments. And I *will take* [*ve'lakachti*] you to me for a people and I will be to you a God and you will know that I am YHVH, the Infinite one, who brings you out from under the burdens of Egypt." Clearly, then, the ancient Passover ritual revolves around the number four, a fact that suggests that on Passover we each begin our own sacred healing journey toward wholeness and freedom.

The four expressions of redemption, the four levels of pardes, the four-letter name of God, and the four worlds all reflect the basic notion that in order to achieve wholeness we must be able to comfortably traverse, embody, and integrate the different aspects of our being.

HEALING MODALITIES IN EACH OF THE WORLDS

The four worlds provide a useful model for approaching healing from a multidimensional perspective. In the following descriptions of the four worlds I have included a brief account of how healing might be approached at each level.

The World of Atzilut, or Emanation

Atzilut, the world of emanation, represents the realm of pure infinite being. It is in atzilut that everything that would be called forth, willed, created, formed, and made is held in potential. The word *atzilut* shares the same root as the Hebrew word *etzel*, which implies nearness. It corresponds to that place within each of us that is always intimately connected to God and to all being. Our soul is rooted in atzilut. No matter how spiritually disconnected we may feel, at the core atzilut level of our being we are always connected to our source. As we say in the morning prayers, "My Source, the soul you have placed in me is pure."

We open up to the realm of atzilut in deep states of meditation or prayer, when we let go of our separate sense of self and relax into the ground of our being. In atzilut, the boundaries of time and space and of subject and object dissolve, and we experience the bliss of devekut, or union with God. Through the expanded sense of awareness we experience when we touch the realm of atzilut, we gain a better sense of perspective on life. We begin to see things from the soul's perspective. Instead of getting caught up in our daily problems and frustrations, we begin to take in the big picture. In this more expansive state we become increasingly intuitive, and we are able to perceive the whole rather than the fragmented parts of reality.

Atzilut can be seen as corresponding to the intuitive function in Jung's typology. Those whose souls are deeply rooted in atzilut are often very intuitive. Operating much like prophecy, intuition enables us to know things without being able to pinpoint exactly how we obtained our knowledge. Intuitive people tend to perceive the whole, or the gestalt, rather than the individual parts. Though we all have intuition, most of us have not learned to pay attention to and honor this faculty. Often we have clear intuitions about important events in our lives, but we ignore them because we haven't learned to trust our intuition. In fact, most of us have learned to mistrust our intuitive knowledge and rely instead on our intellect or on sensate data that can be quantified and verified. Yet, as many of us have learned the hard way, when we ignore our intuitions, we often end up paying a hefty price. Healing work in atzilut enables us to develop and honor our intuition.

To the extent that the different levels of our being are integrated, we can benefit from spiritual healing practices that open us up directly to atzilut. Someone whose being is fragmented, however, may be unable to benefit from these practices. In fact, certain vulnerable people may even be harmed by such practices, as I witnessed during my years living in Jerusalem, where I encountered many people who attempted to climb the ladder of spiritual ascent to atzilut but came crashing down because they were not sufficiently integrated to assimilate the powerful energy or insights they experienced.

The World of Beriah, or Creation

The second dimension, the world of beriah, or creation, refers to the stage of divine unfolding when the very first "something" emerged out of the primordial nothingness. It marks the beginning of the creative process when the divine will to create first became manifest. In the human dimension, beriah refers to the cognitive or thinking realm, where ideas form and begin their creative function, for all creativity begins in pure thought.

Healing in the realm of beriah involves claiming our innate intelligence and harnessing the power of our thoughts. At the highest level it involves aligning our minds with the divine mind, the greater intelligence that is inherent in all life. Healing in beriah also entails letting go of negative thought patterns, like excess self-criticism and pessimism, that inhibit our growth and creativity and minimize our enjoyment of life.

Since so much of our suffering arises out of the stories we tell ourselves about reality, healing in the realm of beriah demands that we let go of our outdated personal myths and narrow belief systems. Our thoughts and beliefs have a profound effect on our lives, for we tend to interpret reality through the lens of our preexisting thoughts and beliefs. We also tend to contribute to the creation of situations in our lives that support our beliefs. If, for instance, we hold on to a belief that we are unworthy of love, we may try to prove this point by continually seeking out partners who betray or abandon us. If we go through life holding on to a belief that people just can't be trusted, we may keep ourselves away from trustworthy people and instead find that we get involved over and over again with people who let us down. While many of our beliefs are conscious, some are quite unconscious. In order to challenge and revise them, we must first bring them into our conscious awareness.

Healing in the realm of beriah also means knowing things truthfully as they are, not as we imagine or wish them to be. To see life clearly, we have to let go of our stubborn attachments, which can cloud our perceptions, for when we are attached to our own desires and ends, we tend to see what we want to see rather than what is.

We must also let go of fixed ideas about things in order to experience each moment of our lives with freshness and clarity. Our fixed notions about the people in our lives, for instance, often cloud our perception of what they say or do to us. I remember recently receiving an e-mail note from someone with whom I had unfinished emotional business. As I read her note, I found myself becoming hurt and angry, for I interpreted her words as rejecting me. When I got past my initial hurt and anger, I sat down to respond to her e-mail. I decided that in my reply to her I would express my true desire, which was for us to become closer to each other. I suggested that we get together to talk and clear the air between us. After composing my note I reread her e-mail only to discover that it was not really rejecting me but actually had been her best attempt to reach out to me. My fixed idea about her, which was based on past interactions, had distorted my understanding of her words in the present moment.

For some people, healing in beriah involves getting out of their heads—overcoming their overreliance on thinking—while for others, gaining greater access to cognitive processes enables them to better regulate their emotional lives.

The World of Yetzirah, or Formation

The world of yetzirah, or formation, describes the stage of creation where all things are successively fashioned, one from another. In yetzirah the raw materials of creation give birth to the multitude of embodied forms. On the human level, yetzirah is associated with feelings and with the power of speech. The two are linked together, for it is through speech that we are able to fully express and articulate our feelings.

Healing in this realm usually involves working through personal inhibitions that block the flow and expression of our true feelings. While some of us may be overly emotional, most of us find it difficult to access our emotions. As children we learned to ignore our feelings, particularly those that we sensed were threatening or unacceptable to our caretakers. We may have learned to replace our undesirable feelings with others that are considered more acceptable. We may use anger to mask our sadness or sadness to cover up our anger. Even our joy and excitement can become muted when we grow up feeling it is not safe to express the fullness of our being. When we are not able to feel and express our true emotions, we lose touch with our vitality and inner essence, and our life force becomes blocked. When this happens, we may become ill or develop painful symptoms that express for us our disavowed feelings.

On the other end of the spectrum there are people who are overly enamored of their feelings and are unable to regulate the intensity or appropriateness of their emotional responses. They become easily overwhelmed by their feelings, and their unrestrained expression of emotions can do great damage to their relationships. These people can benefit tremendously from inner work in the other realms of their being, particularly the cognitive and spiritual dimensions, which can help them attain greater mastery and perspective vis-à-vis their feelings.

As we shall explore in the following pages, learning to identify and express our feelings accurately and in an appropriate fashion liberates us from the unconscious control that unidentified feelings have over us. And when we get in touch with our true feelings, we become more able to navigate our lives with integrity and create lives that express our true being.

The World of Assiyah
Doing and Actualization

The world of assiyah is associated with the physical realm, with doing and actualization. It is in assiyah that our deepest spiritual essence (atzilut), our thoughts (beriah), and our feelings (yetzirah) find expression in embodied form and in action. Since embodiment and self-actualization are key in this realm, healing in the world of assiyah involves overcoming the inner and outer obstacles that block our ability to actualize and embody our dreams and aspirations.

Healing in assiyah also involves nurturing our physical existence. This includes strengthening, balancing, and purifying the body and paying attention to our nutritional and fitness needs. It also involves caring for the environment and all living ecosystems, and living in harmony with our surroundings.

Connecting the Four Worlds

In addition to the healing work that we can do within each of the four realms, we also need to connect the different levels of our being in order to experience life in a fully embodied and holistic fashion.

Our bodies (assiyah) and souls (atzilut) must become interconnected with our thoughts (beriah) and emotions (yetzirah), so that our spiritual, intellectual, emotional, and physical selves support and balance each other.

Connecting the Physical (Assiyah) and Emotional (Yetzirah) Realms

There are a number of tools that can help us weave conduits of connection between these different dimensions of our being. For instance, we can connect the physical (assiyah) and emotional (yetzirah) dimensions of our being by consciously grounding our feelings in the body. All too often we have been trained to ignore our feelings, and so we are unattuned to the way that our feelings are expressed in the body through our posture, muscle tensions, and other somatic expressions of emotion. In fact, many of us have learned to "dissociate," or leave our bodies, as a means of avoiding our feelings. And so when we first attempt to become mindful of how we embody our feelings, what we notice may be not a feeling itself but the way in which our body resists that feeling. As we identify the resistance, we can relax and allow our true feelings to emerge and be expressed. My client George is a good example. Before getting in touch with his anger, he first noticed how he avoided the emotion. He described feeling as though a heavy weight were crushing his chest, restricting his breath. And in fact, George's breathing was frequently very restricted and shallow. By noticing his restricted breathing and describing his bodily felt sense of crushing pressure around his chest, George was able to uncover his buried anger.

This kind of attentiveness to the bodily felt sense of a particular emotion employs the therapeutic method known as *focusing,* which was developed by the psychotherapist and author Eugene Gendlin. Focusing is a helpful tool for weaving connections between the physical, emotional, and cognitive levels of our being. It enables us to discover the feelings that lie hidden just beneath the surface of our conscious minds. By focusing on the bodily felt sense of an emotion, we allow it to fully emerge and be expressed.

As a therapist I am struck by how often people leave their bodies in order to avoid emotions. The most common way we do this is by inhibiting our breath. We simply stop breathing or breathe shallowly in order to avoid our feelings. When I work with clients who are choking off their feelings in this way, I often notice that there is a visible increase in blood flow to their necks. It may appear as though they have a rash around their entire neck region. This apparent rash is the result of blood accumulating around the neck, at the very spot where they are attempting to cut off their feelings. Interestingly, the Hebrew word for neck, *oref,* spelled *ayin-resh-peh,* shares the same three-letter root as the word for pharaoh, *peh-resh-ayin,* only in reverse. Our inner pharaoh often oppresses us by choking off the flow of energy between our heads and our hearts. The neck, which is the narrowest part of the body's frame, can become our personal mitzrayim when we choke off our feelings and restrict our self-expression.

When I notice clients of mine in this state of constriction, I usually instruct them to become mindful of their body and breath, and especially to notice if they sense any tightness around their head and neck. By employing this kind of gentle body-mind awareness, people can learn to release the physical holding patterns they use to avoid feelings. By allowing themselves to breathe, they can typically relax into their feelings. However, when physical holding patterns become habitual, people often develop chronic muscle contractions and other symptoms of stress, including stomachaches, back or neck pain, and headaches. In these cases therapeutic bodywork may be required to release the chronic tightness that holds feelings in check.

As with the neck, many of us instinctually tighten up our abdomens in order to avoid feelings. When we have tender, vulnerable feelings, we may brace ourselves as though we are going to be socked in the stomach and have the wind kicked out of us. By learning to soften our bellies, breathe, and be physically at ease within our bodies, we can allow the ebb and flow of feelings to wash over us like waves at the shore. We can then express our feelings without unnecessary resistance.

Connecting the Spiritual (Atzilut) and Physical (Assiyah) Realms

While most medieval kabbalists sought spiritual enlightenment through highly ascetic practices that devalued the physical realm and the body, many of the Hassidic masters honored the need to embody the spirit. Rabbi Nachman of Breslov, for instance, stressed the importance of the body in spiritual development. In contrast to those mystics who extolled the virtue of *hitpashtut ha'gashmiut,* divestment of physicality, as the highest level of spiritual attainment, Rabbi Nachman considered the body to be a full partner in the attainment of spiritual enlightenment. He taught that the soul must share its most lofty spiritual insights with the body, for the body is also capable of the same degree of enlightenment of which the soul is capable. This is possible, he said, when the body is in a state of purity. Therefore, he taught, it is an act of great compassion to tend lovingly and compassionately to the body's needs, for when we purify and care for the body, we are more able to hold on to our spiritual attainments, for the body's memory of a spiritual state can help restore the soul to its previous level of attainment. To support this notion, Rabbi Nachman cites a passage from the Book of Job and gives it a creative new interpretation: "And this is what is meant by (the passage) 'from my flesh shall I behold God.' (Job 19:26) . . . Through the very flesh of the body one can behold God . . . (for) the human sees and perceives spirit by way of the body."[9]

Rabbi Nachman's embodied spirituality marks a radical departure from the otherworldly, transcendent spirituality we find among many other Jewish and non-Jewish mystics. Spirituality, according to Rabbi Nachman, must be anchored in the physical realm, for ultimately, it is through our earthly vessel—the body—that we come to behold God. If the soul does not share its illumination with the body, we will not be able to hold on to our spiritual insights.

In addition to anchoring spiritual insight in the body, Rabbi Nachman also urged his followers to bring all intellectual insights from Torah study into the heart-space of personal prayer, where it might lead to embodied action. In these personal prayers designed to follow

Torah study, he taught his disciples to ask God to help them embody in action what they had just learned with their minds.

NAMING

Much of what goes on in therapy involves weaving connections between our thoughts and feelings. We do this primarily by "naming" our feelings. In verbally identifying our different feeling states we use the cognitive-contemplative capacities of beriah to hold and contain the more mercurial emotional energies of yetzirah. While an un-named feeling can produce overwhelming anxiety or cause us to act irrationally, a named feeling becomes manageable. Naming enables us to be fully present as witnesses to our feelings without becoming reactive or defensive.

The healing power of naming is something that goes back to our human origins. In the section of the Book of Genesis where God creates the animals, we find that Adam can name each of the animals as he recognizes its essence. In the healing journey of the Exodus, the Israelites must learn the divine name, YHVH, in order to remember their own true names and essence. By learning to name our pre-viously unrecognized feelings in therapy, we reclaim the exiled and unconscious aspects of our being.

Naming also enables us to own our feelings without becoming overly identified with any single one of them. By staying centered in the witnessing self, we can name and compassionately hold all our emotions without becoming overwhelmed by any single state. Thus, we can experience a full range of emotions without letting any one define or control us.

Josie's Story

In my work with Josie, a Holocaust survivor who came to me for help with debilitating migraine headaches, the naming of feelings became a crucial step in healing. Josie had suffered from headaches as a child but had been relatively headache-free until about a year before she came to me, when they started to occur as frequently as two or three times a week. Josie had seen a number of doctors and had been given medications for pain control, but it seemed as though the medications were becoming part of the problem; though they helped in the short run, they seemed to be triggering a classic rebound effect, where the body's withdrawal from the medication triggers another headache. At the point when Josie came to see me she was feeling very depressed and discouraged with Western medicine's handling of her problem. At a friend's suggestion she sought me out as a therapist in hopes of uncovering whatever underlying emotional issues might be contributing to her symptoms. Psychotherapy, for her, was somewhat of a last resort.

Over the course of about a year of intensive weekly therapy, I worked with Josie on two fronts. First, I taught her simple meditation and relaxation techniques that she could use on a daily basis for stress reduction and healing. These practices seemed to reduce the frequency of the headaches. At the same time we also began to search for clues as to the emotional stressors that may have contributed to the onset of her symptoms. In looking back Josie realized that the headaches had begun around the time when her only son was getting ready to leave home for college. As we explored her feelings about this important transition in her life, memories from her own childhood and adolescence began to surface. For the first time in her life, Josie began to talk about some of her traumatic memories from the war, memories of painful separations and losses she had never really explored with another person. In fact, she had attempted to bury these painful memories and leave them behind her, along with the family members she lost in the war.

The most significant trauma that Josie had endured during the war was her separation from her parents. At the age of eleven she was sent off to London to live with a family that took care of her until she was reunited with her parents at the end of the war. Though the family that took her in was loving and caring, Josie suffered from separation anxiety and depression as a result of being traumatically ripped apart from her family and friends.

Throughout her life Josie had remained sensitive to feelings of loss and abandonment as a result of this trauma. All endings and separations potentially triggered feelings of anxiety and depression in Josie, and so it made sense that her son's departure would have a powerful emotional impact on her. Josie and I began to wonder if her headaches were a somatic expression of the pain she was feeling over her son's departure. She realized that she was holding on to a lot of unexpressed grief. In fact, her grief was twofold. She felt an immediate sense of loss over her son's absence from her daily life, and at the same time, his leaving home had restimulated vague, unconscious memories of loss and trauma. When he left her, she was in effect unconsciously reexperiencing the trauma of her own separation from her parents. Through her headaches it seemed that Josie was expressing the unbearable pain she had felt as a child when she was sent off alone to a strange country to live among strangers.

When she was able to name the amorphous psychic pain buried deep inside her, Josie also was able to move the "trauma" out of her body, where it had been seeking expression, and her headaches became less of a problem. Josie's headaches were, in a sense, an attempt to re-member her forgotten pain. When she consciously re-membered her pain, she was able to separate out her current experience of separation from her son, which was a normal, healthy process, from the traumatic separation she had experienced in her own childhood. Therapy, then, enabled her not only to work through her feelings about her son's departure but also to belatedly grieve some of the losses she had endured in childhood but had never been able to face.

If I look at our work together through the lens of the four worlds, Josie was experiencing symptoms in the physical (assiyah) dimension of her being that came on as a distress signal calling attention to the disconnection between her thinking (beriah) and feeling (yetzirah) selves. By finding words for the unimaginable sorrow that she carried deep within her, Josie was able to reconnect these split-apart parts of her self. I learned from my work with Josie that physical symptoms often require work at the emotional level in order to release and unblock the energy behind them.

Symptoms

Their Origins in the Four Worlds

Painful symptoms, like Josie's headaches, often arise when the different levels of our being become disconnected from each other or when we become too focused on one level of our being to the exclusion of the others. Ultimately, our physical symptoms or feelings of distress serve a healing function. They come to call our attention to the lack of balance in our lives and let us know that we need to attend more closely to our innermost self. Sometimes, as Jung once said, a person's symptoms may be their best attempt at healing.

Whenever we approach healing, we need to look at the *whole* person on all four levels of his or her being in order to truly understand the source of his or her distress. And though an intervention aimed at any one of the four levels of being will inevitably have an impact on all other levels, in order to be most helpful it is important to identify the appropriate level at which to intervene. Sometimes it is best to address a problem or symptom on the same level at which it arose, while at other times it can be more effective to address a problem at a different level than the one at which it arose. In chapter 11, for instance, we saw how Judith's depression lifted when she was able to express fully her childhood feelings of grief from her mother's untimely death. (An emotional problem, namely depression, was treated on the emotional level.) With several other clients who were dealing with belated grief, however, I found that it was necessary to combine expressive therapy with therapeutic bodywork in order to release old feelings that had become trapped in the body. In this case, an emotional problem had to be addressed on the physical level before effective work could be employed in treating the depression.

Sometimes physical and emotional problems have their origin in the spiritual realm. Many addictions, for example, such as alcoholism, drug abuse, overeating, and gambling, can mask a deep spiritual hunger or be the result of a crisis of meaning. In addressing these larger issues of meaning, we may be better equipped to help people overcome their difficulties.

THE FOUR WORLDS IN THERAPY

In my work with Sam, a forty-two-year-old man who came to see me about his chronic depression, loneliness, and sense of emotional deadness, the four-worlds healing model provided a particularly effective therapeutic paradigm. When he first started therapy, it seemed as though Sam were wearing an emotional straitjacket. He seemed to live in his head; he spoke in a complete monotone and rarely showed emotion. Sam also appeared to be visibly uncomfortable in his body, frequently holding himself rigidly still and hardly breathing. He gave the impression of being up against a wall, like the person in a circus act who is being used as a target for knife-throwing: one wrong move and he would be dead.

When I shared this image with him, Sam confided that in therapy he felt terrified of having to be spontaneous or show any feelings. He often rehearsed what he was going to say before our sessions in order to feel prepared to respond. When we explored the roots of his anxiety, Sam uncovered memories from his childhood of being repeatedly humiliated by his parents whenever he made a mistake. They often ridiculed his feelings or told him he wasn't really feeling what he said he was feeling. To deal with his parents' cruelty and lack of understanding of his emotional life, Sam had learned to cut himself off from his feelings. Whenever a feeling would arise, he would avoid it by leaving his body.

After several months of therapy, Sam had gained a lot of insight into his problem, but he was still unable to let go of control and allow himself to drop down to his emotions. He still seemed very fragmented and rigid. So I decided to try using the model of the four worlds to help Sam achieve greater self-integration.

Before he could truly feel his feelings, Sam first needed to learn how to ground his emotional experience in the body. Thus, for several months we began each session with a body-focused exercise, in which Sam learned to pay attention to and identify different sensations in his body, like tension or tightness in his shoulders or the sensation of warmth or cold in his chest. After he relaxed and identified the sensations in his body, I asked Sam to pay attention to any feelings or emotions that surfaced. As he did this, he began to notice that whenever a feeling arose, he was assaulted by a hostile inner voice that called him "weak" or "wimpy" for having the feeling. Even when his feeling seemed completely understandable, he found himself fighting this voice that continually tried to humiliate him for simply having feelings. I suggested that Sam visualize this shaming voice as a cartoonlike character, a predictable and unreasonable little guy who meant well but really wasn't being very helpful. By identifying and naming this voice, Sam felt more able to ignore its taunts. Instead of reacting to the voice, Sam could just acknowledge its presence and treat it like an old propaganda channel that incessantly broadcasts a message that he need not listen to anymore.

By repeatedly grounding his feelings in his bodily experience and then naming them, Sam was able to create links between his thinking (beriah), feeling (yetzirah), and physical self (assiyah). In the process he began to feel a greater sense of self-integration. The naming process provided Sam with a way of handling his feelings without being overwhelmed by them, as well as a means of staying connected to his body.

As Sam progressed in this work of self-integration, I introduced the spiritual dimension to our work. During each session, after he grounded himself in his body and named whatever feelings had arisen, I guided Sam into a deeper state of meditation in which he was instructed to see himself from the vantage point of the infinite, from God's perspective. After seeing himself through God's eyes for the first time, Sam broke down in tears. He later explained that his tears were tears of relief and gratitude. Imagining how he might be perceived by God, Sam felt, for the first time, a tremendous amount of compassion for himself, for the person who had experienced so much pain and loneliness in his life. When he viewed himself through God's eyes, he found that he not only was able to feel more self-acceptance but also attained more perspective on his problems. The meditation had reminded him that he was not just his problems and feelings but also a spark of light, a beloved child of the divine.

Over time, I noticed that Sam became more able to tolerate contra-

dictory feeling states. His vulnerable-child self could coexist alongside his adult self, allowing him to be weak and strong all at once. At
the same time, Sam realized that he need not define himself by any
of his parts, for his true essence was connected to a greater, integrated
whole. Ultimately, this is what we each seek to achieve through the
work of self-integration—namely, to be able to experience our full
being in all its richly layered dimensions.

Exercise

Healing in All Four Worlds

The following exercise can be used to facilitate healing in all four
dimensions of being.

Take a few moments to relax and center and become mindful of
your body and your breath. Pay attention to the different parts of
your breath—the in-breath, the out-breath, and the pause between
breaths. As you become more and more relaxed, allow your breathing
to slow down and deepen so that your neshima (breath) can connect
you with your neshama (soul). Feel yourself becoming fully present
as your body becomes ensouled through your breath. Take a moment
to scan your body from toe on up to head, noticing any tension or
discomfort that exists. Try to release any bodily tensions or holdings
by using your breath to send waves of relaxation to the spot that
needs release. Throughout this exercise use your breath as an anchor
for your awareness. If you find your mind wandering, just gently
bring your awareness back to your breath.

Connecting the Somatic Self (Assiyah) and the
Emotional Self (Yetzirah)

Now pick a feeling or problem that you wish to work with, perhaps one you are frequently troubled by, or pick a situation to which
you wish to bring greater insight or resolution. Now try to locate the
feeling or problematic situation in your body. Where do you feel it?
What changes do you notice in your body when you focus on this
problem situation? Try to ground your emotional experiences in your

bodily felt experience of them. It may be helpful to ask yourself, "How old is the *me* who feels this feeling?" By giving the feeling an "age" you may learn more about its origin. As you "name" the feeling, try to witness and experience it without judgment.

Cognitive Restructuring
HEALING IN BERIAH

Now become aware of thought patterns, such as self-judgment, that arise in relation to the feeling you are exploring. What is the habitual stance you take toward yourself around this and other similar feelings? What are your self-judgments about the feeling or situation? How else might you begin to think about the problem feeling? See if you can develop some flexibility in your way of thinking about it. Can you allow yourself to be with the pure feeling state, free of self-judgments and self-blame? See if you can let go of old myths you hold on to about yourself and allow new thoughts and meanings to emerge. Letting go of these old thought patterns frees you from the unnecessary pain that faulty beliefs create. For instance, instead of feeling a painful emotion plus the painful feeling of shame over having the emotion, see if you can just be in the pure feeling state without any self-judgment. Just be openhearted to yourself.

Gaining Ultimate Perspective
ASCENDING TO ATZILUT

Now let all your thoughts and feelings dissolve, focusing instead on pure white light. Imagine a river of white light flowing from the heavens down through your skull and filling your entire being. As you focus on the light, see if you can open yourself to experiencing the light of the infinite, the Or Ein Sof, allowing yourself to dissolve into the great ocean of pure beingness. Spend as much time as you like in this state, allowing yourself to simply bask in God's infinite love and radiant light.

Before you begin to return to your ordinary self, try to see yourself, for a moment, as God sees you—from the perspective of the infinite. See yourself through unconditionally loving eyes and let yourself be filled with deep compassion for the "you" who is grappling with the problem feeling that came to mind earlier in the meditation.

Grounding

Using whatever image is helpful for slowly returning to ordinary consciousness, such as descending a ladder or traveling back to earth through space, slowly return to your body and the physical space where you are. Take some deep breaths, open your eyes, and begin to notice your surroundings.

When you open your eyes and return to ordinary consciousness, you may notice that you have already begun to think and feel differently about the problem you chose to work on. See if you can experience greater spaciousness in relation to the issue, or an increased tolerance for contradiction or paradox.

DIVINE UNIFICATION

The Role of Mitzvot

All too often as we go about our daily lives and routines, we fall into a state of unconsciousness. We act without thinking and speak without reflecting on the feelings that may have prompted us to speak. It's as though our hearts and minds are disconnected from our bodies and we are a million miles from our emotional and spiritual center. From a kabbalistic perspective, these states of fragmentation result from a lack of integration between the different levels of our being.

One of the practices that Jewish mystics devised to enhance awareness and unify heart, mind, body, and spirit is the recitation of *yichudim,* or divine unifications. While these meditative phrases traditionally focus on divine unification—bringing together the transcendent and imminent aspect of divinity—they also serve to unify our own being. By reciting one of these mystical incantations prior to prayer or before performing a mitzvah, or sacred act, we become focused and centered, so that we act and speak with greater kavannah, mindfulness and intentionality. They enable us to unite body, heart, mind, and spirit in the wholehearted act of performing the mitzvah.

Yichudim typically begin with the following phrase, which focuses on unifying the transcendent and imminent, or male and female, aspects of God: "For the sake of the unification of the Holy Blessed One and the Shechinah, with awe and love, uniting the name of YH with VH. . . ." They then conclude by stating the particular mitzvah that one intends to do and the spiritual effect that one hopes to achieve through its performance. For instance, the sacred intention recited before putting on a prayer shawl, or tallit, contains the wish that as one's body is being wrapped in the ritual garment, one's soul should also be wrapped in God's light.

Bringing together the four letters of God's name symbolizes the joining together of the four worlds, for each of the letters of God's name is associated with one of the four worlds, or levels of being. The first letter, *yod,* corresponds to the most hidden and sublime of realms, known as atzilut, or the world of emanation. The first *heh* corresponds to beriah, the world of creation. The *vav* corresponds to yetzirah, the world of formation. And the second *heh* corresponds to assiyah, the world of doing and actualization, which includes the manifest, physical world in which we live.

The mitzvot also aim at joining together the disparate realms. The Hasidic masters point out that the word *mitzvah* itself, which typically is translated as "commandment," also signifies "joining," from the Hebrew root *tzavta,* or joined together. The implication is that the mitzvot facilitate the joining together of the part to the whole. This includes the joining of man to man and of man to God, as well as the integration of the individual person within herself. Mystically speaking, the mitzvot unite the upper and lower worlds, bringing spirit and matter, light and vessel, into harmonious balance. If it is a mitzvah, then even the most mundane physical act becomes a conduit for the flow of divine energy.

The mitzvot also help us ground our highest ideals in concrete action, so that we anchor our beliefs in our actions. Otherwise it's easy to live in our heads, absorbed in our ideas without ever manifesting them in the real world. For example, the many practical mitzvot, or *g'milut chassadim* (acts of loving-kindness), such as visiting the sick and caring for the poor, the elderly, and disadvantaged members of the community, allow us to ground our belief in God's unity in our daily actions. By treating others with compassion, acting as though they are a part of us, we express our belief in God's unity in embodied action.

The spiritual practice of reciting yichudim prior to the performance of a mitzvah can be seen as a mystical version of what Freud and Jung sought to accomplish through analysis. In effect by uniting the first two letters of God's name with the last two letters of God's name, we bring together the hidden (YH) and revealed (VH) dimensions of divinity, for God is both hidden and revealed, *nigleh ve'nistar*.

So it is also in psychoanalytic theory, where the cause of neurosis is understood to be an inner sense of divisiveness, and the path to healing involves the "re-membering" and reintegration of repressed emotions and impulses. Freud believed that when powerful sexual or aggressive impulses become overly repressed or split off from consciousness, they lead to distressing symptoms. Through analysis one learns how to become attuned to the unconscious, so that its contents may be continually assimilated by the ego, for in order to maintain a state of health and wholeness, the conscious and unconscious realms of our being must be continually unified.

Like Freud, the Ba'al Shem Tov also saw memory as an essential component of healing. When he said that "remembering is the source of redemption," he was referring to both meanings of the word *remember*; for in addition to the role of memory in healing, re-*membering* also implies the reassembling of the dis-membered (forgotten) and fragmented parts of the self.

THE DAILY LITURGY

A Journey through the Four Worlds

In Jewish practice, the daily morning liturgy, or *Shacharit* service, is structured as a meditative journey through the four worlds. By reciting the morning prayers one can achieve a sense of balance and integration among the four dimensions of being.

The service itself begins with a series of blessings and readings that focus awareness on the world of assiyah, bringing our attention to the body and the breath. The next section of the morning service, characterized by its heart-opening prayers of praise and thanksgiving, takes us into the feeling realm of yetzirah. This section begins with the *baruch she'amar* prayer, blessing the "One who spoke the world into being" and celebrating the creative power of the word. Next, we enter the world of beriah, the contemplative part of the morning service, beginning with the *barechu,* or call to prayer, which is followed by a series of meditative prayers focused on the ongoing nature of creation, light, and divine love. This contemplative part of the service contains the Shema, the affirmation of divine oneness, and a series of prayers that recount the Exodus and the crossing of the Red Sea. These prayers lead up to the silent standing prayer, or *amidah,* which brings us into the realm of atzilut, or pure spirit. As we stand in the presence of God, we become God's mouthpiece, as it were, and allow God to pray through us.[10] When recited with intentionality, or kavannah, the traditional liturgy can help us become grounded in the different dimensions of our being.

FOUR-WORLDS MEDITATION

For those who find meditation more accessible than prayer, the following guided meditation through the four worlds can be used to embody the four realms of being. This meditation focuses on the experience of *kedusha*—holiness or spiritual transparency—by using the Hebrew word *kadosh* (holy) as a mantra. The meditation is structured like the daily Shacharit liturgy as a journey through the four worlds, from assiyah to atzilut and back again, focusing on bringing holiness into each world or level of our experience.

Take a moment to relax, center, and become attuned to your breath. Let yourself breathe effortlessly, as though you are being breathed by the breath of all life. Now bring your awareness to your body. Allow yourself to experience the holiness of your body.

Now as you breathe in, whisper the sound *ka* just under your breath as you begin to say the word *kadosh*. Having breathed in *ka,* now breathe out *dosh*. Do this three times, breathing in *ka* and breathing out *dosh*. After taking these three breaths, just sit silently for a few minutes and experience your body as a holy, shining vessel of light. Let yourself experience the holiness of your body.

Now turn your attention to your heart-center and once again breathe in *ka* and breath out *dosh*. Do this three times as before and then sit silently and just allow yourself to feel the holiness of an open heart and the holiness life itself.

Now turn your attention to your mind and become aware of your ability to fill your mind with holy thoughts. And once more, take three breaths, breathing in *ka* and breathing out *dosh*. As you do this, allow your mind to become aligned with the divine mind. As you sit silently for a few minutes, make an affirmation to fill your mind today with loving and holy thoughts. Feel the creative power that is unleashed in you when you align your mind with the divine mind.

Now bring your awareness to the space above your head and surrounding your body as you open yourself to the holiness of your neshama, or soul. Once more take three deep breaths, breathing in *ka* and breathing out *dosh*. As you sit silently for a few minutes, let yourself experience spiritual transparency as you contemplate how you might be an instrument of the divine will. Experience how the light of the infinite fills you and all creation. Allow yourself to rest in the world of atzilut, where all things are one and connected with their source.

As you begin your descent from the world of atzilut back to assiyah, imagine that you can take one last whiff of the fragrance of atzilut, like the sweet smell of a flower from the Garden of Eden, and bring that sweetness back with you as you once again pause to align your mind with the divine mind. Sense your heart, open and full. And as you return to your body, try to ground your awareness of the holiness you have sensed in the upper realms within your body, in this world of assiyah.

13

THE MESSIANIC TORAH
Life as Sacred Narrative

Rabbi Hanina, the son of Rabbi Issi, said: Sometimes
God speaks to a person from the hairs on his head.
—*Midrash Bereishit Raba 4:4*

The Torah is eternal and does not exist in time. The
question then arises, How is it possible to tell a story
in an entity that exists outside of time? The truth is
that the story always exists, at all times. Man is also a
microcosm (of the entire universe); therefore, each
story (in the Torah) also exists in man.
—*The Maggid of Mezerich*

When Rabbi Shneur Zalman of Liadi was
on his way to Mezerich to study with Rabbi Dov Baer, the great
Maggid, he was asked why he wasn't instead going to study with
Rabbi Elijah, the Gaon (genius) of Vilna, the most illustrious Torah
scholar of the generation. Shneur Zalman responded that one goes to
Vilna to learn *how to learn* Torah; he, however, was going to Mezerich to learn how to *become* a *sefer Torah* (Torah scroll).

Rabbi Shneur Zalman's response captures one of the unique inno-
vations of Hasidism—namely, the idea that Torah study is not just
about acquiring knowledge but also about personal transformation.
What one knows is not so important as how one embodies that

knowledge in one's life and very being. For the Hasidic masters, the aim was not just to *know* the story but to *become* the story, to live the story fully and deeply in all of one's thoughts, feelings, and actions.

And so among Hasidim, the *ma'aseh*—the tale spun from the real-life stories of saints and simple pious Jews—became as important a focus of study as the ancient sacred texts. Disciples went to the rebbe often to learn the most mundane and ordinary things. When Rabbi Leib Sures, a disciple of the Maggid of Mezerich, was asked what he hoped to learn from his visit to the rebbe, he responded that he intended to learn how the Maggid tied his shoelaces. In other words, he wanted to learn how the rebbe embodied his knowledge in the most ordinary of daily acts.

The radical notion that our lives and actions can become living embodiments of Torah is expressed by Rabbi Yehudah Aryeh Leib of Ger in the opening lines of his Torah commentary, the *Sefat Emet:* "All the sections that tell of the patriarchs are there to show how Torah was made out of their actions. . . . The task of humans is to make this clear, to show how every deed takes place through the life-energy of God . . . for the human being is a partner in the act of Creation."[1]

The Torah, as the *Sefat Emet* points out, does not launch right into the laws revealed at Sinai but begins with the stories of the patriarchs and matriarchs. It begins that way to teach us how, by aligning ourselves with the divine life force, we can transform our lives and deeds into words of Torah, so that our lives become sacred narratives.

REDIGGING THE ANCIENT WELLS OF TORAH

According to Hasidic thought, the dynamic reciprocity that exists between life and sacred writ was captured in the biblical metaphor of the well. As we know, many stories in the Bible take place at a well, or *be'er.*[2] As shepherdesses and shepherds, the matriarchs and patriarchs were all involved in digging and maintaining wells. The well was a meeting place where people gathered in ancient times to converse, share news, and engage in business transactions; it was also the site where many of the patriarchs and matriarchs met their *bash-ert,* or intended marriage partner.

But when the Torah speaks of wells, it is not referring simply to wells of water but also to the deep inner wellsprings of spiritual wisdom—the wisdom of the unconscious that wells up from the depth of our being. This wisdom of the depths is what enables us to penetrate the mysteries of Torah, as well as the very mysteries of existence. Interestingly, the Hebrew word for well, *be'er,* is also used to imply the clarification of meaning, the *be'ur,* that we seek when we engage in the study of a sacred text. Just as the matriarchs and patriarchs each dug wells, revealing sources of life-giving waters, each of us must dig deep to find meaning in the sacred narratives of our lives. The very nature of Torah study is tied into this process of renewal, in which we redig the ancient wells over and over again, each time finding new life and nourishment for the soul through our insights.

Redigging wells is an old tradition in Jewish life. According to Genesis 26:18–19, Isaac "excavated the wells of water that were dug in the days of Abraham his father and were plugged up by the Philistines after Abraham's death. And he [Isaac] called them by the same names that his father called them. And Isaac's workers dug in the riverbed and found there a well of living waters."

Abraham was the first to open up the wells of living waters. Yet his son Isaac had to reexcavate the very same wells that his father had dug in his day. And so it is that each generation must reopen the access-ways to the well of living waters, the Torah. We learn to access these deeper dimensions of Torah (be'ur) when we live by the well (be'er).

But what does it really mean to live by the well? Living by the well of Torah requires that we be attentive to the ongoing flow of the spirit that perennially emerges from the depths of our being. It means being attuned to the wisdom of the unconscious and the mysteries of the soul. As we seek this kind of living relationship with spirit, our Torah study extends beyond the boundaries of the *beit midrash* (house of study) and penetrates every area of our lives. To live by the well is to allow the boundaries that separate our ordinary lives from the sacred dimension to dissolve, so that the divine life force that can be found everywhere, and in everything, may be revealed. We just have to dig beneath the surface, as Rabbi Yehudah Aryeh Leib points out when he writes that, in biblical narrative, "finding wells and underground water sources suggests that Torah, which is referred to as water, can be found in every place (situation) only it is hidden. According to our efforts we can always find, in every situation, the light of the Torah and the inner lifeforce from the Life of all Life (God). . . . And all [these stories] teach that every place has hidden sparks of light. . . . The well symbolizes the hidden point of divinity. We must remove the external covering to reveal the innermost point."[3]

Torah study is essentially about discovering the intersection between our lives and the life of God. It is about living mindfully and awakening to the profound meaning of all existence as a mirror of the divine—of God coming to know God through embodied form. The Jewish people have been engaged in this intimate love relationship with God through Torah for the past three and a half millennia. As with an earthly lover, we have both discovered and transcended ourselves through our relationship with the sacred texts. The Torah has been the repository of the deepest projections of our souls, and like a Rorschach inkblot, it has also revealed the deepest secrets of our souls to us. As God is said to have looked into the Torah in order to learn how to create the world, Jews have used the Torah in order to awaken and find a healing pathway back to God.

The Torah is an evolving body of wisdom teachings that the Jewish people have passed on from generation to generation. Over the centuries it has evolved in its dimensionality. What began as the "heavenly" revealed written word, or *Torah she'bichtav,* evolved into an oral tradition, *Torah she'be'al peh,* when the rabbis discovered that divine revelation spoke within their minds and hearts as they engaged in Torah study, and that their *own* words could become a source of Torah. And in Hasidism we find the beginnings of a new revelatory process in which the boundaries of Torah expanded beyond scripture and commentaries to include our own stories. Hasidism espoused the radical notion that each of our lives is a sacred narrative and that each of our stories is part of the messianic Torah—a future scroll that will be revealed in the messianic era. I like to think of this new spiritual paradigm as *Torah she'be'al guf,* the embodied Torah.

VIEWING LIFE THROUGH THE LENS OF SACRED NARRATIVE

To experience our lives as living embodiments of Torah is to know that our lives have meaning and purpose. It is also a call to live life with greater awareness and mindfulness of the awesome holiness of each moment. Imagine, for instance, if we were to regard every encounter we had in the course of a day as a *parasha,* or chapter of Torah. How might that awareness deepen our ability to be fully present to the moment?

Though I don't think Freud was consciously aware of these kinds of questions, in his discovery of the unconscious he revealed that we are all much like a Torah scroll. In fact, many of the very same interpretive tools (word associations, puns, free association/the juxtaposition of ideas) that once captured the imagination of biblical scholars were transferred by psychoanalysis from the domain of sacred text to the human soul.[4] And, just as the Torah was considered to have both a "revealed" (*nigleh*) and an infinitely vast "concealed" (*nistar*) dimension, so did psychoanalysis make it clear that the unconscious mind is far more vast and complex than the conscious mind. Much like the "seventy faces," or possible meanings, that the rabbis say coexist within every word of Torah,[5] psychoanalysis revealed the multiple and often contradictory voices, impulses, and feelings that can coexist within each individual person. It's no great wonder that so many Jewish people have been attracted to the field of psychoanalysis, for Jews have been engaged in the psychoanalysis of scriptures for aeons.

I know that when I sit with my clients and listen to their stories, attuning myself to all the many nuances of communication—verbal and nonverbal, symbolic and literal, direct and indirect—I often feel as though I am studying a sacred text. And I realize that whatever I am actually picking up is only the tip of the divine iceberg. For ultimately, every person is an awesome mystery, a complete sefer Torah (Torah scroll) in and of herself, with the potential for infinite meaning.

The rabbis once said that a person who studies Torah becomes like an ever-renewing spring. We all can have access to this inexhaustible source of renewal, because each of us, like every detail of creation, has within him a spark of the infinite. This presence of the infinite, which permeates all things, is waiting to be revealed through each of us in our own unique way.

In my own life, the reciprocity between life and sacred text has both influenced and illuminated my way. By projecting myself into the ancient sacred stories over and over again, I have been able to discover and give voice to the deeper dimensions of my being. And by living my life as fully as possible on as many levels as possible, I have begun to experience my own life as a sacred narrative—a living embodiment of Torah. Something always shifts in my experience of life when I view it through the lens of sacred narrative. Instead of the disjointed and often incomplete stories that make up my life, a thread of meaning begins to weave the chapters together, revealing their hidden connections. My personal struggles are no longer simply personal when viewed in a context where the personal reflects the collective and divine dimensions of reality.

At different times in my life, different Jewish myths have guided my journey. In my youth and early adulthood, the miraculous story of the Exodus held deep resonance for my lived experience. During the early years of my spiritual journey, when I lived in Israel, life felt amazingly providential—full of magic and synchronicity. I often felt that, like the Israelites wandering in the desert between Egypt and the Promised Land, I was eating manna from heaven and being guided by the Divine Presence.

As I have grown older, however, I find that Judaism's myths of exile—both divine and human—more closely reflect the challenges I now face on the spiritual journey. The Book of Esther, which we read on the holiday of Purim, is one of the stories of exile that have been helpful guides to me. It was in reading and rereading the Book of Esther over many years that I began to see my own life through the lens of sacred narrative.

The story takes place during the years following the destruction of the first Temple in Jerusalem, when the Jews living in exile in the ancient kingdoms of Persia and Media faced the threat of genocide. As a result of a series of seemingly disconnected events that take place over a nine-year time span, not only are the Jews saved but they also begin to rebuild and renew their national identity. The creation of the holiday of Purim, celebrating their deliverance, marked the beginning of a new Jewish era in which the Torah she'be'al peh, or oral tradition, began to flourish. The age of transcendent miracles and prophecy was coming to a close; God was in hiding; but, at the same time, in this dark night of exile the Jewish people discovered a new dimension of spiritual creativity—their own power to generate Torah.[6]

The story of Esther, according to religious tradition, must be read from a sacred scroll, or a *megillah*, which is slowly unrolled as the rather lengthy Purim plot unfolds. The popular Yiddish phrase, a *gantze megillah*, refers to stories, like the Purim tale, that seemingly go on and on. So without going into a gantze megillah myself, here are some of the important highlights from the tale that may help you understand my obsession with Purim.

The story of Esther begins in the third year of King Ahashverosh's reign when he has a fight with his queen, Vashti, that results in her removal. Ahashverosh then sets out to find a new queen. A beauty pageant is organized and beautiful women from all over the kingdom are brought to the palace to take part in it. Esther, a Jewish orphan whose parents were exiled from the holy land by King Nebuchadnez-zar, is among the women taken against their will into the king's harem. When she is chosen from among *all* the women in the land to be the new queen there is a sense that divine providence must be at work, though the meaning and significance of her mysterious fate will remain unclear for nine long years. During this time, Esther, whose name implies hiddenness (from the Hebrew root *seter*), keeps her true identity hidden until the critical moment when it becomes clear that she can save her people by "coming out" to the king as a

Jewess. This critical moment comes about in the twelfth year of the king's reign, when he is advised by his wicked adviser, Haman, that the Jewish people who live scattered throughout his lands pose a threat. In truth, Haman has a personal vendetta against Mordecai, because of his refusal to bow down to him. In his grandiosity Haman decides to take revenge not just against Mordecai but against his entire people! In a drunken stupor, the king hastily signs Haman's decree aimed at inciting the people of Persia and Media to kill and plunder all the Jews living in the kingdom. This attack was to take place on the day chosen by Haman's lottery, or *purim*.

Upon hearing about the decree from her uncle, Queen Esther finally reveals her true identity to the king and makes an impassioned plea to the king to counter Haman's evil decree, by allowing the Jews to defend themselves against their attackers. At this point the plot reverses itself. The archetypal villain, Haman—symbol of evil incarnate—is hung on the very gallows he built for his nemesis, Mordecai. Mordecai is recognized and rewarded by the king as a loyal servant, and instead of being annihilated, the Jewish people successfully defend themselves against their attackers. The Jews then celebrate their deliverance by creating a new holiday they call Purim, in keeping with the theme of Haman's lots.

Unlike the transcendent miracles found in earlier Biblical tales, the miracle of Purim is considered to be a "hidden" miracle, or *nes nistar*—like the name and identity of its heroine, Esther. Not only are there no overt miracles in the megillah, God's name does not even appear in it, except as a hidden acrostic. When Esther invites the king and Haman to a banquet by saying *"Yavo Hamelech Vehaman Hayom"* (May the King and Haman come today), she inscribes the divine name YHVH into the invitation as if to invite God, the king of kings, to the banquet. Yet all the events that occur in this story, when strung together like beads on a chain, form a sublime serendipity. The God *of* exile is a God *in* exile, restrained and confined to the ordinary course of events yet working behind the scenes and speaking between the lines. In the megillah, the mystical significance of exile is conveyed through the veiling and cloaking of the divine within the ordinary course of events. The megillah teaches us to read secular history as sacred writ, as the slow yet meaningful unfolding of the will of God.

I love the Book of Esther precisely because it is so much like our lives—full of mystery and hidden plot twists. Esther, whose name implies hiddenness, teaches us about God's mysterious pathways in our lives. In the Purim story, what begins as bad luck is, in the end, reversed into good fortune; what initially appear to be chance events in the plot turn out to be providential. While the casting of lots suggests a certain randomness, the unfolding of events in the Megillah reveals that nothing happens by chance alone. Even those events that appear arbitrary or unlucky—part of the cosmic lottery, as it were—turn out in the end to be deeply meaningful.

For years Esther probably struggled to understand why she, a Jewess, had been chosen to be the queen of Persia and Media. Taken against her will to be part of the king's harem, Esther waits nine long years before the mysterious events of her life reveal their significance and meaning. It is only when Esther finds herself in a unique position to save her people[7] that the providential nature of her strange fate becomes clear, as we learn from Mordecai's impassioned words to her: "Who knows if only for the sake of this moment in time, you were chosen as queen" (Esther 4:14). Esther's personal destiny, a complete conundrum until then, suddenly takes on a sense of historic urgency and significance. Suddenly it becomes clear that she must put her life on the line to save her people.

In this stage of my own spiritual journey I, like Esther, find myself struggling to discover the hidden hand of the divine in the many obscure and inexplicable aspects of my life. I must, through my own efforts, weave the threads of meaning that connect my life to the larger whole. In particular I have struggled to make sense of the events that led me to return to the Diaspora after having made aliya to Israel in my youth. Though I had intended to spend my life in Israel, fate brought me back to California, where my destiny has unfolded in ways I could never have imagined. Though I struggle with self-doubt at times, wondering whether I have made the right choices, when I see my own life as though it were a sacred narrative, inscribed on a megillah (scroll), the scattered pieces of the puzzle begin to come together, and a coherent story emerges. This story reveals how all the conscious and unconscious choices I have made, as well as the random, chance events that have shaped my being, come together in a meaningful fashion to reveal my unique essence— what the contemporary Torah scholar and philosopher Rabbi Marc Gafni calls the soul print.[8]

Oddly enough, one of my earliest childhood memories is of winning a contest for the best Queen Esther costume, along with my brother, who came dressed as Mordecai, in the Sunday school Purim carnival. A snapshot of my brother and me dressed in our handmade Purim costumes (thanks to my mother's gift as a seamstress) hung on the hallway wall throughout our childhood. When I look at my life as a sacred narrative, it seems as though that photo were an auspicious signpost, pointing toward a time in my future when I would turn to this story, whose heroine shares my Hebrew name, to make sense of my life. It's as though the seeds of my essential self—who I have become—were already present in that early childhood snapshot. In these moments I have a sense that my life has unfolded exactly as it had to, mistakes and all.

PURIM AND POSTMESSIANIC CONSCIOUSNESS

The story of Esther is read each year on the early-spring holiday of Purim. While often thought of as a children's masquerade holiday, Purim's ritual celebration is rich in mystical wisdom. In the rabbinic tradition it was awarded a special, postmessianic status and was viewed as being as holy as (some say even holier than) Yom Kippur. "In the future," says the Talmud, "when all the holidays become obsolete, only Purim (and some say Yom Kippur) will be observed!"[9] Why all the fuss about Purim? And what is the significance of its "postmessianic" status?

On Purim, the mystics say, we reach the highest level of nondual awareness, where good and evil, sacred and profane, unite to form a seamless unity. God's name may be absent from the Megillah, but this apparent absence simply reflects the reality of God's hiddenness in this world. The Hebrew expression *Megillat Esther* (literally, the Scroll of Esther) is, in fact, a play on the words *megale hester,* meaning "to reveal that which is hidden."[10] The Megillah of Esther is essentially a metaphor for how the hidden hand of the divine, and the hidden aspects of our own souls, are revealed to us. God's presence is indeed concealed in this world, as it is in each of our lives. Yet it is through its very concealment within all things—good and bad, light and dark—that the divine presence is paradoxically revealed, for everything in this world is revealed through its opposite: God's unity is revealed through the multiplicity and apparent duality of creation; good is made possible by the existence of evil; darkness offers light its luminosity; and exile makes redemption a possibility.[11]

This is the paradoxical, crazy wisdom of Purim. What begins as a story about the archetypal battle between the forces of good and evil, light and dark, is transformed by Purim's ritual observance into a celebration of the nondual, for as the rabbis said, "One must become intoxicated on Purim to the point of 'not knowing' the difference between cursed is Haman and blessed is Mordecai."[12] For a people who practice extreme restraint of impulses the rest of the year, this is a rather strange injunction. Though some people take this command literally and get drunk on Purim, the Sefat Emet suggests a mystical understanding of the phrase "to the point of not-knowing." To become intoxicated to the point where one no longer can distinguish between hero and villain or good and evil, says the Sefas Emes, is to transcend all dualism. Intoxication to the point of not knowing—*ad d'lo yada*—also hints that on Purim we must go beyond *knowing* with our minds, for on Purim we transcend the tree of *knowledge* of good and evil and instead reach for the tree of life, or unitive consciousness. Purim, then, is a celebration of that future time when "God will be One and God's name One" (Zachariah 14:9). And in celebrating this holiday we bring that future consciousness into the here and now of our ordinary lives.

To be a person of faith in our day demands that we transcend the tree of knowledge. It means that we have to stop dividing the world into good guys and bad guys and go beyond all dualisms and divisions. Only when we begin to embrace the messianic vision of a unity that is born out of multiplicity will the reconfigured vessel of creation, made up of all the broken pieces, be able to hold the light of the Infinite One.

THE MESSIANIC TORAH

We began our journey into Jewish spiritual healing by exploring several Jewish myths about brokenness and wholeness. But a discussion about Jewish spiritual healing is not complete without examining another theme that captured the imagination of the rabbis—the theme of wholeheartedness. This theme appears most clearly in a midrash associated with the Book of Ruth.

The midrash begins by describing a discussion among several rabbis who were studying scriptures together. Fascinated by the relationship between life and sacred narrative, they begin to wonder about how the lives of biblical characters were transformed into words of Torah, or sacred writ. Their discussion focuses on the lives of three biblical figures they fault with a lack of wholeheartedness. These three figures are Reuven (Joseph's brother), Aaron (Moses' brother), and Boaz (Ruth's benefactor and future husband). Each of these characters, according to the rabbis, acted with apparent generosity, but on some subtle level they held back and failed to give of themselves wholeheartedly.[13]

Reuven, for instance, ostensibly stands up to his brothers when they plot to kill Joseph. He attempts to save his brother by proposing that they throw Joseph into a pit rather than kill him, and he secretly plans to return and rescue Joseph when the brothers are not looking. Reuven's intentions are good, but by not acting more boldly and assertively on his loving impulse, he misses the opportunity to save his brother and to influence history for all eternity. As Genesis 37:29–30 records, he later "returned to the pit and behold Joseph was no longer in the pit; And he rent his garments in grief. And he returned to his brothers and said, 'The boy is not there, and I, where shall I go.'" By not acting wholeheartedly, Reuven will have to live the rest of his life knowing he failed to show up fully for his brother.

When Aaron greets his brother, Moses, upon Moses' return from

Midian after not having seen him for forty years, the Torah says that "he went and met him at the mountain of God and he kissed him" (Exodus 4:27). Though Aaron greets his brother with "joy in his heart," the midrash wonders why, after decades apart, Aaron does not show more affection or excitement. In noting that Aaron's joy seems muted, the midrash suggests that he was holding back. Perhaps he rejoices in his heart but is not able to show his joy with words and deeds. It's not clear from the midrash why this would be so. Perhaps Aaron's personality is simply restrained. Or perhaps he is plagued by mixed emotions—happy to see his brother but unconsciously jealous that his brother and not he was chosen to be the redeemer. Whatever his reason for holding back, the midrash faults him for a lack of wholeheartedness.

When Ruth comes to glean at Boaz's fields she is destitute. Boaz is kind to her and gives her extra grain, yet the midrash claims he could have been so much more generous. He gives, but his giving is measured. Somehow, the midrash seems to be suggesting, Boaz is afraid to show the depth of the love and generosity he feels in his heart. He holds back.

Why do these characters hold back? Why do any of us hold back? Are we simply too embarrassed to show the fullness of our love and true being? Is it because, when we were kids, our parents failed to receive all our gifts of love and exuberance? Do we hold back so as not to risk feeling that old childhood pain of nonrecognition once more? Whatever the cause, the rabbis who wrote this midrash are trying to teach us that we find our eternity only by giving ourselves wholeheartedly to life—and not holding back.

By holding back in this way, all three biblical figures missed an opportunity to influence all eternity through their actions. If only they had known that their actions were being written up in scriptures, laments the midrash, they would have acted more wholeheartedly. According to the midrash,

> Reb Yitzhak said: "We learn from the story of Ruth and Boaz that when a person performs a mitzvah, he should do it with a whole heart. For had Reuven known that his

actions were being written down in scriptures for all times, as the Torah wrote 'Reuven heard and saved him (Joseph) from their hands,' [Genesis 37:22] he would have carried his brother Joseph on his own shoulder straight back to his father! Had Aaron known that his actions were being written down in scriptures, he would have greeted his brother Moses with drums and dance. Had Boaz known that his actions would be written up in the text as 'he gave her a bit of corn,' he would have fed her [Ruth] stuffed veal."[14]

The midrash then goes on to challenge each of us to live our lives with greater mindfulness and openheartedness—to live each moment as though our deeds were being recorded in a sacred scroll, the Torah of the Messiah. According to the midrash, "Rebbe Kohen and Rebbe Yehoshua of Sachnin in the name of Rebbe Yehoshua ben Levi said: In the past a man performed a mitzvah and the prophet wrote it down. Now, when a person performs a mitzvah who writes it? Elijah and the Messiah. And God seals it."[15]

The messianic Torah alluded to in this midrash is the cumulative spiritual work of all the generations. It is composed of the stories of each of our lives, as we live mindfully and wholeheartedly from the depth of our being. Seeing our lives as living embodiments of Torah is an invitation to live life with a greater awareness of the holiness of each moment. Each of us, like the three characters mentioned in the midrash, has the power to influence life for the better through our deeds. This influence reaches out to eternity. Ultimately, every person is an awesome mystery, a complete sefer Torah in and of herself, as Reb Tzaddok Ha'Cohen of Lublin suggests, "from God's perspective . . . the souls of Israel are the intended fruit of creation and they contain within them the entire Torah, only it is inaccessible [*satum*] and the [written] Torah is its interpretation. . . . The [written] Torah itself comes to reveal the depths that are hidden in every single soul of Israel."[16] Essentially, then, *we* are the true revelation of God's in-finite being, "the intended fruit of creation." We contain within us the entire Torah, while the scriptures come "to reveal the depths that are hidden in every single soul."

WHERE TO BEGIN?

In this book I have attempted to share some of the ways that Jewish mystical teachings and mythology have inspired my life and my work as a healer. One of my hopes in writing this book was to inspire you, the reader, to seek out your own personal relationship with the tradition.

Getting started on developing a Jewish spiritual practice can feel rather overwhelming at first. Judaism is so vast; with so many words, ideas, customs, and practices. Where to begin? The Ba'al Shem Tov offers words of advice for getting started on the path. He once said that if you observe even just one single mitzvah or spiritual practice with love and joy, it is as though you have kept the entire Torah. For, as he pointed out, "whenever we grasp hold of any part of [God's] unity, we grasp it in its totality. This is true even when a person holds on to its outermost 'edge.' The Torah and mitzvot emanate from God's essential being which is true unity, so when you observe even a single mitzvah with love and proper devotion, you grasp part of the [divine] unity through this [single] mitzvah."[17] Sometimes, finding just one spiritual practice that we do wholeheartedly with joy can have a profound effect on our lives. This may be what Rabbi Shlomo Carlebach had in mind when he said that sometimes just knowing one holy word or even just one holy letter is enough to open up all the gates of heaven. In the spirit of that one holy letter, I would like to share a short tale I once heard from a Sufi master. Since I cannot recall the names and setting of the story, I have recast it as a Jewish legend.

There once was a poor illiterate Jew named Joseph who lived in Baghdad. His family had been so poor that he never was able to attend school, and so he never learned to read. One day Joseph went to the town *melamed,* the Hebrew teacher, and begged him to teach him the aleph-bet (Hebrew alphabet). The melamed was a compassionate man with heart, and so he agreed to teach Joseph the holy

letters. Using a crude kind of chalk, the melamed proceeded to write
the first letter, the *aleph,* on the practice wall he used with his students. As he finished demonstrating the *aleph,* the melamed told Joseph that this letter, which is essentially a silent letter, was equal to
one. (Hebrew letters also serve as numbers.) Joseph picked up a piece
of chalk and copied the letter over and over again until he perfected
it. The melamed was ready to move on to the letter *bet* (the numerical
equivalent of two), but before he could say a word, Joseph ran off in
delight, singing the praises of *aleph.*

The melamed didn't hear a word from Joseph for two weeks.
Then one day Joseph returned with a big smile and announced that
he was ready to learn the *bet.* The melamed was a bit dismayed that
it had taken Joseph so long to master one single letter, and he began
thinking to himself, "If it took this simpleton two weeks to master
one letter, can you imagine how long it's going to take to learn the
entire aleph-bet!" But hiding his dismay, he said to Joseph, "Okay, so
let me see you write the *aleph.*" As Joseph proceeded to write the
aleph on the practice wall, the cement wall suddenly began to crack
and then shatter to bits. Amazed and awed by the deep wisdom and
spiritual power of this simple, unlearned man, the melamed bowed
in reverence.

To learn the secret of the silent letter *aleph* is to experience the
oneness of all being. This is all we really need to know. With the
wisdom of the silence of the *aleph,* we have the power to shatter
all the walls and remove all the veils that divide us from each other
and from God. As the vessels of creation must shatter to make room
for the light of the infinite, the walls that divide us must inevitably
be brought down so that the light and love of the Beloved One can
be revealed in all its many faces and guises.

EXERCISE

Your Own Sacred Narrative

Look back on your life and pick a segment of your life history, a
chapter that has a certain degree of mystery or one that has remained

unresolved in your mind, a piece of your personal history whose meaning you have struggled with. Imagine that this chapter of your life story is being retold in the voice of a scribe who is narrating and recording your life as sacred text. What happens to your perspective as you begin to view this part of your life as a parasha (chapter) of Torah?

Notes

CHAPTER 1: BROKEN HEARTS AND SHATTERED VESSELS

1. Andrew Harvey, *Hidden Journey: A Spiritual Awakening* (New York: Penguin Books, 1991), p. 54.
2. Zohar 2:184, author's own translation.
3. Rabbi Nathan of Nemerov, *Likutey Moharan II* 282. Collected teachings of Rabbi Nathan's teacher, Rabbi Nachman of Breslov.
4. *Midrash Tehillim Raba* 25:158b, author's own translation.
5. Nahum N. Glatzer, *Hammer on the Rock: A Midrash Reader* (New York: Schocken Books, 1948), pp. 62–63. Based on the *Midrash Ha'Gadol,* Genesis 38:1.
6. Courtney V. Cowart, "Voices from Ground Zero," *Spirituality and Health* (fall 2002): 39.
7. Hayim Vital, *Otzrot Hayim, Sha'ar Hagilgulim I.* Quoted in E. Shore, "Solomon's Request," *Parabola* (fall 2002): 59.
8. Quoted in Daniel Matt, *The Essential Kabbalah: The Heart of Jewish Mysticism* (San Francisco: HarperCollins, 1995), p. 96.

CHAPTER 2: THE BROKEN TABLETS OF SINAI

1. Rabbi Nachman's story, on which my narrative is based, is from the *Sipurei Ma'asiot Hadashim* and is quoted in Howard Schwartz, *Gabriel's Palace: Jewish Mystical Tales* (Oxford: Oxford University Press, 1993), p. 352.
2. This phrase is from Rashi's commentary on Exodus 19:2 ("and Israel encamped there facing the mountain"). In this passage, the Torah uncharacteristically uses the singular form of the verb *to encamp—vayichan.* From this Rashi infers that the people stood together "as one person with one heart" just prior to the revelation.
3. *Midrash Shmot Raba* 29:7.
4. *Midrash Aseret Ha'dibrot.* This ancient midrash was published in Eliezer

Horkonos, *Pirkay d'Rebbe Eliezer* (Jerusalem: Eshkol Books, 1973). A variation on this midrash also appears in the Talmud, Shabbat 88b.

5. Harvey, *Hidden Journey,* p. 38.
6. According to legend, all the Israelites who were present at Sinai were healed. The deaf were given back their hearing, the blind their sight, etc. See Rashi on Exodus 20:15.
7. *Midrash Shmot Raba, Ki Tisa,* author's own translation.

CHAPTER 3: THE WISDOM OF AYIN (NOTHINGNESS)

1. For a more complete discussion of the therapeutic use of ritual for major life transitions, see Estelle Frankel, "Creative Ritual: Adapting Rites of Passage to Psychotherapy for Times of Major Life Transition" (master's thesis, California State University at Hayward, 1982).
2. *Maggid Devarav Le Ya'acov* 54 (Jerusalem: Kollel Mevakesh Emunah, 1963), author's own translation. This book is a collection of teachings from the Maggid of Mezerich, compiled by his disciple, Rabbi Shlomo Lutzker, in 1781.
3. Quoted in Matt, *The Essential Kabbalah,* p. 71.
4. Levi Yitzhak of Berditchev, *Kedushat Ha'Levi, Bereishit (Genesis),* (Jerusalem, 1958), p. 5.
5. Levi Yitzhak of Berditchev, *Imray Tzaddikim, Or Ha'Emet,* translated by Aryeh Kaplan in *Meditation and Kabbalah* (York Beach, Maine: Red Wheel/Weiser, 1982), p. 302.
6. *Bittul ha'yesh* literally means to nullify one's ego or one's "somethingness."
7. *Maggid Devarav Le Ya'acov* 49, author's own translation.
8. Quoted in Mordecai Yosef of Izbitz, *Beis Ya'acov, Parashat Emor,* vol. 3. (Jerusalem: Va'ad Hasidei Radzin, 1975), pp. 239–240, author's own translation.
9. Harvey, *Hidden Journey,* p. 10.
10. Ibid.
11. This story, attributed to Rabbi Isaac of Acco, appears in Rabbi Eliahu Di Vidas's fifteenth-century book *Reishit Chochmah: Shaar Ha'ahavah* (The Beginning of Wisdom: The Gate of Love), p. 63. In its original form, the story is a parable for how single-minded devotion to and love of Torah (likened to a beautiful maiden) can bring one to the enlightened state of loving union with God.
12. *Midrash Otiot d'Rebbe Akiva Ha'Shalem, Nuscha Alef.* Unpublished translation by Rabbi Gershon Winkler.
13. Rabbi Nathan of Nemerov, *Likutey Moharan II* 56, author's own translation.

14. See Eliezer Shore, "Solomon's Request," *Parabola* (fall 2002): 56–59.

15. See Rashi's commentary on Genesis 29:11.

16. This theme, which appears in the *Midrash Bereishit Raba* 40:8, is discussed in the Torah commentary of Nachmanides throughout the Book of Genesis, beginning with Genesis 12.

17. The image of a raindrop falling into the ocean comes from the Maggid of Mezerich. See *Maggid Devarav Le Ya'acov* 66: "When you want to pray to God for something, think of your soul as part (a limb) of the Divine Presence, like a drop of water in the sea. Then pray for the needs of the Divine Presence."

18. Aryeh Kaplan, *Waters of Eden: The Mystery of the Mikveh* (New York: Union of Orthodox Jewish Congregations of America, 1993), pp. 62–67.

CHAPTER 4: HEALING THE SPLIT SELF

1. Martin Buber, *Tales of the Hasidim,* vol. 1, *The Early Masters,* trans. Olga Marx (New York: Schocken Books, 1947), p. 249.

2. This theme, which is integral to the Kabbalah's understanding of the self, is also a key notion in Jung's theory of individuation.

3. Shneur Zalman of Liadi, *Torat Or, Va'Yetse,* p. 44, author's own translation.

4. Quoted in Buber, *The Early Masters,* p. 243.

5. The expression used by the Maggid, "These and these are words of the living God" (*Eilu ve'eilu divray elohim chayim*), is used in the Mishneh in reference to the ancient dialectical debates between the academies of Hillel and Shamai. In all disputes for the sake of heaven, no one opinion can contain the entire truth, for all higher truths are dialectical and paradoxical in nature. Quoted in Buber, *The Early Masters.*

6. Quoted in Arthur Green and Barry W. Holtz, *Your Word Is Fire: The Hasidic Masters on Contemplative Prayer* (New York: Schocken Books, 1987), p. 58.

7. Quoted in Matt, *The Essential Kabbalah,* p. 72.

8. Rabbi Avraham Chaim of Zlatchov, *Orach Le'Chaim on Parashat Ha'azinu.*

9. Mishneh, *Pirkay Avot* 2:4

10. Buber, *The Early Masters,* pp. 199–200.

11. Jean Houston, *The Search for the Beloved: Journeys in Sacred Psychology* (Los Angeles: Jeremy P. Tarcher, Inc., 1987), pp. 192–193.

12. *Midrash Bamidbar Raba* 1:7, author's own translation.

13. Rabbi Yehudah Aryeh Leib, *The Language of Truth: The Torah*

Commentary of the Sefat Emet, trans. Arthur Green (Philadelphia: Jewish Publication Society, 1998), pp. 90–91.

14. The succinct prayer for healing that Moses says on behalf of Miriam became the classic Jewish prayer for healing. "Please God please heal *her*" was understood by the rabbis as referring not just to Miriam but also to the Shechinah, or divine presence—the embodiment of the divine. When we pray for anyone who is sick, it is as though we were praying for God's healing.

15. In Jungian thought we find a similar honoring of the need for a developmental approach to spiritual growth. Until the age of forty, we need to work on developing our egos and our sense of personal agency, whereas after forty, the process of individuation reverses that trend as we begin to surrender our individual local self to what Jung called the larger Self, with a capital S—which represents the totality of being, or the God-self.

16. Rabbi Levi Yitzhak of Berditchev, *Kedushat Ha'Levi, Parashat Ekev.*

17. Green and Holtz, *Your Word Is Fire,* p. 23.

18. The martyrology is a High Holy Day liturgy that describes the deaths of many great Jewish sages at the hands of the Roman Empire. These sages were said to have died for *kiddush hashem*—for the sake of heaven—for they were executed because of their belief in God's oneness.

19. Shunryu Suzuki, *Zen Mind, Beginner's Mind* (New York: Weatherhill, 1973), p. 62.

CHAPTER 5: THE MYTH OF THE EXODUS

1. Michael Lerner, *Jewish Renewal: A Path to Healing and Transformation* (New York: Putnam, 1994), pp. 65–68.

2. Shneur Zalman, *Likutey Amarim Tania,* bilingual edition (New York: Kehot Publication Society, 1984), pp. 247–249.

3. D. W. Winnicott, *Maternal Processes and the Facilitating Environment* (New York: International Universities Press, 1965), p. 60.

4. Stephen Mitchell, trans., *Tao Te Ching: A New English Version* (New York: HarperCollins, 1988), p. 1.

5. John Welwood, *Toward a Psychology of Awakening: Buddhism, Psychotherapy, and the Path of Personal and Spiritual Transformation* (Boston: Shambhala Publications, 2002), pp. 141–147.

6. Mastery of the secret healing power of the holy name became part of the esoteric wisdom of the practical Kabbalah. This wisdom was passed on to only a select few in each generation. The Ba'al Shem Tov, whose

name means literally "master of the good name," belonged to a secret lineage of Jewish mystics who had access to meditative and shamanistic healing practices associated with use of the holy name. Though we no longer have access to these esoteric practices, we can use meditation as a tool for accessing the infinite.

7. Larry Dossey, *Reinventing Medicine: Beyond Mind-Body to a New Era of Healing* (San Francisco: HarperSanFrancisco, 1999).

8. In the writings of the prophets, redemption is often portrayed as a birth process or "delivery." The rabbis also described the ordeals that would precede the final redemption as the birth pangs of the messianic era, or *chevlei mashiach.*

9. *Midrash Tanhuma, Be'Haalotcha,* translated by Noam Zion and David Dishon, in *A Different Night: The Family Participation Haggadah* (Jerusalem: Shalom Hartman Institute, 1997), p. 87.

10. Babylonian Talmud, Sota 11b.

11. Zohar (Parashat Va'era), Exodus 4.

12. Stanislav Grof, *Realms of the Human Unconscious* (New York: E.P. Dutton, 1976), p. 49.

13. Babylonian Talmud, Sota 37a.

14. *Midrash Mechilta, Beshalach* 13. The word that Moses uses for "stand still," *hityatzvu,* is the same verb used by the Torah to describe the Israelites' silent stance at the foot of Mt. Sinai just before they received divine revelation. "And they stood still [*Va'yityatzvu*] at the bottom of the mountain" (Exodus 19:17). A variant form of the same verb is used to denote prophetic vision in several other places in scriptures.

CHAPTER 6: TESHUVAH

1. "Great is repentance for it preceded the creation of the world." *Midrash Bereishit Raba* 1:8.

2. See Buber, *The Early Masters,* p. 241.

3. Zalman M. Schachter-Shalomi, *Spiritual Intimacy: A Study of Counseling in Hasidism* (Northvale, N.J.: Jason Aronson, 1996), p.178.

4. Quoted in V. E. Frankl, *The Doctor and the Soul: From Psychotherapy to Logotherapy* (New York: Vintage Books, 1986), p. 105.

5. "Great is repentance for it brings healing to the world" (Babylonian Talmud, Berachot 34a). "Teshuvah for the sinner is like medicine for illness" (*Midrash Tachkemoni* 44:24).

6. Martin Buber, *Tales of the Hasidim,* vol. 2, *The Later Masters,* trans. Olga Marx (New York: Shocken Books, 1947), p. 228.

7. Martin Buber, *The Way of Man: According to the Teaching of Hasidism*

(New York: The Citadel Press, 1966), pp. 36–41. This story, known as "The Treasure," is attributed to Reb Simha Bunam of Pzyhsha, who was said to have told it to all those who came to him in order to encourage them to look within rather than outside themselves for truth.

8. Earlier kabbalists practiced a much more esoteric and ascetic meditative practice, also called hitbodedut. It demanded intense personal preparation on the part of the initiate because it entailed total ego-annihilation.

CHAPTER 7: REPENTANCE, PSYCHOTHERAPY, AND HEALING

1. In his famous treatise on the laws and practices of teshuvah, Maimonides, the famous Spanish-Jewish philosopher and legalist, includes a lengthy discussion about free will—how every person is given the freedom and power to choose good over evil, to become a tzaddik (righteous) rather than a rasha (evildoer). See chapter 5 in Moses Maimonides, *Mishneh Torah, the Book of Knowledge, the Laws of Repentance* (Jerusalem: Mossad ha'Rav Kook Publishers, 1976).

2. *Midrash Tehillim Raba* 100:2.

3. As we explore the basic steps of teshuvah in the next section of this chapter, you may find that some are familiar to you, particularly if you have ever been involved in recovery work. This is because twelve-step programs adopt many of the classic components of teshuvah in their healing and recovery process.

4. Ben Bokser, *Abraham Isaac Kook: The Lights of Penitance, Lights of Holiness, The Moral Principles, Essays, Letters and Poems* (Mahwah, N.J.: Paulist Press, 1978), p. 49.

5. For a complete description of the stages of repentance see Moses Maimonides, "The Laws of Repentance," in *Mishneh Torah, the Book of Knowledge, the Laws of Repentance,* pp. 207–257.

6. Pinchas H. Peli, *Soloveitchik on Repentance: The Thought and Oral Discourses of Rabbi Joseph B. Soloveitchik* (Mahwah, N.J.: Paulist Press, 1984), p. 95.

7. For an in-depth discussion of the role of mourning in psychotherapy, see Peter Shabad, "Repetition and Incomplete Mourning: The Intergenerational Transmission of Traumatic Themes," *Psychoanalytic Psychology* 10 (1993), no. 1: pp. 61–75.

8. For a more complete discussion of the role of repentance in psychotherapy, see Estelle Frankel, "Repentance, Psychotherapy, and Healing: Through a Jewish Lens" in *Civic Repentance,* ed. Amitai Etzioni (New York: Rowman & Littlefield Publishers, 1999).

9. Moses Maimonides, *Mishneh Torah, the Book of Knowledge, the Foundational Principles of Torah* (Jerusalem: Mossad ha'Rav Kook Publishers, 1976), p. 9.

10. Moses Maimonides, *Mishneh Torah, the Book of Knowledge, the Laws of Repentance,* p. 254.

11. Babylonian Talmud, Sanhedrin 70a.

12. Babylonian Talmud, Succah 52a.

13. Peli, *Soloveitchik on Repentance,* p. 95.

14. *Tzidkat Ha'Tzaddik* 70, author's own translation.

15. *Tzidkat Ha'Tzaddik* 181, author's own translation.

16. Peli, *Soloveitchik on Repentance,* p. 95.

17. Adin Steinsaltz and Josy Eisenberg, *The Seven Lights: On the Major Jewish Festivals* (Northvale, N.J.: Jason Aronson, 2000), p. 58. Rabbi Schneur Zalman offers this interpretation in his explanation of the passage "before YHVH you shall be purified" (Leviticus 16:30), which describes the ancient Yom Kippur rites of atonement. Instead of reading "before YHVH" as referring to a place, he reads it as referring to time. In other words, "before YHVH" means before even God existed. It's a little bit mind-bending to imagine, but according to this interpretation, before there was a world, even YHVH did not yet exist. See *Likkutei Torah, Drushim l'Rosh Hashana* 61a.

18. See Leviticus 16.

19. See Nachmanides' Torah commentary on Leviticus 16:8.

20. Unless the high priest entered the holy of holies spiritually prepared, his life was endangered. According to rabbinic lore, there were occasions when the high priest did not emerge safely from the holy of holies but perished inside.

21. See the conclusion of the Jerusalem Talmud, Ta'anit, for a description of these joyous mating rites.

22. Bokser, *The Lights of Penitance,* p. 85.

CHAPTER 8: THE MYTH OF MESSIANIC REDEMPTION

1. Babylonian Talmud, Sanhedrin 98a.

2. On his maternal side, King David is a descendant of Ruth, who was a convert from the Moabite nation, who, according to scriptures, were descended from the incestuous relations that Lot had with his eldest daughter while in a drunken stupor following the destruction of Sodom and Gomorrah (Genesis 19:37). On his paternal side, King David is a descendant of Peretz, who was born from Yehuda's unconscious sexual relations with his daughter-in-law, Tamar (Genesis 38:29). There is yet

another legend of sexual scandal connected with the birth of King David. According to this legend, David's father, Jesse, intended to sleep with his maidservant the night that David was conceived. When David's mother heard about this from the maidservant, she secretly sneaked into the bedchamber, so that David was then conceived while his father thought he was sleeping with the maid rather than his wife!

3. David commits adultery with Bathsheba and then sees to it that her husband, Uriah the Hittite, is put on the front line in battle, where he is killed. See 2 Samuel 11.

4. See 1 Samuel 15 for a description of Saul's sin.

5. One Hasidic master pointed out how the *gematria,* or numerical value, of the Hebrew word for Messiah, *mashiach,* is 358, equal to that of the word *nachash,* or snake. Thus, the source of evil in biblical myth, the snake, is connected to the source of healing, the Messiah.

6. Babylonian Talmud, Yoma 22b. The expression used here, *kupah shel sheratzim,* implies that one has been made impure by contact with impure creatures.

7. Jerusalem Talmud, Berachot 2:4; *Midrash Eicha Raba* 1:57.

8. Buber, *The Early Masters,* p. 123.

9. C. Jesse Groesbeck, "The Archetypal Image of the Wounded Healer," *Journal of Analytic Psychology* 20 (1975): 122–145.

10. Babylonian Talmud, Megillah 13b.

11. This notion fits well with the theory of dissipative structures formulated by the famous chemist Ilya Prigogine. The basic principle of his theory is that complex structures evolve toward greater complexity when they are exposed to extreme stresses or perturbations that shake up the system, causing a creative reordering and transformation. It is their essential vulnerability or openness to perturbations that enables such complex structures to be transformed, so in a certain sense their fragility is the key to their growth. In contrast, less vulnerable, more insulated structures tend to resist change, and as a result, they are likely to stagnate. For a discussion of how Prigogine's theory of dissipative structures applies to healing, see Larry Dossey, *Space, Time, and Medicine* (Boulder: Shambhala Publications, 1982), pp. 82–97.

12. Babylonian Talmud, Berachot 5a.

13. Babylonian Talmud, Kidushim 40a.

CHAPTER 9: MOVING FROM JUDGMENT TO COMPASSION

1. *Midrash Sifre,* Deut. 49

2. *Midrash Aggadah* 3:1.

3. Matt, *The Essential Kabbalah,* p. 84.
4. Ibid.
5. S. Dresner, *The World of a Hasidic Master: Levi Yitzhak of Berditchev* (New York: Shapolsky Publishers, 1986), p. 64.
6. Philip Goodman, *The Rosh Hashanah Anthology* (Philadelphia: The Jewish Publication Society of America, 1971), p. 168.
7. The basis of this teaching is a saying from the Mishneh, *Pirkay Avot* 1:6: "One should judge every person meritoriously."
8. *Likutey Moharan II* 282 (author's own translation).
9. Ibid.
10. For a deeper analysis of the development of the concept of the Shechinah in Jewish mystical thought, see Raphael Patai, *The Hebrew Goddess* (New York: Avon Books, 1967).
11. Buber, *The Early Masters,* p. 237.
12. Mishneh, *Pirkay Avot* 2:4.
13. Ibn Chaviv, *Ein Yaacov: The Ethical and Inspirational Teachings of the Talmud,* trans. A. Y. Finkel (Northvale, N.J.: Jason Aronson, 1999), p. 12.
14. *Midrash Bereishit Raba* 12:15.
15. Quoted in Nilton Bonder, *The Kabbalah of Envy: Transforming Hatred, Anger, and Other Negative Emotions* (Boston: Shambhala Publications, 1997), p. 173.
16. Elie Wiesel, *Souls on Fire* (New York: Random House, 1972), p. 96.
17. In Hebrew, *"Bamidah she'adam moded, bah modedin lo."* This saying appears in numerous texts, including Babylonian Talmud, Megillah 12b, Sota 8b; *Midrash Bereishit Raba* 9:13.
18. I based my narrative on Rabbi Yerachmiel Tillis's version of the original tale from his Internet correspondence newsletter from Ascent of Safed.
19. Zohar, Emor 99a–100a.
20. It is interesting to note the different names of God that are used in the Hebrew text, for they reflect the different aspects of divinity being revealed to Jonah through God's actions.
21. *Midrash Yalkut Shimoni,* Jonah 551.
22. Babylonian Talmud, Baba Metzia 85a.

CHAPTER 10: WHOLENESS AND THE PARADOX OF HEALING

1. Babylonian Talmud, Eruvin 13b.
2. In Ruth 2:10 both meanings of this root appear in the same verse: "Why have I found grace in your eyes that you have recognized me [*le'hakire-ini*] and I am a stranger [*nochriah*]."

3. A. H. Horowitz of Staroselye, *Avodat ha'Levi, Va-Yehi* 74a (Jerusalem, 1972).

4. Simcha Raz, *The Sayings of Menahem Mendel of Kotsk* (Northvale, N.J.: Jason Aronson, 1995), p. 2.

5. Aryeh Kaplan, *The Bahir Illumination* (York Beach, Maine: Samuel Weiser, 1979), p. 21.

6. After wrestling with the angel and making peace with his brother, Esau, the Torah says that Jacob "came to [the city of] Shechem [Nablus] whole [shaleim]" (Genesis 33:18).

7. On the passage "a simple man (ish tam) who dwells in tents" (Genesis 25:27), Rashi says, *"K'libo kein piv,"* which means Jacob's heart and mouth were congruent.

8. Mordecai Yosef of Izbitz, *Beis Ya'acov, Parashat Va'yeitzei* 1.

9. The fact that Leah had been Esau's intended soul mate appears in the following midrash quoted by Rashi in his commentary on Genesis 29:17: "'And Leah's eyes were tender.' She thought it was her destiny to be [married] with Esau. And [this was why her eyes were tender, because] she was [constantly] crying. . . . Everyone used to say: Rebecca has two sons and Laban has two daughters. The eldest [is destined] for the eldest and the youngest [is destined] for the youngest." Leah's tears over her destiny suggest that we all can change our fate through the power of teshuvah!

10. For a more complete discussion of Jacob's inner transformation, see Aviva G. Zornberg, *Genesis: The Beginning of Desire* (Philadelphia: The Jewish Publication Society, 1995), pp. 144–179.

11. This phrase, which in Hebrew is *"titen emet l'yaacov,"* appears in the Sabbath afternoon prayer *"uva le'tzion go'el."* It originally appears in the Micah 7:20.

12. Yehudah Aryeh Leib, *Sefat Emet, Parashat Toldot.*

13. For a detailed description of the sephirot, see David S. Ariel, *The Mystic Quest: An Introduction to Jewish Mysticism* (New York: Schocken Books, 1988).

CHAPTER 11: FINDING GOD IN ALL THINGS

1. The scriptures say "Adam knew his wife Eve" to indicate that he had sex with her. The Bible uses the same verb—*va'yeida,* from the Hebrew word for knowledge—to describe the conjugal relations between many other biblical couples as well.

2. Chaim of Velozin, *Nefesh Ha'Chayim.* This quote is from the commentary on Gate One, chapter 6.

3. Babylonian Talmud, Berachot 11b.
4. *Midrash Bereishit Raba* 9.
5. Babylonian Talmud, Succah 52a.
6. Ya'acov Yosef of Polonoye, *Toldoth Ya'akov Yosef, Parashat Va'Yechi* 39a, author's own translation.
7. Buber, *The Early Masters,* pp. 237–238.
8. This revision is discussed in the Talmud, Berachot 11b.
9. Babylonian Talmud, Berachot 2a.
10. *Midrash Tanchuma,* Exodus 14, author's own translation.
11. *Shir Hashirim Raba* 5:2, author's own translation.
12. Babylonian Talmud, Shabbat 12b.

CHAPTER 12: THE FOUR WORLDS

1. I heard this version of the tale from my teacher, Rabbi Zalman Schachter-Shalomi.
2. Certain kabbalistic sources consider reality to consist of five worlds, not four. Beyond the realm of atzilut they count Adam Kadmon, the primordial man, as a fifth realm, which is essentially beyond human comprehension. According to this view, the fifth realm, which is associated with the Ein Sof, the infinite, is the source of the other four realms. The doctrine of the four worlds is mentioned in Maimonides' Mishneh Torah, Hilkhot Yesodey HaTorah 3–4. It is also mentioned in the kabbalistic texts *Shaarey Kedushah* III:1–2; and *Etz Chaim, Shaar Kitzur* ABYA 10.
3. The doctrine of the four worlds is based on the image of the four rivers that flowed out of paradise, as described in Genesis 1:10–14, "And a river comes out of Eden to water the garden. And from there it divides up into four heads. The name of the first is Pishon . . . and the name of the second river is Gichon . . . and the name of the third river is the Chidekel . . . and the fourth river is the Perat." This biblical image of the life-giving, ever-flowing waters of paradise was understood by the ancient mystics as a symbol of divinity, for as the infinite becomes manifest in the finite world, it branches out into four distinct dimensions.
4. Rabbi Levi Yitzhak of Berditchev describes the four worlds as stages in God's creative process, likening it to that of an artist. Creation, he suggests, originates with God's desire or will to love: "In relation to the Creator, however, there are no attributes or measurements, because He is infinite. However, it arose in His simple will to create next to Him the attribute of love, in order to share love. . . . And so He brought the concept of love into being like one who lights a candle from another

candle. And this is what is meant by 'the world of emanation' (*atzilut*).
It then arose in His will to create all the worlds, so that His Godliness
would be revealed in this world. This is called the world of 'creation'
(*beriah*). This was His original thought, namely, that his love be revealed
to the world. He then visualized in his thoughts, as it were, how the
world might be constructed, like an artist who has the idea to make
something, but its form is still hidden and stored in his thought. It is
only after he decides to make the thing that he depicts *how* it will be
made, drawing pictures that show which colors and styles he will use
to make it. So, too, the Blessed Creator, as it were, decided which forms
to use for creating the universe. This is called the Universe of Formation (*Yetzirah*) coming from the [Hebrew] word for form (*tzurah*). After
this, He brought His thought from potentiality to actuality, thus creating His universe. This is called the Universe of Doing (*Assiyah*)—for it
is made with boundaries and limits." See *Kedushat Ha'levi, Parashat
Beshalach,* p. 155 (author's own translation).

5. Each of the sephirot exists in each of the worlds, though certain sephirot are considered to be dominent in each world.

6. In *Likutey Moharan II* 67 and *Likutey Moharan I* 56:8 and 14:13, Rabbi
   Nachman associates the four letters of God's name and the four worlds
   with the four foundational elements, or *yesodot,* that make up all creation. The four elements Rabbi Nachman refers to are not the same as
   the four physical elements (earth, air, fire, water); rather, they represent
   dynamic principles that govern the structure of matter itself. A similar
   notion can be found in Rabbi Nachman's discussion of the main causes
   of illness. Basically he suggests that illness is caused by a lack of harmony and balance among the four basic elements within the body, while
   "healing comes about essentially by bringing harmony/balance among
   the elements" (*Likutey Moharan II* 5:1). Rabbi Nachman also writes that
   depression, or a lack of joy, is another key contributing factor to illness.

7. Babylonian Talmud, Chagigah 14b (author's own translation).

8. Ben Zoma's spiritual extremism is also hinted at in another text, the
   midrash *Sifra Kedoshim* 45, which describes a debate he had with Rabbi
   Akiva over the mystical significance of the passage "and you shall love
   your neighbor as yourself." While Rabbi Akiva considered the passage
   to be the most central tenet of Judaism (*zeh klal gadol ba'Torah*), Ben
   Zoma held that another passage, "This is the book of the generations
   of Adam," was an even greater teaching, for Ben Zoma understood this
   passage to mean that all people are as one person—one being with one
   body. In other words, he felt that the essence of Torah was to experience

others as though they were a part of our own very body and being. To love one's neighbor "as oneself" is a holy act, but it implies that one still experiences oneself as a separate being who can love others.

9. *Likutey Moharan I* 22:5–7 (author's own translation).

10. Rabbi David Wolfe-Blank, *Meta-Siddur* (unpublished workbook), describes how the daily liturgy provides a ladder of ascent and descent through the four worlds.

CHAPTER 13: THE MESSIANIC TORAH

1. Leib, *The Language of Truth,* p. 4.

2. Abraham enters into a covenant with Avimelech at the wells of Be'er Sheva (Genesis 21). Eliezer, Abraham's messenger, meets Rebecca, Isaac's future wife, at the well (Genesis 24). Jacob meets Rachel, his beloved, at the well (Genesis 29). Isaac struggles with the Philistines over access to the wells dug by Abraham, his father, but eventually is able to make peace with them (Genesis 26). Moses meets Tzipporah at the well (Exodus 2).

3. Yehudah Aryeh Leib, *Sefat Emet, Parashat Toldoth.*

4. For a discussion of the ways that Freud may have unconsciously drawn on a variety of concepts from the Jewish mystical tradition in his early psychoanalytic formulations, see David Bakan, *Sigmund Freud and the Jewish Mystical Tradition* (Princeton, N.J.: Van Nostrand, 1958).

5. That there are "seventy faces," or possible meanings, for any word of Torah is a popular rabbinic saying, suggesting that scriptures can be understood in many, many different ways. See *Zohar* 1:47 and *Midrash Bamidbar Raba* 13:46.

6. These ideas are based on the writings about Purim of Reb Tzaddok Ha'Cohen of Lublin in his book *Pri Tzaddik.*

7. That Esther was chosen queen against her will is clear from Esther 2:9, which describes her being taken by force: "And Esther was taken to the King's house."

8. Marc Gafni, *Soul Prints: Your Path to Fulfillment* (New York: Pocket Books, 2001).

9. Jerusalem Talmud, Ta'anit 2b.

10. As the scroll is unrolled (spelled *gimmel-lamed-lamed* in Hebrew), the story is revealed (*gimmel-lamed-heh*).

11. Interestingly, the Hebrew word for exile, *galut,* is also related to the root *gimmel-lamed-heh,* which means "to reveal" (see note 10, above). Though God's light is hidden in exile, this hiddenness creates the opportunity for revelation.

12. Babylonian Talmud, Megillah 7b.

13. *Yalkut Shimoni,* Ruth 2:604.

14. Ibid.

15. Ibid.

16. Tzaddok Ha'Cohen of Lublin, *Tzidkat Ha'Tzaddik* 96, author's own translation.

17. *Keter Shem Tov* 111 (teachings of the Ba'al Shem Tov), author's own translation.

Bibliography

Ariel, David S. *The Mystic Quest: An Introduction to Jewish Mysticism.* New York: Schocken Books, 1988.

Bakan, David. *Sigmund Freud and the Jewish Mystical Tradition.* Princeton, N.J.: Van Nostrand, 1958.

Bokser, Ben Zion. *Abraham Isaac Kook: The Lights of Penitence, Lights of Holiness, The Moral Principles, Essays, Letters, and Poems.* Mahwah, N.J.: Paulist Press, 1978.

Bonder, Nilton. *The Kabbalah of Envy: Transforming Hatred, Anger, and Other Negative Emotions.* Boston: Shambhala Publications, 1997.

Buber, Martin. *Tales of the Hasidim.* Vol. 1, *The Early Masters.* Trans. Olga Marx. New York: Schocken Books, 1947.

————. *Tales of the Hasidim.* Vol. 2, *The Later Masters.* New York: Schocken Books, 1947.

————. *The Way of Man: According to the Teaching of Hasidism.* New York: The Citadel Press, 1966.

Chaviv, Ibn. *Ein Yaacov: The Ethical and Inspirational Teachings of the Talmud.* Trans. A. Y. Finkel. Northvale, N.J.: Jason Aronson, 1999.

Dossey, Larry. *Healing Words: The Power of Prayer and The Practice of Medicine.* New York: HarperCollins, 1997.

————. *Reinventing Medicine: Beyond Mind-Body to a New Era of Healing.* San Francisco: HarperSanFrancisco, 1999.

————. *Space, Time, and Medicine.* Boulder: Shambhala Publications, 1982.

Dresner, Samuel H. *The World of a Hasidic Master: Levi Yitzhak of Berditchev.* New York: Shapolsky Publishers, 1986.

Etzioni, Amitai. *Civic Repentance.* New York: Rowman & Littlefield Publishers, 1999.

Frankel, Estelle. "Creative Ritual: Adapting Rites of Passage to Psychotherapy for Times of Major Life Transition" (master's thesis, California State University, 1982).

Gafni, Marc. *Soul Prints: Your Path to Fulfillment.* New York: Pocket Books, 2001.

Gendlin, Eugene. *Focusing-Oriented Psychotherapy.* New York: Guilford Press, 1996.

Glatzer, Nahum N. *Hammer on the Rock: A Midrash Reader.* New York: Schocken Books, 1948.

Goodman, Philip. *The Rosh Hashanah Anthology.* Philadelphia: The Jewish Publication Society of America, 1971.

Green, Arthur, and Barry W. Holtz, trans. *Your Word Is Fire: The Hasidic Masters on Contemplative Prayer.* New York: Schocken Books, 1987.

Grof, Stanislav. *Realms of the Human Unconscious.* New York: E.P. Dutton, 1976.

Harvey, Andrew. *Hidden Journey: A Spiritual Awakening.* New York: Penguin Books, 1991.

Kaplan, Aryeh. *The Bahir Illumination.* York Beach, Maine: Samuel Weiser, 1979.

———. *Chasidic Masters: History, Biography, and Thought.* New York: Maznaim Publishing, 1984.

———. *The Light Beyond: Adventures in Hasidic Thought.* New York: Maznaim Publishing, 1981.

———. *Waters of Eden: The Mystery of the Mikveh.* New York: Union of the Orthodox Jewish Congregations of America, 1993.

Leib, Yehudah Aryeh. *The Language of Truth: The Torah Commentary of the Sefat Emet.* Trans. Arthur Green. Philadelphia: The Jewish Publication Society, 1998.

Lerner, Michael. *Jewish Renewal: A Path to Healing and Transformation.* New York: Putnam, 1994.

Matt, Daniel. *The Essential Kabbalah: The Heart of Jewish Mysticism.* San Francisco: HarperCollins, 1995.

Metzger, Deena. "On Prayer." In *Worlds of Jewish Prayer: A Festschrift in Honor of Rabbi Zalman M. Schachter-Shalomi,* edited by S. H. Weiner and J. Omer-Man. Northvale, N.J.: Jason Aronson, 1993.

Mitchell, Stephen, trans. *Tao Te Ching: A New English Version.* New York: HarperCollins, 1988.

Patai, Raphael. *The Hebrew Goddess.* New York: Avon Books, 1967.

Peli, Pinchas H. *Soloveitchik on Repentance: The Thought and Oral Discourses of Rabbi Joseph B. Soloveitchik.* Mahwah, N.J.: Paulist Press, 1984.

Raz, Hilda. *The Prairie Schooner Anthology of Contemporary Jewish American Writing.* Lincoln: University of Nebraska Press, 1998.

Raz, Simcha. *The Sayings of Menahem Mendel of Kotsk.* Northvale, N.J.: Jason Aronson, 1995.

Schachter-Shalomi, Zalman M. *Gate to the Heart: An Evolving Process.* Philadelphia: Aleph: Alliance for Jewish Renewal, 1993.

———. *Spiritual Intimacy: A Study of Counseling in Hasidism.* Northvale, N.J.: Jason Aronson, 1996.

Schwartz, Howard. *The Captive Soul of the Messiah.* New York: Schocken Books, 1983.

———. *Gathering the Sparks.* St. Louis: Singing Wind Press, 1979.

Shabad, Peter. "Repetition and Incomplete Mourning: The Intergenerational Transmission of Traumatic Themes." *Psychoanalytic Psychology* 10, no.1 (1993): 61–75.

Shore, Eliezer. "Solomon's Request." *Parabola* (fall 2002): 56–59.

Soloveitchik, Joseph. *The Halachik Mind: An Essay on Jewish Modern Thought.* New York: Seth Press, 1986.

Steinsaltz, Adin, and Josy Eisenberg. *The Seven Lights: On the Major Jewish Festivals.* Northvale, N.J.: Jason Aronson, 2000.

Suzuki, Shunryu. *Zen Mind, Beginner's Mind.* New York: Weatherhill, 1973.

Wiesel, Elie. *Souls on Fire.* New York: Random House, 1972.

Welwood, John. *Toward a Psychology of Awakening: Buddhism, Psychotherapy, and the Path of Personal and Spiritual Transformation.* Boston: Shambhala Publications, 2002.

Zalman, Shneur. *Likutey Amarim Tania,* bilingual edition. New York: Kehot Publication Society, 1984.

Zion, Noam, and David Dishon. *A Different Night: The Family Participation Haggadah.* Jerusalem: Shalom Hartman Institute, 1997.

Zohar. London: Soncino Press, 1973.

Zornberg, Aviva G. *Genesis: The Beginning of Desire.* Philadelphia: The Jewish Publication Society, 1995.

ORIGINAL HEBREW TEXTS

Di Vidas, Eliahu. *Reishit Chochmah: Shaar Ha'ahavah.*

Ha'Cohen, Tzaddok. *Tzidkat Ha'Tzaddik.*

Ha'Cohen, Tzaddik. *Pri Tzaddik.*

Horkonos, Eliezer. *Pirkay D'Rebbe Eliezer.*

Keter Shem Tov.

Leib, Yehudah Aryeh. *Sefat Emet.*

Mordecai of Yosef. *Beis Ya'acov.*

Levi Yitzhak of Berditchev. *Imray Tzaddikim, Or Ha'Emet.*

———. *Kedushat Ha'Levi, Bereishit* (Genesis).

Lutzatto, Moshe Chaim. *Yalkut Yediot Ha'Emet,* Ma'amar Ha'choch-mah.

Lutzker, Shlomo. *Maggid Devarav Le Ya'acov.*

Maimonides, Moses. *Mishneh Torah.*

Midrash Mechilta, in *Otzar Ha'peirushim* of the *Malbim.*

Midrash Otiot d'Rebbe Akiva Ha'Shalem. Unpublished translation by Rabbi Gershon Winkler.

Midrash Yalkut Shimoni, Ruth and Jonah.

Midrash Raba, Genesis, Exodus, Eicah.

Nathan of Nemerov. *Likutey Moharan.*

Nachmanides. *Commentary on the Book of Genesis.*

Rashi. *Commentary on the Books of Genesis and Exodus.*

Vital, Chayim. *Shaarey Kedushah* and *Etz Chaim, Shaar Kitzur.*

Continuing Education Units

A board-certified provider of continuing education to MFTs and LCSWs, Estelle Frankel is offering continuing education units based on this book. In order to receive twelve hours of continuing education credit, as required by the California Board of Behavioral Sciences, you must complete a posttest that highlights the clinical applications of salient ideas in this book.

For more information go to www.sacredtherapy.com or e-mail the author at estellefrankel@sacredtherapy.com.

Credits

Index

About the Author

Estelle Frankel is a practicing psychotherapist and a seasoned teacher of Jewish mysticism and meditation. She was ordained as a rabbinic pastor and spiritual guide (*mashpiah ruchanit*) by Rabbi Zalman Schachter-Shalomi. Estelle has taught widely in the United States and in Israel, where she lived for over eight years, and is currently on the faculty of Chochmat Halev Center for Jewish Spirituality. She lives in Berkeley, California, with her husband and two children. This is her first book.